5⁰⁰
C+/1

# *The* CIVIL WAR
# *in the* WESTERN TERRITORIES

*Arizona, Colorado, New Mexico, and Utah*

# The CIVIL WAR
# in the WESTERN
# TERRITORIES

*Arizona, Colorado, New Mexico,*
*and Utah*

☆

by Ray C. Colton

UNIVERSITY OF OKLAHOMA PRESS : NORMAN

LIBRARY OF CONGRESS CATALOG CARD NUMBER: 59-7964

Copyright 1959 by the University of Oklahoma Press, Publishing Division of the University. Composed and printed at Norman, Oklahoma, U.S.A., by the University of Oklahoma Press. First edition.

# Foreword

PERHAPS FEW PEOPLE RECOGNIZE that military campaigns of the Civil War were fought far west of the Missouri River. In view of the remoteness of this region, the sparsity of its population, and the determining significance of the eastern campaigns, such a concept is quite understandable. Nevertheless, it is a fact that from 1861 to 1865 the violent struggle between the states extended into the Western territories of New Mexico, Arizona, Colorado, and Utah, where it assumed further complications with the involvement of the Indians.

Few historians have dealt with the full significance of the role that the Far West played in the mighty conflict between the North and the South. Such writers as Edward Channing, James Ford Rhodes, James Garfield Randall, James Truslow Adams, and James Kendall Hosmer have scarcely mentioned the Intermountain West during the Civil War. Henry Steele Commager in *The Blue and the Gray* related a one-sided, incomplete story under the topic title, "Confederates Win an Empty Victory at Glorieta Pass." E. Merton Coulter, when writing his *Confederate States of America,* briefly sensed the importance of the Far Western theater. It has remained for some of the Western writers to give this area its proper place in Civil War history. Their efforts, however, have been confined to the local limitations of their respective areas. In this study I have undertaken to survey and interpret the significance of the Civil War in the Western region as a whole and place it in perspective.

Confederate leaders planned to annex a corridor from the Río Grande in Texas to the Pacific Coast of California. They expected the Spanish American population of New Mexico to espouse the Southern Cause and California to secede from the Union. Their

v

financiers hoped that the mineral wealth of the West could be won by the Confederacy. Their strategists assumed that the Mormons would join in opposition to the Federal government. Slavery advocates proposed that California, New Mexico, Arizona, Utah, and Colorado, when annexed to the Confederacy, be used for the extension of their system. Southern military leaders planned that the Western Indians would give indirect, if not direct, aid to the defeat of the Union forces. The fortunes of war did not permit this Confederate scheme to materialize, but since Confederate forces actually occupied most of New Mexico and Arizona at one time, the conflict in the Rocky Mountain West should be regarded as a significant campaign in the American Civil War.

It was during the 1860's that Arizona, New Mexico, and Utah received their present boundaries. The Confederates, in their brief period of occupation, carved up the old New Mexican Territory much differently from the boundary lines of New Mexico and Arizona today. Colorado, which became a territory in February, 1861, might have received less under the Confederacy than she has.

Emphasis is necessarily placed upon the military campaigns against the Confederates and the Indians who sought to take advantage of the confusion engendered by the conflict. Details of campaigns, troop movements, and casualties are purposely related, both because of the need of placing such a narrative within the compass of a single study and because these constitute the principal aspects of the war on the distant frontiers.

Ray C. Colton

*Los Angeles, California*
*August 1, 1959*

# Contents

# Illustrations

## MAPS

# *The* CIVIL WAR
# *in the* WESTERN TERRITORIES

*Arizona, Colorado, New Mexico, and Utah*

# War Clouds Over Western America

ON A MAP of the United States at the outbreak of the American Civil War in 1861, one can draw a fairly straight line from the Eastern Shore of Maryland to the northwestern corner of Texas, south of which the Confederate States of America held almost complete sway. Confederate leaders were ambitious to acquire even greater areas. The Territory of New Mexico extended west from Texas to California. This prize, if secured, would place the Confederacy almost on the Pacific Ocean. Jefferson Davis, while secretary of war in President Franklin Pierce's cabinet, had come to understand the importance of the West. With the possibilities of California's seceding from the Union, or at least the southern part of it, and of annexing some of the states of northern Mexico, it was of major importance for the Confederacy to acquire New Mexico.

The potential mineral wealth of the West and the valuable military stores and equipment located in this area were also powerful incentives to the South. The acquisition of this domain was to be brought about principally through conquest, diplomacy, and loyalty to the Southern Cause by soldiers then stationed in the Southwest. The assistance of the Western Indians was counted on. Likewise, the reported spirit of disunion that existed in the Intermountain West and on the Pacific Coast would fit well into the Confederate plans.

Spearheading this scheme were the Texans, who for years had coveted part, if not all, of New Mexico. They considered the Río Grande their western boundary all the way to its headwaters. In 1841 an expedition sponsored by Texas President Mirabeau B. Lamar had been thwarted by New Mexican Governor Manuel Armijo. Conquest of this territory would give them an oppor-

3

tunity to accomplish this ambition and get revenge for the earlier defeat. The invasion would also give the Texans a chance to display their patriotism.

Since the Gadsden Purchase in 1853, Southern leaders, among whom was Jefferson Davis, had fondly hoped to construct a railroad along the thirty-second parallel route from the Southern states to the Pacific Ocean. A corridor to the West Coast would aid in materializing this plan. With the Pacific Slope in their possession through conquest or by alliance with a Western Confederacy, the world would be open to the Confederates, making an effective Union blockade impossible. It would provide an opportunity for Confederate cruisers and privateers to prey upon Union commerce, and it would afford an excellent chance to develop Asiatic trade.

Western minerals were of major importance to the Confederacy. The California gold fields were then in their prime, and rich ore veins in Colorado and Nevada were being developed. There appeared to be immense mineral deposits in the New Mexico Territory, especially in the Arizona section. Prominent Confederate leaders were thoroughly conscious of the potential wealth of this region, as is illustrated by this statement from Lieutenant Colonel John R. Baylor, C.S.A.: "The vast mineral resources of Arizona, in addition to its affording an outlet to the Pacific, makes its acquisition a matter of some importance to our Government."[1]

Of equal value to the Confederates were the military fortifications, supplies, and equipment then in the Intermountain West. On February 18, 1861, General David E. Twiggs in Texas had surrendered all of the property of the United States under his command to the Confederates, and it was the Southern hope to be as fortunate west of the Río Grande. At the outbreak of the Civil War there was a large quantity of military equipment and supplies located in the West, of which the Confederate leaders

[1] U. S. War Department, *The War of the Rebellion: A Compilation of the official Records of the Union and Confederate Armies*, Series I, Vol. 4, p. 23. (Hereafter cited as *O.R.*, I, 4:23.)

U. S. military installations in the territories of New Mexico, Colorado, and Utah early in the Civil War.

were well aware. President Davis was told that the stores, supplies, and munitions of war within New Mexico and Arizona were immense and that the game was well worth the amount of ammunition needed.

The principal military installations in the Rocky Mountain territories at the outbreak of the war in 1861 were Forts Fillmore, Thorn, McLane, Craig, Webster, Conrad, Butler, Marcy, Union, Stanton, Defiance, Fauntleroy, Buchanan, Breckenridge, and Mohave, with garrisons at Santa Fe, Albuquerque, Socorro, Los Lunas, Camp Burgwin, and Tucson in New Mexico (which then included Arizona); Forts Garland, Massachusetts, and Wise in Colorado; Fort Crittenden (formerly Floyd) and Fort Bridger in Utah.

To effect the conquest of the Intermountain West and the acquisition of the fortifications and war materials, the Confederate leaders were anticipating valuable support, and not without reason, from many of the military personnel then with the army in that area. Horace Greeley claimed that Secretary of War John B. Floyd had deliberately sent Colonel William W. Loring of North Carolina, a Secessionist, to command the Department of New Mexico in the critical year of 1861. He and Lieutenant Colonel George B. Crittenden of Kentucky, another Secessionist and a ranking officer in New Mexico, conducted a systematic corruption of their subordinates. Apparently it was their intention to lead their troops into Texas and there turn them "over to the service and support of the Rebellion."[2]

Evidently other officers in that territory had similar motives. Before leaving New Mexico, Colonel Loring received a letter from Major Henry H. Sibley, who had preceded him to El Paso, Texas, in which Sibley implied that he contemplated leading his soldiers into the Confederate ranks. Sibley wrote:

We are at last under the glorious banner of the Confederate States of America. . . . I regret more than ever the sickly sentimentality (I

[2] Horace Greeley, *The American Conflict: A History of the Great Rebellion in the United States of America, 1860–65*, II, 19.

can call it by no other name) by which I was overruled in my desire
to bring the whole command with me. I am satisfied now of the dis-
affection of the best of the rank and file in New Mexico and that we
are regarded as having betrayed and deserted them. I wish I had
my part to play over again; no such peace scruples should deter me
from doing what I considered a bounden duty to my friends and
the cause.[3]

Lieutenant John V. DuBois at Fort Union on February 12,
1861, wrote, "Nothing but secession talked of at the Post. Of all
the officers here only Lt. McRae of North Carolina, Capt. Shoe-
maker, M.S.K. & myself are thoroughly loyal."[4] A month later,
on March 10, he recorded:

I became involved in several very bitter political discussions here
& threatened, if an effort was made to seduce my regiment from its
allegiance, I would assume command myself & fight it out. Propo-
sitions were made to me to go into the southern army & high positions were offered me, but of course declined. . . . The soldiers are
loyal, most of the officers going south themselves, & all the West
Pointers except Longstreet urge their soldiers to remain true.[5]

Those officers who were loyal were trying desperately to hold
the Union forces together. Lieutenant Colonel B. S. Roberts of
Vermont, detecting the disloyal intentions of Lieutenant Colonel
Crittenden, his commanding officer, secured a furlough and hurried from Fort Stanton to Santa Fe. He denounced Crittenden
to Colonel Loring, but to his astonishment he was reproved for
not minding his own business. Until then he had not suspected
that Loring was a Secessionist. Roberts was ordered back to Fort
Stanton, but was able to warn Captain Hatch, commanding at
Albuquerque, and Captain Morris, who was in charge at Fort
Craig.

The great decision finally had to be made by those soldiers

---

[3] *O.R.*, I, 4:55. El Paso, Texas, was at one time known as Franklin, but when
the Civil War began, most of the military commanders referred to it as El Paso.
[4] John Van Deusen DuBois, *Campaigns in the West, 1856–1861*, 110.
[5] *Ibid.*

of Southern sympathies serving in the West. From April 22 until June 8, 1861, the following officers serving in New Mexico resigned their commissions from the United States Army to fight with the Confederate States of America: Lieutenant Joseph Wheeler, Captain Richard S. Ewell, Lieutenant Colonel George B. Crittenden, Captain Carter L. Stevenson, Major Henry Hopkins Sibley, Major James Longstreet, and Captain Cadmus M. Wilcox. On May 13, 1861, Colonel William W. Loring submitted his resignation to the President of the United States, but did not leave Santa Fe until a month later. Before leaving, he placed Lieutenant Colonel Edward R. S. Canby in general charge of affairs in the Department of New Mexico. About this time General Albert Sidney Johnston, commander of the Utah Expedition in 1858 and later in charge of the Department of the Pacific, came through New Mexico on his way to Richmond. Wheeler, Longstreet, Ewell, and Johnston, names which soon became famous throughout the Confederacy, and Sibley, Wilcox, Loring, Stevenson, and Crittenden, also Southern generals with slightly less prominence, were all serving in the West when the war broke out.[6] However, of the twelve hundred regular troops serving in New Mexico when hostilities commenced, only a few joined the Confederate armies.

The Confederate leaders had planned to receive indirect, if not direct, assistance from the Indians in the conquest of the Intermountain West. It was suggested that the Cherokees and Choctaws be used to terrorize the Mexican population of New Mexico. Major E. Kirby Smith considered the Indians north of the Red River as allies of the Confederates. Governor William Gilpin of Colorado informed Colonel Edward R. S. Canby that he had reliable information that more than 64,000 Indians west of the Arkansas River had united with the Rebels. The Indians

[6] Wheeler, Longstreet, and Ewell all became Confederate lieutenant generals. Wilcox rose to the position of major general. General Johnston, while commanding Confederate Department of the West, was killed at the Battle of Shiloh. Loring became a major general. After the war, as Loring Pasha, he became an Egyptian Army general. Sibley, inventor of the Sibley army tent, became a brigadier general and after the war also became a general in Egypt.

were allies of the Georgians in Colorado who were sympathetic toward secession.[7] Bancroft concluded that "the Apaches and Navahos were looked upon, not exactly as partisans of the South, but as a potent factor in the defeat of Union forces."[8] This assumption by the Confederate leaders was borne out by subsequent events. The Indians, by temporarily blocking the mail and burning the supply trains, created in the Intermountain West the necessity of retaining troops which otherwise could be used in other theaters of war.

The Southern leaders were aware that prior to and during the early months of the war the spirit of disunion was not confined to the Confederate states. In the Intermountain West the Union leaders in Colorado could claim about two-thirds of the population, but the Confederates remembered that gold was first discovered in that territory by the Georgians in 1858 and a large number of Southerners had drifted into that area since that time. Governor Gilpin, in a letter to Colonel Canby, placed the number of Secessionists in Colorado at 7,500 and stated that "their plans were to capture Fort Wise and Garland; to surround New Mexico and invade it from the North."[9]

It was assumed by the Confederate leaders that the Mormons in Utah would readily accept allegiance to almost any other government than that in Washington. For years that church had attempted without success to obtain redress through and protection from the Federal government for persecution in Missouri and Illinois. Within three years prior to the outbreak of the Civil War, a United States army, led by General Albert Sidney Johnston, in response to false reports of a rebellion in Utah, had invaded the territory. The Utah Expedition was ill advised on the part of the United States government, costing several hundred lives and at least $15,000,000. It accomplished practically nothing, concluded historian Bancroft, except exposure of President Buchanan and his cabinet to ridicule.[10]

Confederate leaders had planned that New Mexico, especially

[7] *O.R.*, I, 4:96; 1:628; 4:73.
[8] Hubert Howe Bancroft, *History of Arizona and New Mexico*, 686.
[9] *O.R.*, I, 4:73.
[10] *History of Utah*, 538.

9

the southern and western parts of the territory which later became Arizona, would favor disunion. This conclusion was, no doubt, based on information received of the activities of Confederate sympathizers in that territory. A convention was held at Mesilla, in southern New Mexico, on March 16, 1861, at which those present claimed that they represented the people of Arizona and were acting separately from the government of New Mexico. They repudiated the United States government and attached themselves to the Confederate States of America. The Sixth Resolution of this convention read:

Resolved that we will not recognize the present Black Republican Administration, and that we will resist any officers appointed to this Territory by said administration with whatever means in our power. Jas. A. Lucas, President of the Convention, Attest: Ch. S. A. Happin, Secretary.[11]

A convention or mass meeting held at Tucson in the southwestern part of the New Mexico Territory early in August, 1861, not only declared Arizona ready to become a territory of the Confederacy, but elected Granville Oury as a delegate to the Confederate Congress.

Horace Greeley viewed this situation in New Mexico in the following light:

Her Mexican population, ignorant, timid and superstitious, had been attached to the Union by conquest, scarcely fifteen years before, and had meantime been mainly under the training of Democratic officials of pro-slavery sympathies. . . . Her delegate in Congress, Miguel Otero, had issued [Feb. 15, 1861] and circulated an address to her people, intended to disaffect them toward the Union, and incite them to favor the Rebellion.[12]

At the time of the Mexican War the Southern leaders had fully planned on extending slavery into the territory acquired from Mexico as a result of the war or by purchase. This included what

[11] *O.R.*, I, 4:39.
[12] *The American Conflict*, II, 20–21.

is now California, New Mexico, Arizona, Utah, Nevada, and part of Colorado. The Compromise of 1850 restricted this plan somewhat when California was admitted to the Union as a free state, but their hopes brightened with the success of the Confederate Army in New Mexico in 1861 and the early part of 1862. Major T. T. Teel, C.S.A., a staff member in General Henry H. Sibley's brigade, while listing the objectives of the Confederate campaign into the Intermountain West, which had the personal approval of President Jefferson Davis, stated that "with New Mexico, Arizona, California, and Utah there would be plenty of room for the extension of slavery, which would greatly strengthen the Confederate States."[13]

In the meantime, while the Confederacy, realizing the importance of the Intermountain West, was planning its conquest and annexation, the interest of the Federal government was diverted elsewhere, or a full appreciation of the strategic value of this area was lacking, perhaps both. Even as late as May 17, 1861, General Scott ordered ten companies of infantry, then in Utah, the Fifth and Seventh Infantry Regiments serving in New Mexico and four companies of the Tenth Infantry Regiment then in New Mexico and Colorado, a total of approximately 3,400 men, to proceed to Fort Leavenworth, Kansas.[14]

Secretary Caleb Smith of the Department of Interior, however, did sense the importance of the West to the Union cause. On May 11, 1861, he wrote Secretary Simon Cameron of the War Department attempting to impress him with the threatening Confederate danger in this area. He also called attention to the evident disloyalty of certain members of the United States Army in that territory. Secretary Cameron's answer, couched in trite phraseology, stating that "measures have been or will be taken

---

[13] T. T. Teel, "Sibley's Mexican Campaign—Its Objects and the Causes of Its Failure," *Battles and Leaders of the Civil War,* II, 700.

[14] *O.R.,* I, 53:492. Mr. Thomas E. Blades, chief, Records Section, Department Records Branch, Adjutant General's Office, U. S. Army, stated on March 31, 1953, to me that this would total approximately 3,400 men. This estimate is based on the regulation of the U. S. Army in 1861 that there should be 100 men in a company and 1,000 men to a regiment.

commensurate with its importance,"[15] indicates only a casual interest.

On July 15, 1862, Brigadier General B. S. Roberts,[16] in his testimony before the Committee on the Conduct of the War, called attention to the "utter neglect of the Adjutant General's department for the last year to communicate in any way with the commanding officer of the Department of New Mexico," or to answer his urgent appeals for reinforcements, money, and supplies.[17] It was not until 1862 that the strategic importance of this area was fully comprehended by the Washington government.

[15] *Ibid.*, I, 53:90; 1:605.
[16] Referred to previously as Lieutenant Colonel Roberts.
[17] Augustus Allen Hayes, *New Colorado and the Santa Fe Trail*, 165, quotes the report of the Committee on the Conduct of the War, July 15, 1862.

# Confederate Invasion

THE INTERMOUNTAIN WEST in 1861 was a long way from the immediate vicinity of the opening battles of the Civil War. News of the rapid secession of the Confederate states had scarcely reached the West when it was learned that Fort Sumter had been fired upon. Weeks before, when it appeared that war was inevitable, John R. Baylor of the Texas Mounted Rifles, C.S.A., who rose from the rank of captain to lieutenant colonel, made an energetic recruiting campaign from San Antonio to El Paso, Texas, enlisting men to "hunt buffaloes on the plains." Actually they were being recruited to invade New Mexico. The volunteers were required to furnish their own horses, saddles, guns, and ammunition.[1]

By mid-June, 1861, Lieutenant Colonel Edward R. S. Canby, Union commander of the Department of New Mexico, was alerted to the fact that Confederate military leaders were mobilizing near El Paso, Texas, for an invasion of New Mexico. He informed the United States Army headquarters accordingly. To prepare for this invasion and the increasing hostilities of the Indians, Canby moved to enlarge the military personnel in his department. He appealed to Governor Abraham Rencher of New Mexico in June for eleven companies of volunteers. The following month he asked Governor William Gilpin of Colorado for two companies of militia. According to the U. S. Army official report of June 30, 1861, there were only 2,466 men in the Department of New Mexico. Canby sought to combine and coordinate many of the far-flung military installations.

Plans were made to strengthen Fort Fillmore, located about forty miles up the Río Grande from El Paso; Fort Craig, one

1 William A. Keleher, *Turmoil in New Mexico 1848–68*, 147.

hundred miles farther; Fort Union, guarding the supply route from Fort Leavenworth, Kansas; Fort Stanton on the east and Fort Garland commanding the road to Colorado. These forts were to act as centers of defense. On June 16, 1861, Major Isaac Lynde, commanding officer at Fort McLane, was ordered to abandon that fort and move his troops and military supplies to Fort Fillmore, where he assumed command. Fort Breckenridge was abandoned on July 10 and Fort Buchanan on July 23, 1861. Both were located in the western portion of the Territory near Tucson. The troops and supplies which could be easily transported were dispatched to those forts comprising the defense centers.

The Confederate invasion of New Mexico was initiated by the Second Texas Regiment, Mounted Rifles, led by Lieutenant Colonel John R. Baylor, who entered the Territory near El Paso, Texas, on July 23, 1861.[2] They marched up the Río Grande about forty miles and quietly camped during the night of the twenty-fourth within six hundred yards of the sleeping post at Fort Fillmore. The Rebels planned to surprise the garrison at daybreak the following morning, kill or capture the officers in their quarters and take the men prisoners in their barracks. Fortunately for the Yankees, two of the Confederate pickets, who were discharged U. S. Army veterans, left their post and warned the Fillmore garrison. The command awakened, and the fort was saved for the time being. Learning that the Union leaders had been informed of their position, the Texans altered their plans and instead of attacking the fort on the morning of the twenty-fifth, they crossed the river and occupied the town of Mesilla near by.[3] They were welcomed by Southern sympathizers, who as early as March, 1861, in a Secession convention, had declared

[2] Baylor stated that he had only 258 men. However, a claim of about 400 was made by Union officer James Cooper McKee, *Narrative of the Surrender of a Command of U. S. Forces at Fort Fillmore, New Mexico, in July, 1861*, 12.

[3] McKee, *Narrative of the Surrender*, 13–14; Lydia Spencer Lane, *I Married a Soldier*, 107, 121–22. In 1861, Mesilla was on the west bank of the Río Grande. Since then the river has cut a new channel which has placed this town on its east bank.

Arizona, then considered the southern part of New Mexico, a Confederate territory, but no action was taken at that time.

That afternoon Major Isaac Lynde with several companies of soldiers advanced toward Mesilla. Adjutant Edward J. Brooks and Surgeon James Cooper McKee were sent ahead with a demand from Lynde for "an unconditional surrender of the forces and the town" to which the Texans defiantly responded that if Lynde wanted the town, he would have to come and take it.[4] Lynde ordered an attack which resulted in a brisk but indecisive skirmish.[5] He then withdrew his troops to the fort, contending that it was getting dark and that the Confederates were on both sides of them. Baylor, fearing that this might be a feint to draw his men from their position, did not pursue the attackers at that time.

Next morning at the post Lynde gave orders to fortify against an attack. Later, in a moment of panic, evidently feeling, as he had done for some time, that the fort could not be successfully defended, he countermanded with an order to abandon Fort Fillmore and march for Fort Stanton, which was located more than 150 miles to the northeast. A subordinate officer, Captain C. H. McNally, later claimed that three hundred men could have held Fort Fillmore against three thousand of the enemy. In hurried preparation, wagons, buggies, and ambulances were loaded with military and personal supplies, and materials that could not be transported were ordered destroyed. Horace Greeley claimed that in many of the canteens whiskey was substituted for water.[6] This possibly accounts for the extreme thirst of a large number of the Union soldiers the following day.

At 1:00 A.M. on July 27, 1861, Major Lynde, with his entire command, including the wives and children of five officers, evacuated Fort Fillmore, traveling along the Fort Stanton Road. The

---

[4] McKee, *Narrative of the Surrender*, 15.

[5] Lynde places his own men at 380, the Texans at 700. He recorded that three Federals were killed and six were wounded; Confederates, eleven killed and wounded. Baylor reported four of the enemy killed and seven wounded, but did not list any Southern casualties.

[6] *The American Conflict*, 20.

column moved fairly steadily until daylight, but as they trudged along the desert road under a scorching sun, many of the infantry, suffering severely with the intense heat and want of water, began to falter along the way. The command finally came to a halt at San Augustine Springs. By sunrise the Confederates noting the huge dust clouds rising toward the northeast, surmised what had taken place. Baylor immediately directed a detachment of soldiers to take possession of Fort Fillmore and then led his mounted troops in pursuit of the fleeing Yankees. He stated, "The road for five miles was lined with fainting, famished soldiers who threw down their arms as we passed and begged for water."[7]

As the Texans approached the Union forces, Major Lynde, in despair, made a feeble attempt to place his troops in battle formation, but he soon requested terms of surrender from Lieutenant Colonel Baylor. In self-justification Lynde later wrote, "I could not bring more than 100 men of the infantry battalion on parade. . . . Under the circumstances . . . it was worse than useless to resist; honor did not demand the sacrifice of blood."[8]

Baylor, reporting his victory, later wrote:

I was . . . sent for by Major Lynde, who asked upon what terms I would allow him to surrender. I replied that the surrender must be unconditional. To this, Major Lynde assented, asking that private property should be respected. The articles of capitulation were signed and the order given to stack arms.[9]

Most of Lynde's staff did not share his fears and misgivings. The surrender was made under a storm of protest from most of the Union officers. Captain Alfred Gibbs wrote, "Nearly every officer in the command protested against it."[10] Captain J. H. Pot-

[7] Most of the information for this chapter comes from the *Official Record*, I, 4:4–159 and I, 9:488–707.

[8] *O.R.*, I, 4:6.

[9] *Ibid.*, I, 4:19. Characteristic of exaggerations in reporting the enemy's losses and underestimating their own, Baylor claimed 700 Federal troops surrendered to his force of less than 200. In contrast (*O.R.*, I, 4:15) Captain J. H. Potter accounts for only 492 Union soldiers and men involved in the surrender.

[10] *Ibid.*, I, 4:8.

ter angrily remarked, "That d——d old scoundrel has surrendered us!" Post Surgeon J. C. McKee demanded "Major Lynde, I protest against this surrender."[11] Later Dr. McKee bitterly reflected:

Eleven companies . . . of infantry and cavalry, between five and six hundred veterans, well disciplined and drilled troops with two pieces of artillery . . . arms and equipment, some two hundred cavalry horses, mules and wagons and two or three hundred head of beef cattle were unconditionally surrendered. . . . Was there ever such a suicidal, cowardly, pusillanimous surrender as that in all history?[12]

The capitulation also resulted in the loss of Federal drafts amounting to $17,000 held by Captain A. H. Plummer, Lynde's commissary. These drafts, which could have been destroyed, were handed over to the Confederates and, with the exception of $1,000 from U. S. fiscal agents, were collected.[13]

Upon being disarmed and dismounted, the majority of the prisoners were paroled. With only fifty old guns to protect themselves against the Indians, they were compelled to march under terrible privations and hardships to Santa Fe, Fort Union, Fort Wise in Colorado, and then on to Fort Leavenworth, Kansas, and east. Some of the men became mentally deranged during the march from the agony of thirst, while others, to quench it, opened their veins and drank their own blood.

A cry of cowardice and treason arose, not only in northern New Mexico,[14] but in the halls of Congress. On December 4, 1861, the House of Representatives passed a resolution requesting the Secretary of War to report on what measures have been or ought to be taken to expose and punish such of the officers now on parole as were guilty of treason or cowardice in surrendering Fort Fillmore, New Mexico, to an inferior force of Texas troops.

Responding to this resolution, Secretary of War Cameron notified the House that by direction of the President through

---

[11] *Ibid.*, I, 4:13. This contains both Potter's and McKee's statements.
[12] McKee, *Narrative of the Surrender*, 22–23.
[13] Baylor reported that only $9,500.00 was taken.
[14] *Santa Fe Weekly Gazette*, August 17, 1861.

Adjutant General Lorenzo Thomas, General Orders No. 102, Major Isaac Lynde had been dropped from the army rolls on November 25, 1861, for abandoning his post at Fort Fillmore, New Mexico, on the twenty-seventh of July, 1861, and subsequently surrendering his command to an inferior force of insurgents. Captain Plummer was reprimanded and suspended for six months, but all of the other officers were absolved from complicity in the offense.

Lieutenant Colonel B. H. Roberts, commanding at Fort Stanton, upon learning of Lynde's surrender, abandoned the fort on August 2, after attempting to destroy supplies that could not be easily transported. He sent the two companies of infantry to Albuquerque and joined Colonel Canby at Santa Fe with two companies of cavalry. Fort Stanton was occupied later by Confederate troops, but Baylor soon withdrew them to avoid weakening his command by spreading it too thinly. During this time the Texans confiscated, as they had at Fort Fillmore, all the supplies which had not been destroyed or stolen by the Indians and Mexicans. An attempt was made by the Confederates to intercept four companies of United States troops under Captain Moore en route from Forts Buchanan and Breckenridge, in the western part of the Territory, to Fort Fillmore, but learning of the fall of the fort, they cleverly eluded their pursuers and reported to Fort Craig.

The departure of the Union troops from Buchanan and Breckenridge aroused considerable resentment among the settlers in and around Tucson. This gave the Apache Indians an opportunity, with no restraint except from the local citizens, to dash down from the hills to murder, scalp, and pillage. Thieves and bandits lurking along the Mexican border, almost unmolested, could steal, plunder, and intimidate. Sixty-eight Americans in Tucson in the summer of 1861 in a mass meeting voted to make Arizona a part of the Confederacy. Perhaps this attitude stilled what regret the Union soldiers might have felt when they left this area.[15]

[15] Rufus Kay Wyllys, *Arizona: The History of a Frontier State*, 141.

Two indecisive encounters took place in September, 1861, near Fort Craig. A picket skirmish occurred between a company of New Mexican Volunteers under Captain John H. Minks and some Texas scouts under Captain Bethel Coopwood which resulted in the capture of Minks and a small portion of his company. Pursuit of the Confederates by one hundred regulars from Fort Craig under Captain R. M. Morris culminated in a short skirmish in which victory was claimed by both forces.[16]

The Union and Confederate forces now renewed their efforts. The Texans had completed their first objective by successfully establishing a base of operations in the planned invasion of the Intermountain West. On August 1, 1861, Lieutenant Colonel Baylor, flushed with victory, issued a proclamation in the name of the Confederate States of America establishing the Territory of Arizona to include all of that portion of New Mexico south of the thirty-fourth parallel, north latitude, extending from Texas to California. He organized a military government and named himself governor. Mesilla was designated as the capital. At this time Baylor was joined by Brigadier General Albert Sidney Johnston, with a party of officers who had resigned from the United States Army and were en route from the Pacific Coast to Richmond, Virginia. Baylor tendered to General Johnston the command of his forces, which was accepted. Johnston remained in command until there was no further need for his services.

The evacuation of Fort Fillmore and the subsequent surrender by Major Lynde was a staggering blow to the North in the Rocky Mountain West. Department Commander Lieutenant Colonel Canby considered Lynde's report "in all respects as unsatisfactory," but reported that "this news has roused the people of New Mexico from their apathetic condition."[17] Galvanized to action, Colonel Canby on August 2, 1861, the day after Baylor's proclamation, requested four more companies of Volunteers from Henry Connelly, newly appointed governor of New Mexico. The

16 *O.R.*, I, 4:26–32. Canby reports: Enemy losses—11 killed, 30 wounded; Union—3 wounded. Baylor records: Enemy—4 killed, several wounded; Confederate losses—2 killed, 8 wounded.
17 *Ibid.*, I, 4:2.

Governor responded by issuing a proclamation on September 14, calling for the immediate organization of a territorial militia and urging the citizens to volunteer in the expulsion of the Texans. On September 8, Colonel Canby had asked Governor Gilpin of Colorado for four to six companies of troops.

Express messengers arrived in Denver, Colorado, on January 7, 1862, carrying dispatches from Canby requesting all mounted troops to hasten immediately to Santa Fe and other posts in New Mexico in defense against the approaching Texans. Two companies of miners and frontiersmen were recruited and drilled near Cañon City, Colorado. Known as Dodd and Ford companies, after their commanders, they marched to Fort Garland in December, 1861, where they were mustered into the United States Army as companies A and B of the Second Colorado Volunteers. These were the first Colorado units to leave the Territory for war service. In midwinter they proceeded to Santa Fe. Company A (Dodd's) trudged down the Río Grande to Fort Craig. Company B (Ford's) was assigned to Fort Union.

On August 11, Canby informed the Assistant Adjutant General in Washington that the greatest exertions were being made to organize a respectable Volunteer force, but progress did not meet his expectations. Five days later he complained to the Assistant Adjutant General in St. Louis:

> Of the thirty-two companies that I have called for to replace the regular troops that have been ordered out of the country, only nineteen have been organized, and several of these are below the minimum organizations prescribed by the War Department. . . . I question very much whether a sufficient force for defense of the Territory can be raised within its limits, and I place no reliance upon any volunteer force that can be raised unless strongly supported by regular troops.[18]

Meanwhile, Army Headquarters at Washington, although still anxious for the withdrawal of the regular troops from New Mexico, were willing to wait until the volunteers were properly

[18] *Ibid.,* I, 4:65.

organized to replace them. Colonel Canby was not only concerned about sufficient troops, but he was hampered by lack of money to pay his men and purchase much-needed supplies. On November 18, 1861, he informed the Paymaster General that "The military operations in this department have for several months past been greatly embarrassed . . . by want of funds. . . . Many regular troops have not been paid for more than twelve months and the volunteers not at all."[19]

In addition to being handicapped by a lack of troops and funds, Canby was faced with Indian trouble. On December 1, 1861, he reported that the Navahos, Apaches, Utes, Kiowas, and Comanches were becoming more daring in their inroads and incursions. During the Civil War, the military leaders on both sides in this area were harassed by the Indians. Regardless of how pressing the Indian situation was, Canby realized his paramount problem was preparing a defense against the Confederate troops from Texas.

In the meantime, Henry Hopkins Sibley, now a brigadier general, commissioned to raise and command an army to be known as the Confederate States of America Army of New Mexico, was busily preparing a brigade in Texas. Following his resignation from the United States Army, he had gone to Richmond, where he had persuaded President Jefferson Davis that New Mexico was the natural gateway for an expedition that would result in the acquisition of New Mexico, Arizona, Colorado, and probably California.

On July 8, 1861, he was instructed by Adjutant and Inspector General S. Cooper, C.S.A., to proceed without delay to Texas and "in concert with Brigadier General Van Dorn" to organize, from the Texas troops, two full regiments of cavalry and one battery of howitzers and such forces as he deemed necessary. He was charged with the responsibility of driving the Federal troops from New Mexico and of securing all the arms, supplies, and materials of war that could be taken from the enemy territory. If successful, he was to organize a military government

[19] *Ibid.*, I, 4:75.

within the Territory. He was to be guided by circumstances and his own good judgment.

Arriving in Texas in August, Sibley made his headquarters in San Antonio and called for volunteers for the New Mexican campaign. The organization and equipping of the brigade moved along fairly well, but there were some discouragements and delays which Sibley attributed to the inefficiency of the Texas militia, competition with troops going east of the Mississippi, deficiency in arms, and lack of funds. The three regiments raised were designated as the Fourth, Fifth, and Seventh Texas Volunteer Cavalry. Among the brigade staff officers as Assistant Adjutant General was Alexander M. Jackson, former secretary of the New Mexican territorial government. The Fourth Cavalry was commanded by Colonel James Reily, assisted by Lieutenant Colonel William R. Scurry. The Fifth Cavalry was led by Colonel Thomas Green with Lieutenant Colonel Harry C. McNeill second in command. The Seventh Cavalry was commanded by Colonel William Steele with Lieutenant Colonel J. S. Sutton next in authority.

The Volunteers were equipped with a variety of firearms which included squirrel rifles, bear and sportsmen's guns, single- and double-barreled shotguns, bowie knives, and lances. In addition to the small arms, the Texans possessed six mountain howitzers. By late fall, 1861, the brigade had been mustered into the Army of the Confederate States of America, disciplined and drilled in preparation for the invasion of New Mexico. A member of the expedition proudly wrote: "Three thousand five hundred of these men were the best that ever threw leg over horse. . . . All-around men, natural-born soldiers, they were under twenty-five, with a liberal sprinkling of older ones who had seen more or less service on the frontier."[20]

On November 16, 1861, Sibley reported to General Cooper that he was ready to assume in person the command of all Confederate forces in the Territory of New Mexico and to conduct the military operations there and in Arizona. The scarcity of

[20] Theophilus Noel, *Autobiography and Reminiscences of Theophilus Noel,* 57.

water between San Antonio and El Paso made it necessary to follow a well-planned itinerary. Reily's regiment left San Antonio on October 22, Colonel Green's regiment took up the march on November 2, and Colonel Steele's regiment left for El Paso on November 20.

While General Sibley's forces were reaching their stride, Lieutenant Colonel John R. Baylor, the self-appointed governor of this newly proclaimed Confederate Territory of Arizona, anxiously wrote Sibley on October 24 that 2,500 Union troops were moving south and that he proposed to fall back if necessary. He urgently requested that reinforcements be sent to him as soon as possible. He reported the rumor that Union General E. V. Sumner was on his way with 2,000 regular troops from Guaymas, port city of Sonora, Mexico, to meet the Federal troops from northern New Mexico. Baylor was also concerned at the hostility of the New Mexicans. On October 25, he informed Sibley that the Mexican population was decidedly northern in sympathy and would join the enemy at the first opportunity. He felt that nothing but a strong force would keep them quiet, and he pleaded that reinforcements could not be set up too soon.

In mid-December General Sibley arrived at El Paso and took command of all Confederate forces in that area. He established his headquarters at Fort Bliss, a former United States fort in Texas.[21] Baylor was to remain as civil and military governor of Arizona. On December 20, 1861, Sibley addressed a proclamation to the people of New Mexico stating that "an Army under my command enters New Mexico to take possession of it" in the name of the Confederate States of America. "By geographical position," he continued, "by similarity of institutions, by commercial interests, and by future destinies," the Territory "pertains" to the Confederacy. The United States, according to Sibley, had already failed, and the arms of Confederate States had been crowned in victory. He assured the protection of life and

21 The site of Fort Bliss during the Civil War has been marked with a granite monument at the corner of Magoffin Avenue and Willow Street in El Paso. A replica of the old fort has been built on a part of the present Fort Bliss in northeastern El Paso.

property and told the citizens to go quietly about their peaceful avocations. He promised that such forage and supplies as would be required by his army would be purchased in open market and paid for at fair prices. He threatened those New Mexicans who joined the Union forces. He guaranteed the Territory a strong and lenient government under the Confederacy and abolished the Federal taxes in New Mexico. He appealed to his old comrades-in-arms still in the Union ranks to renounce their allegiance to the usurpers of their government and liberties and to join him in the colors of justice and freedom. He further stated, "I am empowered to receive you in the service of the Confederate States; the officers on their commissions, the men upon their enlistments."[22]

Sibley at this time may have been ready for the invasion, but Canby was faced with some serious difficulties. The morale in the Union forces in New Mexico was at a low ebb in the fall of 1861. Canby claimed that the principal cause of this was that the Federal soldiers had not been paid for more than a year. This neglect, he maintained, had caused a great deal of suffering and general dissatisfaction and had almost put an end to raising more troops. A few weeks later, in January, actual revolts did occur among some units of the native Volunteer militia at Fort Union and Camp Connelly. These were suppressed, and the escaped mutineers were pursued into the mountains. In desperation Canby made an unsuccessful attempt to borrow money for the government. Later, in order to obtain funds, he agreed with his chief commissary and chief quartermaster to pay all back bills with treasury notes bearing interest. He urgently requested Washington to redeem these promissory notes. Many of the leading capitalists and merchants of the Territory had pledged their credit for the repayment of the loan.

As late as January, 1862, Canby was not sure whether the Confederate attack would be made by way of the Río Grande or the Pecos River in the eastern part of the Territory. The different approaches were closely watched and the troops were

[22] *O.R.,* I, 4:89–90.

located so that they could concentrate at the vital points in twenty-four hours. He considered his regular soldiers in excellent condition, but he was doubtful regarding the stability of the New Mexican Volunteers. Governor Connelly, who had married into a prominent local family, on the other hand, had confidence in the native troops. By the end of 1861, the Governor estimated that there were 4,000 New Mexican militia and 1,500 regular soldiers stationed in various parts of the Territory.

In February, 1862, Colonel Canby reported from Fort Craig that 3,000 Confederates were moving up the Río Grande and that with the New Mexican militia he had 4,000 troops ready. The native population had now become more "animated."[23] Canby had been notified previously by an El Paso informant that the Southerners were poorly provisioned and armed. Their only hope was to invade New Mexico quickly to procure provisions. Sibley had on his staff an officer to receive confiscated property and had been supplied by Judge Simeon Hart, a Confederate capitalist, with a list of New Mexican capitalists who had property worth confiscating.

Sibley's soldiers may have been short on provisions, but many of them were experienced fighters. Among them were veterans of the Mexican and Indian wars. The Texans entertained a wholesome respect for the Union regular soldiers, but for the New Mexican militia they had only derision for a foe whom they had been bred to despise. Canby also had some crack veterans in his command, but there must have been some of his troops who were not so effective, as subsequent fighting demonstrated.

On January 27, 1862, while at Fort Thorn on their way up the Río Grande, Sibley ordered Captain Sherod Hunter, formerly of Baylor's command, with a company of Confederate cavalry, west to establish a post at Tucson for the "protection of . . . Western Arizona and . . . opening communication with Southern California."[24] Their arrival on February 28, 1862, at this old Spanish frontier outpost and occupation of the town

23 *Ibid.*, I, 9:632.
24 *Ibid.*, I, 4:170.

was hailed by the entire population, according to Hunter's official report.

On February 16, 1862, the Confederate army advanced up the Río Grande to within one mile of Fort Craig and challenged its Union garrison to an open-field fight. Colonel Canby declined the offer, reporting later to Washington that by so doing he hoped to bring on the battle in a position where his New Mexican troops, in whom he had little confidence, would not be obliged to maneuver under enemy fire. The Texans then withdrew seven miles below the fort and on the nineteenth they crossed to the east bank of the river. General Sibley's purpose was to bypass Fort Craig, which he felt was too strong to assault with his light artillery, and force a battle on ground of his own choosing at a ford in the river about six miles above the post. On the twentieth, while the Confederates were making a "dry camp" protected by a deep ravine about one and one-half miles east of the fort, Canby sent a detachment of Federal troops across the river and engaged the Texans in a brief skirmish. One Volunteer regiment, to the disgust of Canby, had been thrown into confusion by a "few harmless shells." This incident and the approach of darkness made it inexpedient to continue the attack.[25]

At times there is humor as well as tragedy in war. On the night of the twentieth, Captain James Graydon, known as "Paddy," who commanded a Union spy company, devised a plan which he thought would cause panic in the Confederate camp. With three or four men he lashed wooden boxes filled with howitzer shells to the backs of two old mules and crossed from Fort Craig to the east side of the river. Near the Confederate picket line, the fuses of the shells were lit and the mules headed toward the camp. However, to the consternation of "Paddy" and his pals, the mules turned around and followed the fleeing spies. The

[25] Raymond McCoy, "The Battle of Valverde," *New Mexico Magazine*, Vol. XXX, No. 9 (1952), 24. Fort Craig, now in ruins, located about four miles east of U. S. Highway 85, about thirty miles south of Socorro, New Mexico, consisted of twenty-two adobe and lava-rock buildings, occupying an area of about ten acres which was enclosed with an earthen and adobe wall pierced with holes for use of guns by the defenders of the fort.

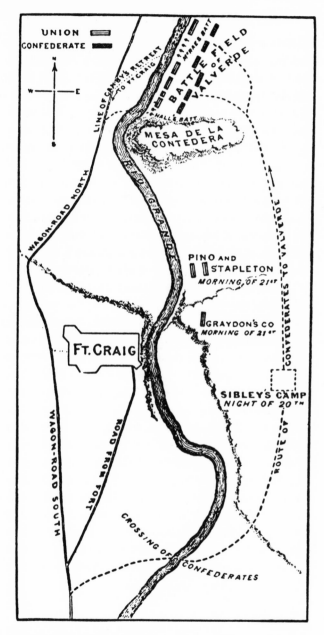

Map of the Fort Craig locality, showing the relative situation of the battlefield of Valverde to the fort. (From *Battles and Leaders of the Civil War* [1887].)

shells exploded well away from the men, but the Rebels awoke and manned their guns. Graydon's party made its way back to the fort minus two mules.[26] That same night about two hundred Confederate horses and mules broke away for want of water and were captured by the Union guards and brought into the post. The loss forced the Texas Fourth Regiment to abandon a number of wagons with supplies, blankets, and records.

The Battle of Valverde, fought on February 21, 1862, was the first major conflict between Union and Confederate forces in the Intermountain West. The Confederate army on the field that day consisted of all or portions of the Second, Fourth, Fifth, and Seventh Texas Mountain Volunteer Regiments and artillery under Captain T. T. Teel and Lieutenant John Riley.[27] The Federal forces at Valverde and at Fort Craig, February 21, were composed of the First, Second, and Third U. S. Cavalry, portions of the Fifth, Seventh, and Tenth U. S. Infantry, parts of the First, Second, Third, Fourth, and Fifth New Mexican Volunteers, Graydon's spy company, a company of Colorado Volunteers, and about one thousand hastily collected, unorganized militia.[28]

At 8:00 A.M., while a detachment of Sibley's men made what he termed "a strong threatening demonstration on the fort," the main body of Texans marched north toward the ford in the Río Grande at Valverde ("green valley"), about six miles above the post. When the Confederate movement was observed at Fort Craig, Colonel Canby ordered Colonel Benjamin S. Roberts with a detachment of regular and Volunteer cavalry to dash up the west bank and resist the efforts of the Rebels to cross the river and cut the supply route to the fort. He was followed immediately by artillery and infantry detachments. Graydon's spy command and several companies of mounted New Mexican militia under Colonels Miguel G. Pino and Robert H. Stapleton had

[26] George H. Pettis, "Confederate Invasion of New Mexico and Arizona," *Battles and Leaders of the Civil War,* II, 105–106.

[27] Sibley reported there was a total of 1,750 Texans engaged, while the enemy had 3,500 on the field, 1,200 of whom were regulars.

[28] Canby reported a Union total of 3,810 men on the field and at Fort Craig; Confederate Army, 3,000 men, reduced to 2,600 by sickness and absent detachments.

previously crossed the river directly east of the fort to scout the movements of the Confederates.[29]

When Colonel Roberts, with his men, arrived at the river crossing, they found that a Confederate detachment of 180 troops under Major Charles L. Pyron, Second Texas Regiment, had already reached the river. After watering their horses, the Rebels then occupied a large grove of cottonwood trees near the stream. The battle opened when Major Thomas Duncan, with four companies of Union cavalry, crossed the river, where they dismounted. Rapid firing immediately began. After a sharp and spirited skirmish, the Texans were driven back from the cottonwoods to higher ground. This permitted Roberts to set up his artillery, consisting of four field guns of Captain Alexander McRae's battery and two twenty-four-pound howitzers under Lieutenant Robert H. Hall, on the west bank of the Río Grande. At 10:00 A.M. the Federal guns commenced firing across the river at the Confederates advancing from the southeast toward the stream. The Union batteries were supported by Captain David H. Brotherton's company of the Fifth U. S. Infantry and Major Duncan's skirmishers.[30]

About an hour later, Lieutenant Colonel William R. Scurry, with half of his Fourth Texas Regiment, accompanied by a light howitzer battery under Lieutenant John Riley, arrived on the field. A bitter rifle and artillery fire developed, during which the Rebels made a desperate effort to retake the cottonwood grove, but without success. Around noon, Roberts was reinforced by the arrival of a Yankee infantry battalion under Captain Henry R. Seldon, including troops under Captains Benjamin Wingate and P. W. L. Plympton, and a company of Second Colorado Volunteers under Captain Theodore H. Dodd. Colonel "Kit" Carson's Regiment (eight companies) of New Mexican Volun-

[29] Valverde Battlefield is located about three miles east of U. S. Highway 85, approximately 100 miles south of Albuquerque, N. M., and 170 miles north of El Paso, Texas. It is bordered on the west by the Río Grande River, with San Marcial Lake near by, and on the south of Black Mesa (*Mesa del Contadero* in battle reports), which rises about three hundred feet in the air.

[30] Sibley wrote that Pyron had 250 men when the fighting started.

teers arrived soon after and were sent on up the west side of the river to forestall a threatened flanking attack by five hundred Confederate cavalrymen. Captain Seldon's command was ordered to wade the Río Grande farther upstream and charge the Texans with bayonets. This Rebel detachment had occupied a wooded area on the Union left. Reaching the eastern bank of the river, the water-soaked Yankees drove the Confederates from their position. Seldon's detachment was then faced with a furious counterattack by Captain W. L. Lang's company of lancers, Fifth Texas Regiment. The charging horsemen were quickly hurled back with severe losses.[31]

Ovando J. Hollister, a Colorado private, describing the charge which was directed at the Second Colorado Volunteer Infantry, located on the extreme Federal left, wrote that each Texan was armed with a lance having a blade three inches wide and twelve inches long, mounted on a nine-foot shaft. A red guidon was tacked to each lance to "drink the blood" of the victim impaled. Coming in three columns at full speed, "they looked as if the Devil had set them on end." As they approached, Captain Dodd shouted, "They are Texans. Give them Hell. And they did." Some of the lancers came near enough to be transfixed and lifted from their saddles with bayonets, but the "greater part bit the dust" before their lances could be used. Only three Texas lancers remained unhurt, while forty-two dead horses were strewn over the battlefield.[32]

Confederate Colonel Thomas Green reported that the lancer charge was "one of the most gallant and furious charges . . . ever witnessed in the annals of battles." His fellow-officer, Lieutenant Colonel Scurry, related that the "desperate courage [of the lancers] was ineffectual against great odds and superior arms." These two companies suffered the greatest loss during the battle, proportional to their numbers, of any units in their respective armies.[33]

[31] *O.R.*, I, 9:489–90, 495, 514, 518–19.
[32] Ovando J. Hollister, *Boldly They Rode*, 110.
[33] Scurry and Green recorded that the lancer charge was made at 3:00 P.M., while Roberts' report indicated that it occurred about 1:00 P.M.

Meanwhile, most of the troops of both armies were drawn up on the battlefield. The Northern forces were grouped on both sides of the Río Grande. The Southern lines extended parallel to the enemy east of the river. Some of their detachments were posted several hundred yards back from the river. General Sibley, claiming illness, retired to an ambulance behind the lines at 1:00 P.M. and turned the command during the battle over to Colonel Thomas Green.[34]

After Seldon's Union column had forced the Confederate right wing and the Colorado troops had repulsed the Texas lancers, Colonel Roberts felt secure in moving the Federal artillery to the east bank of the river, where McRae's batteries were posted on the Union left and Hall's howitzers on the right. The Yankee artillery then renewed the cannonading, which, with the rifle fire from Seldon's and Duncan's commands, forced several Confederate units back behind the sand hills. The Rebels rallied and renewed their assault with vigor. A sloping approach toward the river from the south and east, covered with trees and ridges of sand farther back, permitted the Southern officers to concentrate their men almost unobserved.

The arrival of Texan Captain T. T. Teel on the Rebel's right wing at 1:00 P.M. with the guns of his battery precipitated an artillery duel. The Yankee fire was so heavy that Teel's gun crews were soon reduced to five men, and the Captain was compelled to assist in ramming and loading the guns. A Federal cannon ball, exploding under one of his guns, set the grass on fire, but he and his reduced crew still held on as best they could. Later, when more of the Confederate batteries arrived on the field, Teel was dispatched with them to assist Major Pyron, who was hard pressed on the Texas left wing. Because of the shorter range of the Rebel guns, it was eventually decided to reserve their fire until the Yankees came within their range. By this time three Confederate guns were disabled.

[34] Ralph E. Twitchell, *Leading Facts of New Mexican History*, 377, stated that he was told by a Confederate soldier who fought at Valverde that Sibley was so drunk that day that he couldn't direct the Southern troops.

Colonel Edward R. S. Canby remained at Fort Craig until afternoon, when he became satisfied that the battle plans of the Confederates were developing. The entire Texan force, with the exception of a camp guard, was then moving toward the river crossing at Valverde. Canby recalled Pino's New Mexican regiment from its scouting position opposite the fort with orders to advance up the west bank of the river to the battle area. Then, leaving a detachment to guard the post, Canby proceeded with a company of cavalry and the remaining section of McRae's battery to the battlefield. Arriving about 2:45 P.M., he assumed full command. After making a reconnaissance, he determined to force the left side of the Confederate line with the Union right and center and through a pivot movement drive the Texans from the field. Carson's New Mexican regiment and Pino's troops, who now had reached the west bank opposite Valverde, were both ordered to cross the river and join the Union forces on the east side. However, five companies of the New Mexican Volunteers under Pino, himself a brave man, refused to cross the stream.

While the Federal army was maneuvering under Canby's orders, the Confederates, screened by woods and sand hills, reorganized their forces with a desperate resolve to charge the Union batteries. Concealing their movements, the Southerners formed two storming parties. These were not discovered by the Union leaders until a yelling mass of 250 Rebels, under Major Henry W. Ragnet, armed with shotguns, squirrel rifles, revolvers, and lances, charged down the hill on foot at Lieutenant Hall's batteries on the southern end of the Union line. This charge was repulsed with a heavy loss to the Confederates through support given these batteries by Major Duncan's dismounted cavalry, regular infantry under Captains Wingate, Ingraham, and Brotherton, Graydon's spy company and part of "Kit" Carson's New Mexican Volunteers. Whitford claimed that Carson shot several of his own men who attempted from cowardice to desert and run.

The results were different on the Union left. Suddenly about

750 shouting Texans, armed like their fellow-fighters on their left with death-dealing double-barreled shotguns, rifles, pistols, and machetes, charged on foot about seven hundred yards down the slope through a storm of grape-shot, canister, and musketry toward McRae's batteries, which were supported by Captain Plympton's battalion of regulars and that part of Pino's Volunteers who had crossed the river. The Rebels were directed and cheered from the rear by Lieutenant Colonel Scurry. Major S. A. Lockridge led the charge. As they neared the guns, a Confederate officer shouted, "Surrender, McRae, we don't want to kill you!" In response, this gallant officer, with one arm shattered, leaning against the breech of one of the guns, replied, "I shall never forsake my guns."[35] Lockridge placed his hand on the muzzle of the same gun. Both raised their revolvers, fired at each other, and fell dead across the gun, their blood flowing along its surface. There was a furious hand-to-hand fight with revolvers, clubbed rifles, bayonets, and knives,[36] but part of the Union support, consisting of two companies of regulars and of Volunteers, soon fell back in spite of severe orders from Colonel Canby. Captain Wingate's battalion, swinging hurriedly from support of Hall's batteries to support of McRae's, helped to check temporarily the charging Rebels, but they rapidly regathered their forces and dashed on, and were soon in full possession of McRae's batteries.

Colonel Canby, whose horse had been shot from under him, could see that further Union action was futile. He ordered all of his troops which were still on the east side of the Río Grande

[35] William Clarke Whitford, *Colorado Volunteers in the Civil War*, 64–65; *O.R.*, I, 9:490, 520. *Santa Fe Weekly Gazette*, August 22, 1868, related that Captain Alexander McRae was from a prominent North Carolina family, but remained loyal to the Union although his family disowned him. In 1867 his grave, which had been unattended by his family for five years, was opened by the United States Army and his remains were taken across the country and reburied, with honors, at West Point, his alma mater.

[36] Pettis, "Confederate Invasion," *Battles and Leaders of the Civil War*, II, 108; Whitford, *Colorado Volunteers*, 140. Confederate Captain T. T. Teel, years later, claimed there was no duel between McRae and Lockridge. After they had removed McRae's body from the gun, they found all chambers of his revolver loaded.

to cross to the west bank and return to Fort Craig. The lost battery and the guns of Captain Teel were then turned on the retreating Union forces. Several Union soldiers were killed or wounded while in the stream. The Confederates captured, in addition to McRae's batteries, a considerable amount of small arms, provisions, and equipment.[37] The Union retreat, covered by Captain H. R. Seldon with four companies of the U. S. Fifth Infantry, across the river and back to the fort by the regulars and Colorado Volunteers was accomplished in fairly good order, but many of the New Mexican troops, according to Canby, were "in the wildest confusion." More than one hundred men from one regiment deserted from the field.[38]

The battle was a victory for the South, but the losses were about the same, each side losing in killed and wounded more than two hundred men. In proportion to the number of troops engaged, the casualties in the Battle of Valverde were unusually high. Colonel Roberts reported they were unexampled in any battle fought on this continent. The reports of the losses on both sides are at variance. Even the leaders on each side disagreed. The facts probably lie somewhere between the two extremes.[39]

Each army spent the next two days under flags of truce, taking

[37] *O.R.,* I, 9:520. Whitford, *Colorado Volunteers,* 138, related that at the close of the New Mexican campaign, Sibley's retreating men dragged McRae's battery, consisting of four twelve-pound and two six-pound brass guns back to Texas. Five of the guns, known as the Valverde Battery, were later used in General "Dick" Taylor's Confederate Army. The sixth, the barrel of which long retained the bloodstains of McRae and Lockridge, was left at El Paso because of a shot-weakened axle.

In August, 1953, Mr. Maury Kemp, a local historian of El Paso, informed me that the gun remained at the City Hall until the Mexican Revolution of 1911, when it was stolen at the suggestion of an American, Dr. Ira A. Bush, and taken across the Río Grande to Juárez, Mexico. There it was used by Madero's troops against those of Díaz. Later it was returned to the San Jacinta Plaza, El Paso, where it remained until World War II, when it was hauled away in the scrap drive.

[38] *Ibid.,* I, 9:491.

[39] *Ibid.,* I, 9:493, Colonel Canby reported Union losses as 68 killed, 160 wounded, 34 missing. Captain Gurden Chapin, I, 9:634, Federal losses, 62 killed, 140 wounded; enemy, 150 killed, 450 wounded. Dr. Basil Norris, I, 9:647, Union losses, 56 killed, 147 wounded, 17 of whom died later. General Sibley, I, 9:506, enemy losses, 300 killed and wounded; Confederates, 40 killed, 100 wounded. Colonel Thomas Green, I, 9:521–22. Confederate losses, 36 killed, 150 wounded; enemy, 350–400 killed and wounded.

care of their wounded and burying their dead on the battlefield near the Río Grande. Colonel William Steele, carrying a flag of truce for the Confederacy, went to Fort Craig personally to request medical and hospital supplies for the wounded men. These were furnished at once by Canby's orders. The wounded Union soldiers were taken to Fort Craig. The Confederate wounded were taken up the river to Socorro and Albuquerque.

Efforts to place the responsibility for this defeat brought conflicting reports from the various Union leaders. Colonel Canby claimed that the immediate cause was the refusal of the native militia and Volunteer regiments to cross the river and support the Federal left wing. "The battle was fought," he reported, "almost entirely by the regular troops (trebled in number by the Confederates) with no assistance from the militia and but little from the volunteers." He stated also that large numbers of the militia and Volunteers had deserted, but that this added to rather than diminished their strength.[40] He further explained that the Confederate Army, in addition to having superiority in numbers, also had superior mobility of its force, which was all mounted. Captain Gurden Chapin reported, "No dependence whatever can be placed on the natives; they are worse than worthless; they are really aids to the enemy, who catch them, take their arms, and tell them to go home." Major James L. Donaldson wrote that the New Mexican Volunteers could not be relied on because of their "traditional fear of the Texans" and that they would not face them in battle. Governor Henry Connelly, who was at Fort Craig during the battle, partially absolved the native troops which he claimed followed the example of two regular companies that had refused to charge.[41]

Colonel Canby and his staff were not without blame. Captain George H. Pettis wrote that it was almost the unanimous opinion of the officers at Fort Craig that it would have been a Union victory if Colonel Canby had remained at the fort, leaving Colonel Roberts in command on the field. Colonel Roberts blamed

[40] *Ibid.*, I, 9:487.
[41] *Ibid.*, I, 9:942, 634, 636, 638.

35

the misfortunes of the battle on his fellow-officers, who did not seize the position near the ford as ordered. An officer on "Kit" Carson's staff contended that victory was within their grasp at Valverde, but the battle was lost by mismanagement.[42]

An important factor in the defeat of the Union forces, reported by General Sibley, was the spirit, valor, and determination of the Texas troops, who with double-barreled shotguns charged on and captured the Federal batteries. The ferocity of the Confederates chilled the courage of the Union regulars as well as putting to flight the New Mexico Volunteers and militia. In April, 1862, Canby, by then a brigadier general, was authorized to discharge the New Mexican Volunteers whenever he deemed it necessary to do so. Governor Connelly admitted in his report to Secretary Seward that the militia could best be used in preparing their lands for the coming harvest.

Immediately after the battle, General Sibley and Colonel Canby consulted their officers about the next move. The following morning Sibley sent Lieutenant Colonel Scurry, Lieutenant Tom P. Ochiltree, and Captain D. W. Shannon under a flag of truce with a demand for the surrender of Fort Craig. Colonel Canby defiantly refused. Whitford reported that the commission considered the fort too strongly defended to be taken by assault or siege at the time. The Texans were deceived about the number and caliber of the real cannon mounted on its bastions. Some of these were metal, but the large-sized ones were wooden "Quaker guns."[43] Confederate deserters stated that during a council among Sibley's men, two days after the battle, some of the more daring officers pressed for an attack on the fort, but the enlisted men refused to place their lives in such imminent danger, contending that such a move would bring defeat and dispersion of the whole invading force.

General Sibley and his staff were now faced with the alternatives of attacking Fort Craig, turning back, or marching up

[42] Hayes, *New Colorado*, 170.
[43] Whitford, *Colorado Volunteers*, 68. Tom P. Ochiltree later became governor of Texas and a member of Congress.

the Río Grande. They were in a precarious situation. There was a shortage of food and military supplies. Finally, it was decided to march up the river, supplying the army with what could be confiscated from the Union commissary stores and garrisons along the way, as well as what could be secured from the native population. The Southerners had little fear of the Northern forces at this time. But a quarrel developed between Sibley and Lieutenant Colonel Baylor which ultimately weakened the Confederate leadership in New Mexico and Arizona. Baylor called Sibley an "infamous coward and a disgrace to the Confederate States." He accused him of having doubled himself up in an ambulance during the Battle of Valverde and hoisting a hospital flag over it for his protection.[44]

The Federal forces were in serious difficulties. The victorious Confederates were not only threatening to overrun the whole territory, but were now between Fort Craig and its source of supplies. Canby admitted defeat, but emphasized that he and his men were not dispirited. The Union leaders had three choices of action: first, to hold Fort Craig, await the arrival of reinforcements, and block the enemy on a retreat from northern New Mexico down the Río Grande; second, to abandon the Fort and throw its garrison above the Texans to impede their progress and later unite with any Union troops that might be found above; third, to bring on another battle with the Confederates in the immediate vicinity. Canby and his officers agreed upon the first plan. The New Mexican Volunteers and militia were sent north in front of the Confederates to impede and obstruct their movements.

The Texans, having formulated their plan of action, rapidly moved north up the river on their invasion, where provisions such as "breadstuff and meat" could be procured. At Socorro, on February 25, the remnant of the Second Regiment of New Mexican Volunteers under Colonel Nicolás Pino surrendered and took the oath of neutrality administered by the Confederates. In advance of the Confederate column were the Union quartermaster

[44] Richard E. Sloan and Warren R. Adams, *History of Arizona*, I, 257.

and commissary officers with orders to remove or destroy any Federal property that might fall into the hands of the invaders. There was a large store of supplies at Albuquerque under Captain Herbert M. Enos, assistant quartermaster. When he learned on March 1 that the Confederates were only thirty-five miles away, he ordered all of the ammunition and ordnance supplies that could be loaded in what wagons were available taken to Santa Fe. Early the following morning, the buildings containing the supplies that could not be removed were set on fire, but before the destruction was completed, many of the provisions were rescued by the local inhabitants. Three of the wagons were captured en route by deserters from the militia and Volunteers.

Arriving at Albuquerque on March 2, 1862, the Texans raised their flag in the plaza and took possession of the town in the name of the Confederate States of America. Four Confederates appeared at Cubero, sixty miles west of Albuquerque, and demanded the surrender of the post. The garrison of forty-two New Mexican Volunteers surrendered without firing a shot, thus permitting sixty muskets, three thousand rounds of ammunition, and other ordnance supplies to fall into the hands of Sibley's men. Having secured all of the available supplies in and near Albuquerque, Major Charles L. Pyron was dispatched with his command to Santa Fe, where the most valuable and useful supplies were located.

Major J. L. Donaldson, Union quartermaster, commanding a small force at the capital, anticipated this move and, on March 4, sent forward to Fort Union a train of 120 wagons valued at $250,000. These were escorted by the entire Federal force at Santa Fe. Most of the buildings containing the remaining government stores were then fired, Donaldson giving strict orders that none should be destroyed that would endanger the safety of the city by fire. Governor Henry Connelly was compelled to abandon Santa Fe also and establish temporarily the territorial government at Las Vegas.

On March 10 the vanguard of the Confederate Army entered the capital. Either deliberately or coincidentally, this group

Brigadier General Henry H. Sibley, commander of the Confederate forces in New Mexico, 1862.

Brigadier General Edward R. S. Canby, Union commander, Department of New Mexico, 1861–62.

Fort Craig in ruins.

Western entrance of Apache Canyon, New Mexico, in 1906.

*From Whitford's* Colorado Volunteers

was composed of eleven former residents of Santa Fe, who had joined the Texans at Mesilla. Three days later Major Charles L. Pyron's command arrived in the city, and the Confederates hoisted their flag over the Old Palace, which then served as the governor's mansion. On March 13, General H. H. Sibley issued a proclamation at Albuquerque addressed to the "People of New Mexico" which was distributed throughout the area now occupied by the invaders. In it he proudly called attention to the Confederate victory at Valverde, which he claimed proved the truth of his assertions in his first proclamation on December 20, 1861, regarding the powers and ability to accomplish the purposes which he then had declared. He offered amnesty to all of those New Mexicans in the Federal Army who would lay down their arms in ten days. He stated that the conduct of his expedition since entrance into the Territory attested to the honesty and integrity of its purposes. He promised protection to the citizens and urged them to go back to their homes and their respective vocations.[45]

During their march from Valverde to Santa Fe, none of the Texan detachments met with any armed resistance, but they were disappointed by the cool, even hostile, attitude of a majority of the local people. The invaders largely subsisted "on the country" as they passed through. Especially at Albuquerque, Cubero, and Santa Fe, all available commissary stores, forage, and clothing supplies were seized by the Confederates, thereby providing a supply for about three months. The conquerors exacted money and confiscated property from New Mexican families known to favor the Federal cause. Two Armijo brothers, who were Southern sympathizers, placed their merchandise valued at $200,000 at the disposal of Colonel Sibley's troops.

The *Santa Fe Weekly Gazette*, which was controlled by the Confederates from March 22 until they retreated from the capital, later charged that the seizures were "strangely inconsistent" with Sibley's proclamation of December 20, 1861. On the same page and in the column adjoining the General's proclamation of

45 *Santa Fe Weekly Gazette*, April 26, 1862.

39

March 13, there was printed a report that the stores of Messrs. Clark and Spiegelberg Brothers had been appropriated by the Texans. It related that many Albuquerque citizens had left their homes for quarters in which they could feel more secure. It also reported that the General, while in Santa Fe, had ordered the seizure of all funds in the territorial treasury, and accused him of appropriating the money for either his "private use or for some other purpose."[46] Governor Henry Connelly, whose home ninety miles from Santa Fe was despoiled of its entire contents, bitterly condemned the Texans for their exactions and confiscations from the local citizens. Citing Don Pedro José Perea, a gentleman eighty years old, as an example, the Governor related that he and his three sons were threatened with personal violence by the Confederates if their demand for a large sum of money was not met.[47]

Theophilus Noel, a Confederate soldier in Sibley's expedition, later became ashamed of their actions during this phase of the invasion. He wrote that at Albuquerque the torch was applied to more than six million dollars' worth of commissary, quartermaster, and medical supplies without reason, except that the Texans were getting drunk on the confiscated whiskey and their commander was never sober. He related that at Santa Fe the "burning act was repeated where in less than five days we were suffering the agonies of starvation from our own acts of vandalism."[48]

The Confederate campaign had reached its zenith. The major portions of New Mexico and Arizona were now under Southern control. The capital, Santa Fe, and most of the towns of the territory were dominated by the conquerors. With the supplies running low and the majority of the New Mexicans indifferent to the Southern cause, if not actually hostile, the invaders could not remain idle. General Sibley determined to advance on Fort Union, northeast of Santa Fe, and if possible capture its great

[46] *Ibid.*, April 26, 1862.
[47] *O.R.*, I, 9:651–52.
[48] Noel, *Autobiography*, 61–62.

stores of military supplies. Sibley had supervised the construction of the arsenal and storage buildings at that post a few years before. With the exception of Fort Craig, this fort was the last remaining obstacle of importance to the Confederates' obtaining possession of nearly all of New Mexico, and its conquest would mean a step nearer to the mines in Colorado.

The military fortunes of the Union forces in the Intermountain West, on the other hand, were at their lowest ebb. Colonel Canby had requested reinforcements repeatedly. Finally the Federal government and the commanding generals in the Middle West were becoming conscious of the seriousness of the Confederate invasion of New Mexico, but the delay was almost disastrous. On February 10, 1862, Major General David Hunter at Fort Leavenworth, Kansas, requested Acting Governor Lewis W. Weld of Colorado to send all available troops to Colonel Canby.

On March 20, Secretary of War Edwin M. Stanton approved the suggestion of Major General H. W. Halleck at St. Louis, Missouri, that reinforcements be sent to Canby in New Mexico. The next day Halleck recommended that a column of four to five thousand men be sent to New Mexico and that Colonel Canby be made a brigadier general. Captain Gurden Chapin, on February 28, reported from Santa Fe to General Halleck that "It is needless to say that this country is in a critical condition. . . . A force of Colorado Volunteers is already on the way to assist us, and they may possibly arrive in time to save us from immediate danger."[49]

[49] *O.R.*, I, 9:634.

# 3

## Colorado to the Rescue

WHILE THE Confederate Army was preparing to attack Fort
Union, the First Regiment of the Colorado Volunteers was
marching rapidly from Denver. Colorado had been settled by
pioneers from the North and the South. At the outbreak of the
Civil War, the Territory was torn between the two factions.
On April 24, 1861, the Stars and Bars of the Confederacy were
run up over the store of Wallingford and Murphy on Larimer
Street in Denver. A belligerent crowd gathered. Samuel B. Logan, a Union supporter, promptly climbed on top of the building
and tore the flag down. For a few tense minutes it looked as if
a local civil war would result, but with the Union men in majority the crowd subsided without bloodshed. This was the first
and last time the Southern emblem waved over Colorado, and
this waving was so brief that it failed to remove the wrinkles
from the flag. The incident brought the Union spirit out with
full force.

Colorado's first governor, William Gilpin, arrived at Denver
on May 27, 1861. He realized that prompt and decisive action
was necessary to save the Territory for the Union and to supply
troops to resist the threatened invasion of the Confederates
through New Mexico. He appointed a military staff and authorized the purchase of arms and ammunition from local citizens.
He ordered the arrest of Confederate sympathizers, who were
also buying guns.[1] The Governor sent Samuel S. Curtis, son of

[1] William J. Barker, in "The Forgotten War for the West," *Denver Post*
(Magazine Section), November 6, 1949, wrote "Actually, the Confederate sympathizers accomplished very little. They managed to break up a few Union enlistment meetings, obtained a miscellaneous pile of weapons which were not
standard and therefore virtually useless for war. The raids they attempted on
wagon trains made for better Union propaganda than anything else. By the fall

General S. R. Curtis, to distant Fort Laramie for military supplies. Early in the summer of 1861 a request was made to the Secretary of War for permission to organize several companies of infantry or cavalry to be used in the service of the North. For some reason this request was ignored. Nevertheless, the Governor, in co-operation with several prominent citizens, went ahead with plans to organize a militia.

In July, 1861, recruiting offices were opened in towns and mining camps throughout the Territory. A military campsite was selected about two miles south of the center of Denver which was called Camp Weld in honor of Territorial Secretary Lewis L. Weld. Barracks were built on it at a cost of $40,000, exclusive of the labor of the soldiers. Eight hundred thousand feet of lumber and thirty thousand bricks were used in the construction.[2] Ten companies were raised to comprise the First Regiment of the Colorado Volunteers. John P. Slough, a Denver attorney, was commissioned colonel and Samuel F. Tappan, lieutenant colonel. John M. Chivington, the presiding elder of the Methodist church in Denver, refused the offer of chaplain, preferring a strictly fighting position. He was then chosen major. Reverend J. H. Kelher was appointed chaplain and Dr. John F. Hamilton, surgeon.[3] The *Rocky Mountain News* of October 24, 1861, described the daily camp program as follows:

Reveille at daylight, and breakfast call at 7 o'clock. Guard mount at 8 and company drill at 9 A.M. Battalion drill at 2½ P.M., and Dress

of 1861 most of those favoring the Southern cause dropped away and joined the Confederate armies."

[2] The site of Camp Weld is marked today with a granite slab and a tablet at West Eighth Avenue and Vallejo Street, Denver, Colorado.

[3] John P. Slough was originally from Ohio, where he was a Democrat member of the legislature. His part in recruiting Denver's Company A and his activity in forming the regiment, led to his appointment as colonel. Samuel F. Tappan, appointed as lieutenant colonel, had been recruiting captain in Central City's and Black Hawk's Company B. John M. Chivington, also from Ohio, six feet, five, and "strong as a bull elephant," was appointed major and later colonel. He possessed a powerful voice which could be heard Sunday mornings "three blocks from the Methodist Church." He was known as the "fighten preacher" against whom the Devil had "mighty poor odds."

Parade a half hour before sundown. Tatoo at 8½ P.M. and at 9 lights are extinguished and all visitors withdraw from camp.

The men of the regiment were for the most part well qualified for military duty in the West. Their lives on the frontier had made them hardy, individualistic, self-reliant, and accustomed to danger. They were loyal to the Union and eager to go to the front, but they did not take kindly to the restraints of military discipline when there was no fighting to be done. Often, individuals and even groups of men were placed under arrest for insubordination, disturbing the peace in Denver, petty larceny, and activities bordering on mutiny. The final order to march was welcomed by all, preventing perhaps the disintegration of the regiment. The regulation government military equipment failed to arrive for some time, thus compelling nearly every man to drill with different kind of gun. When the specified arms did arrive, they were few in number and inferior in quality. Late in the autumn of 1861, three companies of the Colorado First Regiment were dispatched under the command of Lieutenant Colonel Tappan to Fort Wise, two hundred miles southeast of Denver. The seven other companies remained at Camp Weld with Major Chivington directly in charge.

One of the most serious problems that faced Governor Gilpin was that of financing the militia. The Federal government had not placed a war fund at the Governor's disposal. He therefore met the emergency in the method that he felt to be proper and justified, issuing negotiable drafts on the national treasury which were readily acceptable in Colorado on the presumption that they would be paid when they reached Washington. Some of them were even passed as currency. A total of about $375,000 worth was issued. When the drafts reached Washington, they were repudiated by the Federal government. Eventually, a large part of these drafts were paid, but Governor Gilpin was dismissed for overstepping his authority.

When it was learned in Denver that Sibley's army was advancing from Fort Bliss, Texas, an attempt was made to induce

Major General David Hunter, commander at Fort Leavenworth, Headquarters Department of Kansas, of which Colorado was a part, to order more Colorado troops to the assistance of Colonel Canby in New Mexico. It was not until February 10, 1862, more than a month later, that General Hunter sent the following dispatch to Acting Governor Lewis L. Weld:

> Send all available forces you can possibly spare to reinforce Colonel Canby, commanding Department of New Mexico, and to keep open his communication through Fort Wise. Act promptly and with all the discretion of your latest information as to what may be necessary and where the troops of Colorado can do most service.[4]

On February 13, 1862, orders were received at Camp Weld for the First Colorado Volunteer Regiment to prepare to march. This news was received with great enthusiasm, and preparations for departure were eagerly made. The troops at Camp Weld marched out of Denver on February 22, the day following the Union defeat at Valverde. The other companies of the regiment under Tappan departed from Fort Wise on March 3. The First Colorado now consisted of the following companies and their respective commanders: Company A, Captain Edward W. Wynkoop; B, Captain Samuel M. Logan; C, Captain Richard Sopris; D, Captain Jacob Downing; E, Captain Scott J. Anthony; F, a cavalry unit, Captain Samuel H. Cook; G, Captain William F. Wilder; H, Captain George L. Sanborn; I, mostly Germans, Captain Charles Mailie; K, Captain Samuel H. Robbins.[5]

The dreary march in freezing weather was made through a section of the rugged Rocky Mountains where little more than a rough path or broken wagon road existed until the Santa Fe Trail was reached. It was not until the companies from Camp Weld had reached Pueblo and those from Fort Wise had arrived at old Fort Bent, both on the Arkansas River, that it was learned that the Union troops had been defeated at Valverde and that the Confederate columns were triumphantly marching

[4] *O.R.*, I, 9:630.
[5] Whitford, *Colorado Volunteers*, 48–50.

up the Río Grande. Leaving behind everything except actual necessities, the Colorado troops advanced as rapidly as they could. Although they had to trudge through several inches of snow, they were able to travel about forty miles a day. The columns were united on the Purgatoire River, near the present city of Trinidad.

In the evening of March 8, after a strenuous day of toilsome climbing Raton Pass, they were met by a courier from Colonel G. R. Paul, commander at Fort Union, with the startling information that General Sibley's troops were already in possession of Albuquerque and Santa Fe. The Rebels were now planning to attack that fort, in which there were only about eight hundred Yankee regulars and New Mexican Volunteers to defend it. On a stirring appeal to the regiment to render speedy aid to Fort Union, all of the men expressed their willingness to continue without delay. Carrying only their arms and blankets, they pushed on in the darkness over a rough, unfamiliar route, thirty miles to the Cimarron River. Here they were compelled to halt from sheer exhaustion. They had marched sixty-seven miles since the morning before and ninety-two in the previous thirty-six hours. Some of their animals, pulling the baggage wagons, dropped dead in their harness because of overwork and underfeeding. Only one or two companies were mounted for scouting purposes. Most of the men walked the entire distance. After a brief rest, the Volunteers proceeded on through bitter cold and a mountain hurricane. Arriving at Fort Union on March 10, they were welcomed by Colonel Paul and his men and by Governor Henry Connelly.

The Colorado Volunteers had made the phenomenal march of over four hundred miles in thirteen days. The Governor, in reporting the arrival of Colonel Slough with 950 men, stated that from all accounts they could "be relied upon." He added that the New Mexican militia had all dispersed.[6] The Colorado Regiment remained at Fort Union for twelve days, during which time they were supplied with regulation uniforms, arms, and

[6] *O.R.*, I, 9:645.

ammunition from the government stores. Daily drills were held, but again, because they were endowed with such rugged energy, the Volunteers found it hard to endure the routine and discipline of garrison life. The tendency toward lawlessness still existed among some of them. One evening while in the act of arresting Sergeant Philbrook for drunkenness and noise, Lieutenant Isaac Gray of B Company was shot in the face, but later recovered. Philbrook was subsequently court-martialed and executed.[7] Colonel Canby, who had not learned of the arrival, on March 16, of the Pikes Peakers from Denver, instructed Colonel Paul to hold Fort Union if at all possible and to destroy Fort Garland in Colorado if the enemy moved north.[8]

Upon arrival at Fort Union, Colonel Slough assumed command of all of the troops at that post through the seniority of his volunteer commission. His claim of authority was a blow to Colonel Paul's ego. Paul requested Army Headquarters in Washington to grant him a promotion to brigadier general. There also arose a difference of opinion between Slough and Paul regarding the interpretation of Colonel Canby's orders. Colonel Paul claimed that Canby's orders meant that all troops were to remain at Fort Union until further instructions were received from the Department commander toward effecting a junction between the Federal forces in northern and southern New Mexico.

Colonel Slough maintained that he was empowered by Canby to be governed by his own judgment and discretion. He held that his instructions permitted him to act independently against the enemy if he was joined by a sufficient force. He claimed that his orders were to harass the enemy, obstruct their movements, and cut their supplies. He contended that by advancing over approximately the same route the Confederates would travel to reach the fort, the Union forces could defend it as well as by staying at the post. Such action would also draw the enemy away from Santa Fe and thus protect it from depredation. In

7 *Rocky Mountain News*, March 27, 1862; Hollister, *Boldly They Rode*, 53–56.
8 *O.R.*, I, 9:653.

spite of Colonel Paul's protest, on March 22, 1862, the Union army began its march toward Santa Fe by way of Las Vegas.

Colonel Slough's command as it left Fort Union consisted of all of the First Regiment of Colorado Volunteers, Ford's company of the Second Colorado Regiment, a battalion of the U. S. Fifth Infantry under Captain W. G. Lewis, a detachment of cavalry from the First and Third U. S. Cavalry, commanded by Captain George W. Howland, one company from the Fourth New Mexican Volunteers, artillery composed of a battery of four guns under Captain J. F. Ritter, Fifteenth U. S. Infantry, and four mountain howitzers, commanded by Lieutenant Ira W. Claflin. This made a total of 1,342 men, of whom about 75 per cent were from Colorado. A small number of regulars and New Mexican Volunteers, considered sufficient to guard the fort, were left under the command of Colonel Paul. Two days later this army arrived at Bernal Springs, about fifty miles southwest of the fort.[9]

Meanwhile, the Confederates were looking forward eagerly to the capture of Fort Union. They considered that they could win a fairly easy victory, unaware that the Colorado troops were in New Mexico. General Sibley anticipated little interference from Colonel Canby and his men, who had been bypassed at Fort Craig. Major Charles L. Pyron of the Second Texas Mounted Rifles, after leading the Rebel vanguard into Santa Fe, was reinforced with four companies from the Fifth Texas Cavalry under Major John S. Shropshire, and then moved toward Fort Union. Colonel William R. Scurry with the Fourth Texas Regiment and the First Battalion, Seventh Texas Mounted Volunteers, commanded by Major Powhatan Jordan, were dispatched to Galisteo, northeast of Albuquerque. These forces were to be united on the road between Santa Fe and Fort Union. Colonel Thomas Green with the remaining part of the Fifth Regiment, being handicapped for lack of transportation, was held back a few days to check any movement from Fort Craig.

[9] Most of the information for this chapter comes from the *Official Report*, I, 9:509–654.

# 4

# Glorieta, the Gettysburg of the West

TWENTY MILES SOUTHEAST of Santa Fe, at the southern tip of
the Sangre de Cristo Range in the Rocky Mountain cordillera,
nature has carved a passageway known as Glorieta Pass, which
extends for several miles from northwest to southeast. Early
Spanish settlers called it *La Glorieta* because of the dense and
beautiful growths of cottonwood and pine trees along the arroyos
and up the slopes. Apache Canyon, named after the powerful
tribe of Indians which terrorized the Southwest for decades, cuts
through the hills at the western section of the pass. Glorieta Pass,
compared to the Brenner Pass in the Alps, has been a gateway
through the New Mexican mountains for centuries. The fleet-
footed Indians anciently learned its value as they roamed over
the mountains and deserts. The Spanish explorers, *padres*, and
colonizers tramped along its pathway. Then followed the Americans of the era of "Manifest Destiny"—pathfinders, fur traders,
soldiers, pioneers, and supply trains.

The Santa Fe Trail cut through Glorieta Pass and across
Apache Canyon on its last lap toward the early metropolis of
the Southwest, Santa Fe. Along this historic trailway the Union
and Confederate armies met head on in the "Gettysburg of the
West." The two battles—known in the Official Army Records as
"Apache Canyon," fought on March 26, 1862, and "Glorieta,"
on March 28, 1862—were of major importance in the struggle
for control of the Intermountain West during the war between
the states. These engagements were the turning point during the
war in saving this area for the Union; yet neither of the supreme
commanding officers participated. Colonel Edward R. S. Canby,
commander of the Department of New Mexico, United States
Army, was at Fort Craig and remained there until April 1.[1] Briga-

[1] *O.R.*, I, 9:658.

49

dier General Henry H. Sibley, commanding the Confederate States Army of New Mexico, was either in Santa Fe or Albuquerque when the Battle of Glorieta was fought.[2]

On March 25, at 3:00 P.M., Major John M. Chivington of the Colorado Volunteers, with a detachment of 418 infantry and cavalry troops, left Bernal Springs for Santa Fe, where he planned to surprise and expel the small force of Confederates reported to be in control there. After marching thirty-five miles, this vanguard, at midnight, arrived and camped at Kozlowski's Ranch, about halfway between Bernal Springs and Glorieta Pass. Here Chivington learned for the first time of the presence of the enemy in the immediate vicinity. Rebel soldiers had visited that place earlier in the evening. At 2:00 A.M. on March 26, Lieutenant George Nelson, with twenty cavalrymen, sent out to find and capture the scouts, completed his mission without firing a shot, near the entrance to Glorieta Pass at Pigeon's Ranch. The prisoners were brought back to the Union camp and thoroughly questioned. It was learned that General Sibley's advance forces were at the far end of the pass and expected to march the following day against Fort Union.[3]

At 8:00 A.M. Chivington's entire force moved forward from Kozlowski's Ranch[4] toward Glorieta Pass with the intention of striking the Texans before they had a chance to attack Fort Union. Marching steadily, the Yankee column passed Pigeon's Ranch[5] and entered Glorieta, reaching its summit about 2:00 P.M.

[2] *Ibid.*, I, 9:541; Hayes, *New Colorado*, 169, reported that he interviewed a barber who had shaved Sibley twenty miles from the scene of action on the morning of the Battle of Glorieta. He added that Sibley "seems to have been supplied [perhaps for medicinal purposes] with whiskey."

[3] Hollister, *Boldly They Rode*, 59; Whitford, *Colorado Volunteers*, 82, 84. Among these were Lieutenant McIntyre, formerly of Colonel Canby's staff, who had deserted at the Battle of Valverde, and Captain Hall, formerly of Denver.

[4] Whitford, *Colorado Volunteers*, 84–85. This ranch was owned by Martin Kozlowski, a Polish refugee and U. S. Army veteran, who complimented the Union troops thus: "When they camped on my place, and while they made my tavern their hospital for over two months after their battles in the canyon, they never robbed me of anything, not even a chicken."

[5] *Ibid.*, 85. This ranch, which served as a hotel for travelers along the Santa Fe Trail, was owned by Alexander Valle, a Franco-American who had been nicknamed Pigeon from his peculiar and amusing style of dancing.

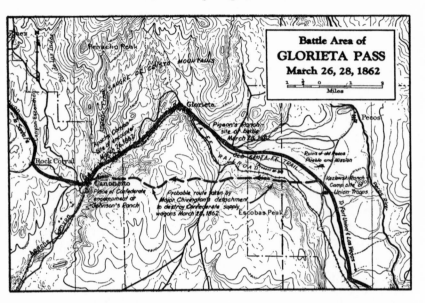

The Union advance guard, while descending the opposite slope in a thicket of trees and bushes, unexpectedly came upon a scouting party of thirty mounted Confederates, whom they captured without any casualties. One of the Colorado pickets came rushing back to the main group with a Rebel lieutenant as a prisoner, shouting, "We've got them corralled this time. . . . Hurrah for the Pikes Peakers."[6]

The Federal troops moved forward hurriedly, but cautiously, down the trail. Meanwhile, Major Charles L. Pyron with the main body of his command had left their camp at Johnson's Ranch, now called Canyoncito, at the west end of Glorieta Pass, and marched up the Santa Fe Trail for about two hours. Suddenly both forces faced each other, approximately one-third of a mile apart, in a long open space in the Apache Canyon proper. The Texas column unfurled in defiance its red flag with the lone star and set up in the road two howitzers supported by mounted infantry. Chivington's detachment had no artillery with it. The Confederate gunners immediately began to fire shells and grape-

[6] Hollister, *Boldly They Rode*, 61; Whitford, *Colorado Volunteers*, 85–86.

51

shot in the direction of the Northern troops, who crowded in some confusion to the left, out of range of the guns.

Vigorous measures taken by Major Chivington restored order among his men. Captains Edward W. Wynkoop and Scott I. Anthony with their Colorado infantry companies were deployed to the left on the mountainside among the evergreen trees. Captain Charles J. Walker with a company of regular cavalry dismounted soon joined them. Captain Jacob Downing, with his company of First Colorado troops, was dispatched to the irregular mountain slope on the Union right. Captain George W. Howland, with his company of regular cavalry, and Captain Samuel H. Cook, with his mounted company of Colorado Volunteers, were held in reserve to charge on the Texas artillerymen in case that battery showed signs of retreat. The remaining Volunteers and regulars were posted in front along the road.[7]

The rapid fire of the Yankee skirmishers upon the flanks of the Rebel lines made their position along the road precarious. The Confederates withdrew hurriedly down the canyon about one and one-half miles, where the mountain sides narrowed in, providing more protection. Captain Howland failed to follow his orders to charge the retreating Texans. The Federals collected their scattered forces and followed cautiously. As the Rebels retreated, they crossed a sixteen-foot log bridge over an arroyo about twenty feet deep. They then destroyed the bridge to cut off immediate Yankee pursuit. Near the bridge site the canyon turned abruptly to the left, with a steep, rocky bluff arising like a bastion directly in front, providing a natural defense. The Confederate battery was placed on a mound at the base of the bluff and a large number of riflemen were posted around the artillery and among the rocks and trees along the canyon slopes around it.

As the Northerners advanced, they were blasted by the retreating Texans with cannon ball from the road and with buckshot and rifle bullets from the rocks on both sides of the canyon. Approaching within an eighth of a mile of the battery, Chivington

[7] *O.R.*, I, 9:530–31; Whitford, *Colorado Volunteers*, 88–89.

began executing a plan for assaulting this natural fortress. Captain Downing's Colorado Volunteers and Captain Howland's regular cavalry, dismounted now, were ordered to climb the steep, rough mountainside on the Union right above the Confederate skirmishers. With close, incessant firing, they were to drive the Rebels out of the bottom of the canyon. Captains Wynkoop and Anthony, with their Colorado troops, were to outflank the Texans on the Union left. Captain Cook's mounted Volunteers were placed in reserve out of range of the howitzers with orders to charge at a given signal. The remaining Union infantry and cavalry, dismounted, were to keep up a steady fire of musketry from the bottom of the canyon in front of the enemy.

Major Chivington was in the midst of the fighting with a pistol in each hand and one under each arm. Dressed in full regimental uniform, he was a conspicuous target, but he must have had a charmed life. A Texas officer taken prisoner related that he had emptied his revolver at the Major three times and then ordered his company to fire a volley at him, but he had galloped on unhurt through the storm of bullets.[8] "Zat Chivington," said Alexander Valle (Pigeon), "he poot 'is head down, and foight loike mahd bull."[9]

After a contest of about an hour, the Federals gradually forced the Confederates back. By this time Captain Downing and his men had nearly flanked the Texans on the Union right. At the propitious moment, the mounted Company F of the Colorado Volunteers, with piercing yells, led by Captain Cook and Lieutenants Nelson and Marshall, charged down the road, compelling all of their 103 horses to leap across the deep gulch at the bridge site. One fell backward into the arroyo, injuring the rider for life. Then, amidst shot and shell from in front and the surrounding hillsides, the Colorado cavalry charged three times back and forth through the wavering ranks of the Texans. The Confederate artillerymen were too fleet-footed down the canyon to

[8] Hollister, *Boldly They Rode*, 62.
[9] Hayes, *New Colorado*, 168. Hayes claimed that Pigeon personally gave him his version of the two battles.

be overtaken. Captain Downing with his men and Lieutenant Reuben F. Bernard, with regular cavalry dismounted, poured a sharp fire from the right which drove the Texans up a canyon to the left of the main canyon. Here the Colorado Volunteers under Captains Wynkoop and Anthony captured a large number of prisoners. However, since evening was coming on, further pursuit was abandoned.

A Confederate soldier under Major Pyron vividly described part of this battle as follows:

> On the 26th we got word that the enemy were coming down the canyon in the shape of two hundred Mexicans and about two hundred regulars. Out we marched with two cannon expecting an easy victory, but what a mistake. Instead of Mexicans and Regulars, they were regular demons, that iron and lead had no effect upon, in the shape of Pike's Peakers. . . . Up the canyon we went for four miles, when we met the enemy coming down at double quick, but the grape and shell soon stopped them, but before we could form in line of battle their infantry was upon the hills on both sides of us, shooting us down like sheep. . . . They had no sooner got within shooting distance of us, than up came a company of cavalry at full charge, with swords and revolvers drawn, looking like so many flying devils. On they came, to what I supposed certain destruction, but nothing like lead or iron seemed to stop them, for we were pouring it into them from every side, like hail in a storm. In a moment these devils had run the gauntlet for half a mile and were fighting hand to hand with our men in the road. . . . How some of these men who charged us ever escaped death will ever be a wonder to me. Our men who were fighting them in the road were soon obliged to retreat and the fight was over.[10]

O. J. Hollister, a Colorado cavalryman, in describing the encounter as he saw it, related the following incidents:

[10] Hollister, *Boldly They Rode*, 167–68. Excerpts from a letter written on April 20, 1862, by George M. Brown, a paroled Texas prisoner at Socorro, New Mexico, to his wife. It was to have been carried by a friend, James Davis, but was found by Lieutenant Risley, California Volunteers, at Mesilla, New Mexico, and was later published in the *Denver News*, from which Hollister copied it.

Pigeon's Ranch, scene of the Battle of Glorieta, March 28, 1862. Photographed in 1880.

Chivington's Rock, on Glorieta battlefield.
Photographed in 1880.

As soon as the order to charge left the Major's mouth, we were on wing. . . . The old United States musket cartridges, containing an ounce ball and three buck shot began to zip around our heads. . . . We met a redoubled shower of lead, rained on us from the rocks above. . . . The fire from the small arms was indeed terrific, and discharging a few shots of our revolvers at the rocks above, we dashed around the point, broke through the centre, trampled down their reserve, and passed away beyond the fight in pursuit of the coveted artillery. But it was too fleet foot for us. . . . The Texans, terrified at the impetuosity of the attack, broke and fled in every direction.[11]

This same Union trooper also told how his captain, Samuel H. Cook, who was struck in the thigh by an ounce ball and three buckshot during the charge, whose horse had fallen on him forty yards farther on, who had also received a bullet in the foot, made light of his agonizing wounds to hearten his men. Lieutenant Marshall, another cavalry officer, lost his life when a prisoner's musket discharged while Marshall was breaking it over a rock. Private Lowe, after being unhorsed, leaped into an arroyo for protection, only to be confronted by a stalwart Texas captain with a loaded pistol who "guessed Lowe was his prisoner." The private sprang on the captain like a cat, and after a violent struggle, the officer was disarmed and marched to the Union rear. Cavalrymen Boone and Dixon captured fifteen men in an old house where the Confederates could have held out against fifty. After one Texan had surrendered, he deliberately shot Captain Logan, who was already wounded in the face, the bullet striking Logan in the arm. The captain then aimed his gun and mortally wounded the Confederate.[12]

Major Chivington and his men, not knowing how near the Confederate reinforcements might be and having no cannon to oppose those of the Texans, gathered up the Union dead and wounded, as well as several Rebel wounded left on the field,

11 *Ibid.*, 63–64. The U. S. musket cartridges referred to here could have been some of those surrendered by General Twiggs in Texas, or they may have been captured by the Confederates in New Mexico.

12 *Ibid.*, 63–67.

and returned through Glorieta Pass to Pigeon's Ranch, where they camped for the night. A rear guard of Union cavalry remained in Apache Canyon until later that night. The defeated Confederates returned to their camp at Johnson's Ranch. That evening Major Pyron sent a request, under a flag of truce, for the privilege of burying their dead and caring for their wounded, which was agreed to by Chivington.

The Battle of Apache Canyon occupied only about three hours, but the fighting was furious while it lasted. Reports on the casualties on both sides are at variance. The statements on the Confederate losses in dead, wounded, and captured vary from 131 to 223. The total Union casualties have been placed between 21 and 29.[13]

During the morning of March 27, Union troops under Major Chivington buried their dead in an open field near Pigeon's Ranch and attended to the needs of their wounded. One wing of the ranch house was converted into a hospital. The Confederate prisoners were started toward Fort Union under guard. During the night, the Union forces had been strengthened by three hundred infantry and cavalrymen from Bernal Springs, where Colonel Slough held his reserves in case a further advance on Fort Union should be attempted by the Texans. Fortunately, for Chivington's men were short on rations, a quantity of flour and corn was found in a building near Pigeon's Ranch which had been stored there by the Confederate commissary officer. This was confiscated and converted into morning rations by the hungry men. The water supply from the well at Pigeon's Ranch was not sufficient for all of the men and their horses, and, consequently, all of the troops, except the wounded and their attendants, returned in the afternoon to their main camp at Koz-

---

[13] *O.R.*, I, 9:531, Chivington reported: Federal losses, 5 killed, 14 wounded, but he does not list those missing; Confederates, 32 killed, 43 wounded, and 71 taken prisoner. Hollister, *Boldly They Rode*, 66–77, stated: Federals, 5 killed, 13 wounded, 3 missing; Texans, 16 killed, 30 to 40 wounded, 75 prisoners. Twitchell, *New Mexican History*, 382, wrote: Confederates, 35 killed, 43 wounded, 71 prisoners; Union, same as Chivington's report. *History of Denver*, 75, states: Confederates, 40 killed, 75 wounded, 108 prisoners; Union, 13 killed, 13 wounded, 3 missing. General Sibley or Colonel Scurry gave no figures for this fight.

lowski's Ranch, where there was more water. Here at 11:00 P.M. on the twenty-seventh, Colonel Slough united all of his forces following a hurried march from Bernal Springs.

During the Battle of Apache Canyon, in the afternoon of March 26, Major Pyron dispatched a fast courier to Colonel William R. Scurry, encamped at Galisteo, a distance of about sixteen miles, informing him of the critical situation in which Pyron's command was involved. He urged immediate relief. Scurry notified his men of Pyron's circumstances, and in ten minutes the Confederate column was formed with orders to march. The baggage train, with a detachment of one hundred men, was sent forward by the regular road, while the main army, in the cold night air, marched directly over the mountains toward the scene of the conflict. At 3:00 A.M. on the twenty-seventh, Scurry and his men reached Pyron's encampment at Johnson's Ranch, Canyoncito, at the western end of Glorieta Pass. Chivington and Pyron had agreed to suspend hostilities until 8:00 A.M. that morning. After that time Scurry expected an attack. As soon as daylight permitted, he made a thorough reconnaissance of the area and then stationed his troops to guard every approach to the encampment.

The Texans remained at this position until the morning of March 28, when Colonel Scurry and his staff decided to march forward and attack the Union forces. Leaving his supply train with a small wagon guard in order not to impede progress, Scurry ordered ahead his command, which consisted of seventeen partially filled companies from the Texas Fourth, Fifth, and Seventh Regiments, an independent company of Volunteers, and a battery of three guns. In command under Scurry were Majors Charles L. Pyron, Henry W. Ragnet, and John S. Shropshire. There was a total of approximately 1,100 men.[14] Reaching the

---

[14] Various estimates of Scurry's command: Hollister, *Boldly They Rode,* 71, recorded 1,800 men; Colonel Slough, *O.R.,* I, 9:534, 1,200 to 1,400; Scurry, *O.R.,* I, 9:543, stated there were "600 fit for duty;" General Sibley, *O.R.,* I, 9:541, reported 1,000. The figure given by Gertrude A. Harris, *A Tale of Men Who Knew Not Fear,* 47, of 1,100 and the same number by Whitford, *Colorado Volunteers,* 99, appears to be about the correct estimate.

eastern decline of Glorieta Pass on the Santa Fe Trail about one mile west of Pigeon's Ranch and six miles east of the Confederate camp at Johnson's Ranch, Scurry halted his troops. His advance guards had notified him that Union forces were near by. After making a hurried examination of the Federal position, Scurry arranged his troops in battle formation.

While the Federal troops were encamped at Kozlowski's Ranch about twenty-seven miles from Santa Fe, it was learned through spies that the Texans had been strongly reinforced and were in Apache Canyon and at Johnson's Ranch beyond. The Union officers planned a daring expedition. Major Chivington with about 430 men was to take the road in a circuitous route toward Galisteo for a short distance, then climb across the mountains south of Glorieta Pass to reconnoiter the Confederates and harass them from the rear.[15] Colonel Slough with the remainder of his command was to move against the Confederates directly through the pass.

On the morning of March 28, 1862, after assigning a detachment to guard the supplies, the two Union columns left Kozlowski's Ranch for the purpose of ascertaining the position of the Confederates and harassing them as much as possible. Slough's men consisted of six companies of the Colorado Volunteers, reduced somewhat by guard detail and other duties, part of a company of New Mexico Volunteers, two small detachments of regular cavalry, and two batteries of regular artillery. There was a total of approximately 700 men.[16] At 9:00 A.M., Slough's division left its encampment, the cavalry in advance, then the infantry, the artillery, and a supply train of at least one hundred wagons with their guards in the rear. By 10:30 A.M. this column had arrived in the vicinity of Pigeon's Ranch, a distance of about five miles. Here the companies broke rank, and the infantry stacked arms in the road. Canteens were filled from the well, which would be the last opportunity for water before reaching the western end of Glorieta Pass. Some of the men

---

[15] *O.R.*, I, 9:533–34.
[16] Whitford, *Colorado Volunteers*, 101; *O.R.*, I, 9:657.

visited the wounded who had been left at the ranch following the battle two days before.

Meanwhile, Colonel Slough sent the cavalry, under Captain Gurden Chapin, Seventh U. S. Infantry, forward to reconnoiter the enemy. The horsemen had only proceeded about three hundred yards when they came rushing back with the news that the Texans were in position to attack about eight hundred yards in front, concealed among the trees. The Yankee troops were hastily reassembled, seizing their firearms as they formed in rank. Preliminary orders were issued, but before the men could be organized into battle formation, grapeshot and shell from the Rebel guns came crashing through the tops of the trees over their heads.

The opening clash of the Battle of Glorieta, or Pigeon's Ranch, as it has sometimes been called, occurred in Glorieta Pass about half a mile west of Pigeon's Ranch. It was a difficult place for an encounter. A rough gorge cut through the mountains with the wagon tracks of the Santa Fe Trail running along the bottom. The floor and the walls of the canyon were perforated in places by deep gulches and arroyos. The ground rose abruptly on each side with huge boulders and clumps of juniper and pine trees interspersed.

The fighting, for the most part among the rocks and trees, in what Colonel Slough termed "bushwhacking," was general and furious.[17] Cavalry could not be used. During the entire battle the regular cavalry under Captain George W. Howland was held in reserve, never moving except to fall back and keep out of danger. Company F, the cavalry unit of the Colorado Volunteers, was dismounted and fought as infantry. Rifles and small arms accurately fired by the expert marksmen on both sides produced bloody results. The roar of the muskets and the artillery was incessant. The Federal troops were forced to adopt defensive tactics during most of the engagement. From the opening of the battle to its close, the odds were against the Yankees. The Rebels were superior in number and had the opportunity of

[17] *O.R.*, I, 9:533.

choosing the battlefield. Nevertheless, every inch of ground was stubbornly contested. In no instance did the Northern forces fall back until they were in the greatest danger of being flanked and surrounded.

Had Colonel Scurry known of the Union inferiority, it is almost certain that he would have made his battle plans differently. The experience of two days before at the Battle of Apache Canyon had made the Confederates more cautious. The engagement raged for over six hours, beginning with the Confederate bombardment at about 11:00 A.M.[18] Alexander Valle, or "Pigeon," described the beginning of the battle thus: "Goovernment mahns vas at my ranch and fill 'is cahnteen viz my viskey (and Goovernment nevaire pay me for zat viskey); and Texas mahns coom oop, and soorprise zem, and zey foight six hour by my vatch, and my vatch vas slow!"[19]

As the battle opened, Colonel William H. Scurry deployed his infantry and dismounted cavalry across the canyon from a fence on their left up into the pine forest on their right. Major Charles L. Pyron was sent to the right side of the Confederate line, Major Henry W. Ragnet commanded the center, and Colonel Scurry for a short time took over immediate command of their left. Lieutenant James Bradford, commanding the artillery, was ordered to take a position on the brow of a ridge and commence firing immediately on the advancing Federals. Early in the fight Bradford was severely wounded and carried from the field. His horses were shot down, and his men were forced to retreat with a three-gun battery as Lieutenant Kerber, with Company I, First Colorado, charged down upon them from the hillside. When Scurry discovered that the guns had been withdrawn, he hastily ordered two of them back to the front. A short pause was made to reunite the Confederate forces which had become scattered.

Following the opening salvos from the Rebel guns, the Yankee troops formed in their respective ranks as quickly as possible.

[18] *Ibid.*, I, 9:535, 541; Frank Hall, *History of the State of Colorado*, 282, stated that the battle raged incessantly for nine hours.
[19] Hayes, *New Colorado*, 169.

Earlier in the day Lieutenant Colonel Samuel F. Tappan had been assigned the immediate command of most of the Colorado Volunteers and regular army artillery in Colonel John P. Slough's column. Responding immediately to Slough's orders, Tappan sent at double-quick time the batteries under Captain John F. Ritter and Lieutenant Ira W. Claflin to a position on a slight elevation, in and to the left of the road, about four hundred yards from the Texan lines. Captain Richard Sopris with his Company C, Colorado Infantry, was assigned to support Ritter. Captain S. H. Robbins with K Company of the Colorado troops was ordered to support Claflin. The Confederate artillery fire was promptly returned by the Federal batteries. Captain Jacob Downing with Company D, First Colorado Volunteers, was deployed to the Union left, and Lieutenant Charles Kerber with Company I, First Colorado, was ordered to the right. Each company was to occupy the hillsides, for the present, as skirmishers. The other companies of infantry with the cavalry were held in the rear, farther down the pass, as reserves and to protect the supply train.

Captain Downing and his men, as they took their position, fought desperately, meeting a larger force of Texans. This company was almost overpowered and surrounded, when, fortunately Captain William F. Wilder saw the critical situation, and with a detachment of his Company G, First Colorado, came to the relief of Company D, extricating it from what might have been almost annihilation.

Colonel Scurry suddenly discovered Company I, Colorado Infantry, the German company, led by Lieutenant Kerber, advancing partially concealed up a gulch toward the left flank of the Confederate rear. Scurry dashed with his column about two hundred yards across a clearing into the gulch among the Federal troops. With both sides using pistols, knives, clubbed muskets, and bayonets, a desperate and deadly hand-to-hand conflict ensued. Company I, greatly outnumbered, stubbornly fell back, leaving behind in dead and wounded many of their number. Among these were Lieutenant John Baker, who had led his company along the gulch to a point opposite the Texan artillery on higher ground to his left, and then drawing his sword and waving it, had called to his men, "Let's capture the guns!" At that instant he was struck with a musket ball.[20]

On the opposite flank of the Confederate line, Major Pyron's column, reinforced from the center, fiercely attacked Captain Downing's company, pressing it back with considerable losses in killed and wounded. One part of this company had encountered a masked cannon firing grapeshot with deadly effect. The Federal officers, concerned by these temporary reverses and conscious that they were outnumbered by a determined foe which they expected would charge, ordered their troops to gradually fall back about four hundred yards to a position near Pigeon's Ranch. A line was again formed, which extended from a rough ledge of rocks on the Union right across the valley, over an arroyo, and up on a wooded rocky bluff on their left. Captain Downing's men took the new position to the left. Lieutenant Claflin's battery of regular army gunners was stationed on the top and the western slope of the bluff. Captain Ritter's regular artillery occupied the middle section of the Union lines. Ritter was still supported by Captain Sopris with his Company C, Colorado Infantry. Later they were joined by Captain W. F. Wilder with Colorado Company G, most of whom had been held in reserve until this time. Lieutenant Kerber's Company I, assisted by the cavalry under Captain Walker, occupied the right flank of the Federal line.[21]

In the shift, Captain Ritter's battery was first placed south of the road, where it was exposed to a galling fire by the enemy's muskets and artillery without being able to return it effectively. Since the Texan big guns were some distance away and shel-

---

[20] *O.R.,* I, 9:536–38; Whitford, *Colorado Volunteers,* 107. Colonel Tappan reported that Baker, after being severely wounded, was beaten to death by the enemy on the field after the battle that night with the butt of a musket and his body stripped of his clothing. Hollister, *Boldly They Rode,* 73, wrote that this hideous act was committed by vagabond Mexicans who had followed the Confederate forces.

[21] Whitford, *Colorado Volunteers,* 108.

tered by trees and the Union ammunition wagons were hard
to reach, Ritter felt it advisable to return to the wagon road on
the Santa Fe Trail with his battery. Here Lieutenant McGrath
of Ritter's staff was fatally wounded. After a few rounds, Ritter
moved again. This time he took a position nearly in front of
Pigeon's Ranch, where he established one six-pound gun in the
road and flanked it with smaller guns. The limber boxes were
sent back and forth to the rear to be replenished.

As the Union forces fell back, the Texan artillery advanced
and, planting their guns on a ridge, again opened fire. The
Yankee gunners from both Claflin's and Ritter's batteries responded with spirit and effectiveness. The cannonading lasted
for three hours. A Rebel gun was dismounted by a round shot
from a Federal cannon which struck it directly in the muzzle.
Another Confederate gun was disabled and a limber box blown
up by a case shot. At the same time riflemen from Companies D
and I had picked off most of the Texas gunners. Thus during
the latter part of the battle the Confederates were compelled
to rely mainly upon their infantry and dismounted cavalry in
continuing the engagement. Their hope to reach and break the
Federal line could only be realized through sheer pressure of
superior numbers in manpower and repeated charges.

At this time the Union command realized the necessity of
occupying a hill to the left of their batteries in order to prevent
the Texans from outflanking them and destroying the Federal
supply train along the Santa Fe Trail a short distance in the
rear. Such a move would also give Lieutenant Claflin's battery
more support. Lieutenant Colonel Tappan with seventy men
advanced to the summit of the hill and took a position in front
and to the left of their artillery. He extended his line of skirmishers for nearly three-quarters of a mile in a half-circle, and
at nearly a right angle to the road occupied by the Union train
of one hundred wagons. This position, commanding the valley
in part, was held by the Yankees for four hours, during which
time several groups of Rebels attempted to ascend the hill, but
were thrown back.

Meanwhile, Colonel Scurry, having been reinforced by two companies of fresh troops, rearranged his line in three divisions, on the ridges abandoned by the Federals, for another assault. Endeavoring to determine the exact positions now held by the Yankees, Scurry dispatched several squads of men toward the Northern line at different points to draw fire. The Union force then extended from a grove of trees to the north on the Confederate left, behind a long adobe wall, beyond a rocky precipice, and over the top of a bluff south of Pigeon's Ranch. The Texan squads were easily driven back. One of these detachments was dressed in the uniform of the Colorado Volunteers. Lieutenant Colonel Tappan, anticipating the arrival of Major Chivington's expedition from the Confederate rear at any time, permitted the Rebels dressed in blue to advance within a short distance of his line, but when they were recognized as Texans, orders were given to fire on the impersonators.

Colonel Scurry then ordered a battalion of Confederate troops under Major John Shropshire to advance on their right among the pines and to attack vigorously the left wing of the Union line. Major Henry W. Ragnet, with similar orders, was dispatched to the Confederate left. Major Charles L. Pyron was to assist Ragnet. Scurry with the remainder of the command was to charge in front. Noticing a delay on the right, he left his column at the center, and upon reaching these troops, he found that Major Shropshire had been killed just as the movement started. When the Texas column neared the Union line, Private George W. Pierce, Company F, Colorado Volunteers, had darted from the ranks, killed and disarmed Major Shropshire, at the head of his battalion, and had taken prisoner Captain D. W. Shannon, who was hurriedly delivered to Captain Gurden Chapin, U. S. Army, in the rear.

Colonel Scurry at once took command of the Confederate right and ordered a general charge. The Texans made a furious attack, but met with such resistance from the Federal skirmishers that they were forced to fall back temporarily. Joined by his own men from the center, Scurry renewed the charge farther down the field toward the road and was again repulsed by the Northern riflemen and artillery. Colonel John P. Slough was near the front line, doing all that he could to repel the Rebel onslaught with numerically inferior troops. The Federal officers, cool and collected, stubbornly held their ground. Lieutenant Clark Chambers, Company C, First Colorado Volunteers, was mortally wounded while inspiring his men by voice and example.[22]

Majors Ragnet and Pyron with their Texas detachments were dispatched to the Confederate left, across an arroyo, up a rugged slope, and to the summit of a hill which borders the battlefield on the north. Colonel Slough, anticipating this move, had previously strengthened the Union right flank with additional infantry. Captain Ritter, in response to orders from Captain Chapin, hurriedly moved his Federal battery from the road in front of Pigeon's ranch house across a ravine to the other side of the canyon, where he set up his guns. Lieutenant Claflin was commanded to descend the bluff on the south and arrange his mountain howitzers near Ritter's artillery. The supporting Northern infantry effectively protected the artillery shift. The Union big guns again blazed away at the advancing enemy.

The Rebel troops under Ragnet and Pyron, upon reaching their assigned position, began a furious and steady onslaught. They would fire their rifles and double-barreled shotguns and then rush forward, dodging from tree to tree and from rock to rock until they came into close quarters with the Yankees. The outnumbered Federal infantry delivered volley after volley in response, yielding ground only inch by inch as they were pushed back to the ledge of rocks extending northward from Pigeon's Ranch.[23] "Here the conflict was terrible," reported Colonel Scurry. "Our men and officers . . . pushed forward among the rocks until the muzzles of the guns of the opposing forces passed each other."[24] Some of them shot at each other from the opposite sides of the clumps of cedar bushes.

[22] Hollister, *Boldly They Rode*, 70, reported that Lieutenant Colonel Tappan sat on his horse during the charge, leisurely loading and firing his pistols as if rabbit hunting.

[23] Whitford, *Colorado Volunteers*, 111.

[24] *O.R.*, I, 9:544.

Scurry, seeing the advantage that had been gained for the Texans by this contest on his left flank, united the main forces from the right and center of his line. The Confederate aim was to capture the Federal batteries, as they had done from Colonel Canby's forces during the Battle of Valverde, and to drive the Union skirmishers from the ledges which they had recently occupied. With the brim of their slouch hats falling over their foreheads and with deafening yells, the Texans charged toward Ritter's and Claflin's batteries.[25] A furious fire of grapeshot, canister, and exploding shell from the Union artillery and a galling fire from the Northern infantry in the canyon and from the surrounding elevations forced the attackers back each time.[26]

The Confederates charged the Federal position five times, but were repulsed with heavy losses each time. During an interval between two of these attacks, a German officer in the Colorado Volunteers, which were supporting the Union batteries, shouted in broken but emphatic English to his men standing in a huddle near the artillery, "Poys, lay down flat dere; does you vant to go died?"[27] At one time, when the Texans were within forty yards of the Federal guns, Lieutenant Claflin ordered his men to cease firing. Captain Samuel Robbins and Company K, First Colorado, part of the artillery support, arose from the ground "like ghosts," delivered a deadly musket fire into the approaching enemy, and charged with bayonets, scattering the wavering column. On another occasion, Claflin gave orders to double-shot his guns. Since they were only small, brass howitzers, when they were fired, one of the gun carriages capsized and fell down into a gulch. Members of Colorado Company K lifted it out of the ravine, thus saving it from being captured by the enemy.

[25] Hall, *History of the State of Colorado,* 281; Whitford, *Colorado Volunteers,* 111.

[26] Whitford, *Colorado Volunteers,* 111. *The Rocky Mountain News,* June 10, 1862, reported that the Texans claimed the bullets used by the Colorado Volunteers were made of poison lead. A sample was sent to the state analyst of Massachusetts, who said that they were not. This newspaper then humorously commented that the lead was from Tappan and Company, Central City, Colorado, referring to Lieutenant Colonel Tappan and his men.

[27] Whitford, *Colorado Volunteers,* 112.

The fighting at this time was more deadly than any of these soldiers had yet witnessed. Both sides suffered severely. The Confederate officers—Major Ragnet, Captain Charles Buckholts, and Lieutenant Charles L. Mills—were all killed near the close of the battle. Major Pyron's horse was shot from under him. Colonel Scurry's cheek was twice bruised, drawing blood, by a minié ball, and his clothing was torn in two places by bullets. Scurry reported later to Sibley that the fire of the enemy was so hot that all of the Texas "field officers upon the ground were either killed or touched."[28]

A pathetic incident occurred in the Federal ranks in connection with the death of Major Ragnet. A boy, just reaching manhood, serving with the Colorado Volunteers, told his captain, Jacob Downing, in the forenoon that he had dreamed that he had been shot through the heart during the battle. Captain Downing cheerfully told him that it was a mere fancy produced by a bad dream. In the course of the engagement, the Captain detailed the youth with others to conduct some prisoners to the camp at Kozlowski's and did not expect him to return to the battlefield. Late in the afternoon, to the Captain's surprise, the boy was in his place on the bluff above Pigeon's Ranch. A fellow-soldier told him that if he still wanted to get into the fight, to see if he could hit the Confederate officer, who was on a horse about forty rods away. The boy took deliberate aim with his rifle and fired. Major Ragnet fell mortally wounded. A Texan sharpshooter, observing this action, instantly discharged his rifle at the youth. The bullet struck the boy's gun, glanced from it, and pierced his heart. Turning to Captain Downing at his side, he gasped, "I told you something would happen."[29]

While this part of the battle was in progress, a detachment of Texans gained possession of a rocky hill on the Union right and poured a destructive fire into the side of the Federal batteries, wounding and killing some of Captain Ritter's gunners. The artillery with the supporting infantry then withdrew a short

28 *O.R.*, I, 9:541–45.
29 Whitford, *Colorado Volunteers*, 112, 114.

distance in good order and took a new position where the supports were entirely sheltered from the enemy fire. The supply train was stationed about forty yards to the left. Here the Confederates made their last charge upon the Union guns, endeavoring also to reach the supply train, but they were again driven back with a loss and confusion among their troops.

Soon after 5:00 P.M., Colonel John P. Slough ordered his forces to fall back gradually to their camp at Kozlowski's Ranch. The supply wagons and the pieces of artillery, well guarded, began one after another to withdraw. Some of the Federal troops objected to this order and were reluctant to leave the battlefield. They were eager to move against the Confederates and complete the work of the day through a counter-offensive either to force a Confederate surrender or to start them on a retreat toward Santa Fe. Yet to Colonel Slough the object "to reconnoiter in force" and to "harass" the enemy had been accomplished.[30] Colonel Scurry reported to General Sibley that "another victory" had been "added to the long line of Confederate triumphs," but on another occasion he wrote that his troops that day were "forced to halt from the extreme exhaustion of men, who had been engaged for six hours in the hardest contested fight it had ever been my lot to witness."[31] Actually, the soldiers on both sides were so exhausted and crippled by the battle, during which they had received neither rest nor refreshment, that neither could effectively continue the fighting.

About the same time that Colonel Slough issued his orders to withdraw, Colonel Scurry received information from the Confederate rear of the destruction of his supply train. He immediately ordered that a flag of truce be taken to the Union commander. An ambulance carrying a white flag was driven down the Santa Fe Trail from the west through the Rebel and Yankee lines. Major Alexander M. Jackson alighted when the carriage reached Captain Jacob Downing and Captain John F. Ritter, whose units had remained on the battlefield for some time after

[30] *Ibid.*, 114; *O.R.*, I, 9:533.
[31] *O.R.*, I, 9:544.

the order was given to fall back to the Union camp. Jackson, former secretary of the Territory of New Mexico, an ardent Secessionist, personal friend of President Jefferson Davis, and an adjutant in the Confederate Army of New Mexico, conveyed a request for the suspension of hostilities until noon the following day, in order to care for the wounded and bury the dead. He was thrust back into the vehicle and compelled by Captain Downing to be driven blindfolded to the Union Field Headquarters at Kozlowski's. Here he met Colonel Slough, who granted the request for an armistice, which was subsequently extended until the morning of the second day.

A crushing blow had been dealt to the Confederates through the destruction of their supply train by the Federal troops under Major J. M. Chivington. This detachment, which separated from the main Union column in the early morning of the Battle of Glorieta, was composed of the following: Captain W. H. Lewis's battalion (regulars) with Captain A. B. Carey assisting him in command, consisting of 60 men; Companies A and G, Fifth U. S. Infantry, Lieutenants Barr and Norvell in charge; Company B, First Colorado Volunteers under Captain Samuel M. Logan and Lieutenant Jacobs; Company B, Second Colorado Volunteers with Captain James H. Ford and Lieutenant De Forest leading; Company A, First Colorado, with 68 men under Captain Edward W. Wynkoop and Lieutenant Shaffer; Company E, First Colorado, 71 men, commanded by Captain Scott J. Anthony and Lieutenant J. A. Dawson; and Company H, First Colorado, about 80 men under Captain George L. Sanborn and Lieutenant B. N. Sanford.[32] James L. Collins, a civilian, accompanied the group by his own request. Lieutenant Colonel Manuel Chávez, New Mexican Volunteers, was selected as a guide. In all there was a total of about 430 officers and men.

Major Chivington and his men left their camp at Kozlowski's Ranch at 8:30 A.M., marching along the Santa Fe Trail. An hour later they left the main road. Then, for five hours in a circuitous route south of Glorieta Pass, they struggled over a rugged, track-

[32] *Ibid.*, I, 9:538.

less terrain which took them along narrow defiles, over rocky ledges, across a high mesa, and through dense thickets of piñon pines and cedar bushes. About 1:30 P.M., they arrived at the crest of the mountain overlooking the Confederate encampment at Johnson's Ranch, now Canyoncito. A Texan sentinel stationed as a lookout by Colonel Scurry, was captured. While en route, about 11:00 A.M., the detachment heard cannonading to their right from the direction of Pigeon's Ranch which indicated that fighting had begun between Colonel Slough's and Colonel Scurry's forces.

The Yankee expedition spent an hour carefully examining the situation at the Rebel camp more than one thousand feet below. From this height it appeared that there were stationed in the area around the ranch buildings about eighty wagons with one large gun mounted on a knoll. Approximately two hundred men, left to guard the camp, moved leisurely about. Having satisfied himself that no formidable difficulty existed to prevent an attack upon the encampment, Major Chivington determined to descend the mountain with his men and burn the Confederate supply train. The order to charge was given, and the troops hurried down the precipice. They crawled, slid, and were lowered by ropes and leather straps while carrying their guns. As they descended, the crashing of loosened rocks down the bluffs and among the trees aroused the attention of the Texas troops in camp. The defenders fired several shots from the six-pound cannon at the oncoming Federals, but without effect. Chivington's men, yelling like wild Indians, were not long in reaching the base of the mountain.

The engagement was short and decisive. Some of the frightened Confederate teamsters and camp guards hurriedly mounted horses near by and dashed out of camp toward Santa Fe. Others retreated quickly into the canyon to the east. It is not difficult to account for the almost defenseless condition of the camp. The flank movement of the Union troops was entirely unanticipated by the Confederate leaders. When Colonel Scurry left that morning, he had detailed a much larger force to protect their supplies and animals than the Federals found upon their arrival. The Texan captain who was placed in command of the camp on the departure of Scurry later related that two companies of German immigrant soldiers, among those assigned to him, broke away when they heard the cannonading at the front. They shouted that they had enlisted to get glory by fighting, not in guarding mules and provisions. It was almost impossible to restrain them as they ran out of camp through Glorieta Pass, where they joined the other Texas troops on the battlefield. These were probably the reinforcements that Colonel Scurry received in the middle of the afternoon.[33]

Upon nearing the Confederate camp, Captain Edward W. Wynkoop, with his Colorado troops, was deployed to the mountainside to silence the Confederate guns by "picking off" the gunners. This was done adequately with a single volley from the rifles of Wynkoop's men. Captain W. H. Lewis, U. S. Army, assisted by Lieutenant B. N. Sanford, Colorado Company H, with their men, captured and spiked the six-pound cannon, using a steel ramrod. Then they jammed an iron ball into its muzzle and tumbled the gun carriage off the knoll, smashing the wheels in pieces. They set fire to a quantity of ammunition and a limber box for this gun which was found hidden in a small gully near by. As it exploded, Lieutenant Sanford came dangerously close to losing his life. They also searched the buildings and ravines close by for concealed Texans, taking them prisoner whenever they were found.[34]

The remainder of Chivington's command surrounded the wagons and ranch buildings and rushed in to destroy the wagons. The vehicles were all heavily loaded with ammunition, clothing, food, medical supplies, and forage for the animals, all necessary equipment for a small army on the march and in camp. Under the circumstances, very little from this large quantity of stores could be carried away by the captors. The Union commander could see that the only practical thing to do was to destroy the

[33] Whitford, *Colorado Volunteers*, 118, 119.
[34] *O.R.*, I, 9:539; Whitford, *Colorado Volunteers*, 119–20.

71

supply train completely, rendering it useless to the Texans. All the wagons in the supply train were then burned with their entire contents.[35] A Confederate prisoner wrote in a letter to his wife, "Our whole train of seventy wagons was burned by the enemy. In one of the wagons was that trunk of clothing you sent me." He was compelled to rely on his Union captors for wearing apparel during the succeeding months that he was in New Mexico.

While the Northern troops were watching the smoldering ruins of the train, a Confederate messenger on horseback dashed out of a ravine back of Johnson's ranch house, turned suddenly into the mouth of Glorieta Canyon, and rode at top speed through the pass toward the eastern end where the battle was raging. Whitford claimed that it was very possible that the information he gave to Colonel Scurry caused the flag of truce to be sent to Colonel Slough.[36] During the destruction of the train, one of the wagons containing ammunition exploded, severely wounding Private Simon Ritter, Company A, First Colorado, the only Yankee hurt in the expedition. Five Federal soldiers, taken prisoner in the forenoon in the battle between Colonel Slough's and Colonel Scurry's forces, were found in the camp and released. They gave a vivid account of the battle, the first information Chivington's detachment had received concerning the furious fighting at the front except the distant report of the big guns.[37]

There remained a task, disagreeable to most Western frontiersmen who appreciated good horses and mules, necessary in order to complete the entire destruction of the Confederate property in the camp. In addition to those few animals which were used by the escaping teamsters and camp guards, there were approximately five hundred horses and mules in a corral near the camp. Some of these were used by the officers and the cavalry and some to pull the wagons. Most of the Sibley brigade was orig-

[35] *Ibid.*, I, 9:539; *Santa Fe Weekly Gazette*, April 26, 1862.
[36] Whitford, *Colorado Volunteers*, 118–19.
[37] *O.R.*, I, 9:539

inally mounted. The animals could not be removed over the rugged mountain to the Federal camp, so they were all bayoneted. A Northern soldier who was present said, "It was a pity to kill them, but we could do nothing else with them." The Union leaders reasoned that if they permitted the animals to live, they would enable their owners to prolong the Confederate campaign.[38] Regarding this loss to the Texans, a Confederate trooper wrote, "It went hard with the boys to walk, as we were all well mounted when we came to this country."[39]

During the destruction of the camp, three Confederate soldiers were killed, several wounded, and seventeen were taken prisoner. A rumor circulated among the Federal troops before they left the wrecked camp that a large Rebel reinforcement was rapidly approaching from Galisteo, the former Texan encampment. It was therefore decided by the Union commanders not to march back to Kozlowski's Ranch by way of Glorieta Pass, but to travel the same route they had followed in coming, thus avoiding the danger of being caught in a trap between two divisions of the Confederates. It was late in the afternoon when the Yankee expedition had finally climbed the precipitous slope down which they had charged a few hours earlier. On the way up, it was noticed that four wagons filled with military stores hidden behind a knoll outside of the main camp had been overlooked during the destruction. Four men volunteered for the task of going back to burn them, which was accomplished within an hour's time.

Upon reaching the summit of the mountain, Major J. M. Chivington was met by Lieutenant Alfred S. Cobb, Company C, First Colorado, with a message from Colonel John P. Slough ordering Chivington to hasten back with his command to support the main Union column.[40] A discussion arose over which route should be taken. Colonel Chávez refused to take the responsibility as guide for any way other than that which was followed before.

[38] Whitford, *Colorado Volunteers,* 121.
[39] Hollister, *Boldly They Rode,* 169.
[40] *O.R.,* I, 9:539.

At this time Padre Ortiz, from a small settlement near the Pecos church ruins, rode into their midst on a white horse and addressed the officers in Spanish. He volunteered to lead them to their camp over the mountains alongside Glorieta Pass, and warned them that if they returned by the old trail, they might meet some of Colonel Scurry's troops. Colonel Chávez, who knew the priest and understood what he said, advised Chivington to accept his services. Through intense darkness, over steep ridges and through narrow defiles, along a pathless route, the priest led the column safely to the main road from the point where the troops had turned into the Galisteo trail that morning. At 10:00 P.M., the expedition, suffering from extreme thirst and fatigue, rejoined their comrades at the Union camp at Kozlowski's Ranch, who welcomed the victors and listened to the account of their achievements. Chivington's report made clear the reason that Colonel Scurry had sent the flag of truce.[41]

The accurate number of casualties in the Battle of Glorieta is hard to determine because of the wide variety of figures given. There is reason to believe that the two commanders on the battle-field, Union Colonel John P. Slough and Confederate Colonel William R. Scurry, in comparison with the estimates of other writers, underestimated their own losses and exaggerated those of their enemy. Colonel Slough, in his official report, placed the Union losses in killed, wounded, and captured at 83 men, and the Confederates at 275, with a total loss of 350 in the two battles, Apache Canyon and Glorieta. Colonel Scurry officially reported that the Texan losses were 36 killed and 60 wounded, without mention of those taken prisoner. He estimated that the Federal dead exceeded 100, but made no calculation of their wounded or prisoners.[42] Some writers reported the Confederate casualties as high as 581 men and the Union losses at 150.[43] Because of the

---

[41] *Ibid.*, I, 9:539; Whitford, *Colorado Volunteers*, 123.

[42] *Ibid.*, I, 9:535, 545.

[43] Hollister, *Boldly They Rode*, 76, Confederates, 281 killed, 200 wounded, 100 prisoners; Union, killed 49, wounded, 64, prisoners 21. Harris, *A Tale of Men*, 51 (a Texas author) Confederates, lost about 500, or one third, of their men. Federals, likewise, sustained a severe blow. Hayes, *New Colorado*, 170,

difference in tactics employed at Glorieta—the Confederates on the aggressive and the Union forces on the defensive—the Texan casualties would logically be more apt to be the higher. Probably the truth lies somewhere between the extremes reported.

March 29 was spent in burying the dead and caring for the wounded. Most of the Union dead from the Battle of Glorieta were interred in the open field east of Pigeon's Ranch by the side of those who had fallen on March 26 in Apache Canyon. The Confederates were laid side by side in a large trench excavated on a level spot across the arroyo just west of the ranch near a high ledge of rocks. Pigeon's Ranch was again used for a hospital, this time by the Confederates. At one corner of the corral at the ranch fifteen Texans who died in the hospital were buried. The Union wounded were moved to Kozlowski's Ranch.

Each side claimed that it had won a major triumph. The possible defeat of Colonel Slough's troops was turned into a victory by the stunning, fatal blow that Chivington's detachment had inflicted on the Confederates at Johnson's Ranch. The rear of Colonel Scurry's forces was ruined, and a further advance was made hopeless. The demoralized Texans, after staying at Pigeon's Ranch for two days and nights following the battle, without blankets or shelter and practically without food, retreated on foot during the armistice to Santa Fe in search of provisions. Scurry wrote, "I have not slept for three nights, and can scarcely hold my eyes open."[44] Two hundred Confederate wounded were left at Pigeon's. The Rebel soldiers not only suffered for want of food, blankets, and clothing, but were dangerously low in ammunition. There was an average of no more than ten rounds for each man.

At Santa Fe, Colonel Scurry in a letter to General Henry H. Sibley[45] and in a proclamation to the Confederate soldiers report-

Union, 150 killed, wounded, and missing; Rebels, 300 to 400 killed and wounded, 93 prisoners. *History of Denver*, 75, Union, 134 killed and wounded; Confederates, 251 killed, 200 wounded, 100 prisoners. *Santa Fe Weekly Gazette*, April 26, 1862, Union, 38 killed, 54 wounded, 17 prisoners; Confederates, 80–90 killed, 100 wounded, over 100 prisoners.

[44] *O.R.*, I, 9:542.
[45] *Ibid.*, I, 9:541.

ed that "another victory" had been added to a long list of Confederate triumphs. Several weeks later the *Santa Fe Weekly Gazette* sarcastically chided:

> We have frequently heard the remark made by military men after a successful battle that they could not stand another such victory, but now we have an instance in which one claimed victory has proved the destruction of an army and rendered it necessary for them to attempt to evacuate the Territory which they had invaded.[46]

Meanwhile, Colonel G. R. Paul back at Fort Union had bitterly complained to the Adjutant General in Washington of Colonel John P. Slough's aggressive attitude. He wrote, "My object in this communication is to throw the responsibility of any disaster which may occur on the right shoulders."[47] At Fort Craig, Colonel Edward R. S. Canby, who was overly cautious, also reported to Washington that the Federal troop movement under Colonel Slough against the Confederates in northern New Mexico was premature. Canby stated that it was at variance with his instructions and might involve serious consequences.[48]

In contrast, Governor Henry Connelly of New Mexico in his report to Secretary Seward praised Colonel Slough with his Colorado troops "for this favorable result in our struggle with the Texan invaders."[49] Whitford claimed that Slough's decision to strike the Confederates immediately, even though Colonel Paul vigorously objected, was "veritably and unmeasurably wise."[50] Captain Richard Sopris, Company C, First Colorado Volunteers wrote:

> We have saved this Territory and perhaps Colorado by coming here. Colonel Slough deserves a great deal of credit for our success. Had we remained at Fort Union until the enemy came up, I believe

---

[46] April 26, 1862. Both the Proclamation and the newspaper's answers are printed in the same issue.
[47] *O.R.*, I, 9:652.
[48] *Ibid.*, I, 9:658.
[49] *Ibid.*, I, 9:662.
[50] Whitford, *Colorado Volunteers*, 81.

we would have lost many more men than we did; but as it is, we cut the enemy up so badly that they are leaving the Territory, and there are none of them north of Albuquerque.[51]

With the realization that the destruction of the Confederate supply train at Johnson's Ranch by the Union detachment under Major J. M. Chivington was one of the chief contributing factors in turning the Rebels back at the Battle of Glorieta, a bitter controversy developed later over who should be honored—the Volunteers or the regulars of the Union Army. Bancroft praised the Union troops who were on this expedition and stated that Major Chivington "made himself the hero of the war."[52]

Colorado historians, in general, when describing this outstanding achievement of the Yankee troops, have praised Major Chivington for his aggressive leadership.[53] James L. Collins, publisher of the *Santa Fe Weekly Gazette,* claimed in his newspaper that he was in charge of the burning of the Texan supply train.[54] Major Chivington, in his official report of the event, indicated that Collins had accompanied the expedition at his own request, but stated that "he [Collins] did not burn the train or cause it to be done."[55] A Colorado soldier, signing himself "Union" (probably Captain Jacob Downing), who fought under Chivington, in a report to the *Rocky Mountain News* on the Battle of Glorieta, eulogized Chivington for his leadership in destroying the Texan supply train. This columnist branded as "false and unjust" the claims of Collins that the train was burned under the latter's direction.[56]

The controversy over who should receive the honors was eventually taken to the New Mexican Territorial Legislature,

[51] *Rocky Mountain News,* May 3, 1862. Excerpts from a letter written by Captain Sopris at Gallestillo [Galisteo], New Mexico, April 12, 1862.
[52] Bancroft, *History of Arizona and New Mexico,* 697.
[53] Hall, *History of the State of Colorado,* 281; Hollister, *Boldly They Rode,* 72; LeRoy R. Hafen, *Colorado and Its People,* 306; Wilbur Fisk Stone, *History of Colorado,* 715; Whitford, *Colorado Volunteers,* 115–23.
[54] April 26, 1862.
[55] *O.R.,* I, 9:539.
[56] *Rocky Mountain News,* June 10, 1862.

which adopted a resolution on January 23, 1864, that did not mention Major Chivington but asked the President of the United States to promote Captains William H. Lewis and Asa B. Carey to the rank of major for their "meritorious and distinguished services in attacking the rear guard of the Rebel army, in Apache Canyon, and in destroying the entire train and commissary stores."[57] On March 8, 1864, the *Río Abajo Press* praised Captain Lewis without mentioning Captain Carey, his fellow-officer, as follows:

> The people of the Territory are grateful to the Colorado Volunteers for largely contributing to the rescue of New Mexico from the rebel invaders. . . . At the same time we object to Col. Chivington's strutting about in plumage stolen from Captain William H. Lewis, 5th U. S. Infantry.

This newspaper further contended that on March 28, 1862, while the Confederate invading expedition was being met in front by the Union forces under Colonel Slough, a detachment of Federals, under Major Chivington, made a detour to reconnoiter from a mountain. Someone suggested attacking the Texan rear guard and destroying their supply train. After two hours' persuasion, Major Chivington consented to the attack. Captain Lewis led the assault and destroyed the train and supplies while Chivington viewed the scene from afar. Chivington was made colonel, "while Lewis should have been made a General," concluded this newspaper, for an event in which a "defeat was probably changed into a victory." Regardless of where the credit should have gone, the destruction of the Confederate supply train did contribute to the defeat of Colonel Scurry's army and the ultimate retreat of the Confederate forces to Texas.

Whitford contended that the Texans in their weakened condition following the Battle of Glorieta could not have renewed the engagement as Colonel Slough had expected them to do at the time the truce was arranged. Nor could they have made

[57] *New Mexico Territory, Legislative Assembly Laws with the Joint Resolutions, 1863–64,* 124.

much resistance to an attack from the Northern army had the Union commander attempted to intercept their retreat to Santa Fe. The effect of the battle on General Sibley and his advisers was soon made evident by their recognition of the fact that they had failed to attain their objective in New Mexico and by their decision to send the skeleton of their army back to Texas as soon as possible. Stone wrote that the Confederates' dream of a union with the Far West and control of the Intermountain Western territories was rudely dispelled. The Texans were compelled to retreat ignominiously to Santa Fe, where preparations were made for the withdrawal of their entire force from the Río Grande Valley to Fort Bliss in Texas.[58]

Immediately following the truce, Colonel Slough and his troops were ready to renew their campaign against the Confederates, but on March 30, the second day after the Battle of Glorieta, a written command from Colonel Edward R. S. Canby, Union commander of the Department of New Mexico, was received by Slough ordering him to fall back to Fort Union to protect it from any possible enemy attack.[59] When the Federal troops reached the fort, they found that it was not in the least danger of being assaulted. In the meantime, Colonel John P. Slough had forwarded his resignation to Canby in disgust at not being permitted to follow up the advantages which the Union forces had gained at Glorieta by capturing or dispersing the Confederate troops under Colonel Scurry.[60] Slough's officers and men were thoroughly in agreement with him in this feeling of exasperation. Hollister wrote:

[58] Stone, *History of Colorado,* 716.

[59] *O.R.,* I, 9:659.

[60] Whitford, *Colorado Volunteers,* 127. Colonel Slough later went to Washington, was commissioned a brigadier general, and was placed in command of the Military District of Alexandria, Virginia. After the Civil War, he was appointed chief justice of the Territory of New Mexico. On December 15, 1867, he was shot and killed by W. L. Rynerson, a member of the territorial legislature, who had unwisely introduced a resolution censuring Slough for alleged unprofessional conduct. *Santa Fe Weekly Gazette,* in various issues from December 21, 1867, to May 2, 1868, gives a detailed report on Slough's death, Rynerson's trial, and "unjust acquittal."

Flushed with an honorable and complete victory, his brave troops eager to complete the destruction of the enemy, Col. Slough read the dispatch brought by Capt. Nicodemus in dismay. He could not destroy the order; it had been too openly delivered to leave any room for evasion. To obey it was to let the enemy, broken and disheartened, escape; to refuse was to subject himself to court martial and disgrace. He issued the order for the backward movement, but resigned his commission.[61]

Governor Connelly also felt that it was a mistake to lose this valuable opportunity. On April 6, 1862, he informed Secretary Seward that "had our troops advanced the day after the battle it would have led to the entire capture or dispersion of the enemy's forces in the neighborhood of Santa Fe."[62] The *Santa Fe Weekly Gazette* likewise expressed disappointment at the Federal order to fall back after the Battle of Glorieta. It claimed that

The retreat gave a virtually vanquished enemy an opportunity to come to Santa Fe and recuperate from losses to which he had been subjected. Had pursuit been made at that time our forces would have met little if any resistance and the Texans would have been so completely routed and broken up that their retreat out of the Territory would have been precipitate.[63]

[61] Hollister, *Boldly They Rode,* 74.
[62] *O.R.,* I, 9:660.
[63] April 26, 1862.

# 5

## Confederates in Retreat

IN THE EVENING of March 29, 1862, the Confederate survivors of the Battle of Glorieta began to arrive at Santa Fe in squads and companies. A few of the men rode, but most of them walked, hobbling along in shoes which were nearly worn out. Most of them had only the clothing that was on their backs and were without blankets or food. All available supplies and equipment in the capital not already confiscated were seized by the Texans. Blankets and camp equipment meant for the Indians which had been cached before the occupation by James L. Collins, U. S. superintendent of Indian Affairs, were found and appropriated. Other items from the cache were taken and sold, the money being pocketed by the Confederates. Private citizens were forced to provide supplies and clothing for the destitute army. Business among the merchants was suspended, and the stores were closed.

Meanwhile, Colonel Canby had remained at Fort Craig during the five weeks following the Battle of Valverde on February 21, 1862, waiting and hoping for reinforcements and supplies from Fort Union. When the food supply ran low, the troops were placed on short rations. Canby and his men occupied a rather helpless and vulnerable position. The Confederates held Santa Fe, Albuquerque, and Socorro to the north. Forts Fillmore and Bliss to the south were likewise in the possession of the Southern forces. No help could be expected from California for months. As a result, no supply trains could get to Fort Craig from any direction, and its garrison faced the possibility of slow starvation. This critical situation and the dispatch from the north informing him of Colonel Slough's aggression against the Confederates compelled Canby to take action.[1]

[1] *O.R.*, I, 9:658.

81

On April 1, Colonel Canby marched out of Fort Craig leading 860 regular and 350 volunteer soldiers. He placed Colonel Christopher ("Kit") Carson, with ten companies of New Mexicans, in charge of the fort in his absence. Canby's plan was to unite his men with the Union troops in northern New Mexico and then compel the Rebels to withdraw from north of Fort Craig.

While en route, traveling up the Río Grande near Socorro, the column met "Doc" Strachan, a resident of Albuquerque, with an important dispatch from the Union commander of the Northern District. The message was read aloud to the troops drawn up in a hollow square. It notified Colonel Canby that during a fierce engagement between the Confederate and Union forces, the Texans had lost their whole train of supplies. Considering themselves in a very precarious situation, the Rebels had commenced their retreat to Texas. The whole Yankee column, from the commanding officer down to the lowest private, gave three rousing cheers. The Texans in charge of the hospital at Socorro, seeing the column in line and hearing the cheers, probably thought Colonel Canby intended to storm the town. They quickly hoisted the hospital flag and sent a delegation to advise Canby that there were only a few able-bodied Confederate troops in town who were acting as guards and nurses of the sick and disabled Texans.

General Henry H. Sibley with his Confederate brigade was also in a critical position. Forts Union and Craig contained all the subsistence supplies in the Territory with the exception of the fast-dwindling supplies already confiscated and what had been hidden by the native population in order to avoid seizure. He had no money with which to purchase supplies except Confederate currency, which was not accepted by the local people. He could not advance toward Fort Union since the Federal troops in that area would throw back any forces that he might send. His army was not strong enough now to attack Fort Craig. Accordingly, it was determined by the Confederate high command to retreat from the Territory if Colonel Canby would allow them to do so.

After having occupied Santa Fe for nearly a month, the Confederate forces evacuated the capital on April 5 and 6 and marched toward Albuquerque, leaving behind their sick and wounded. The Union troops re-entered the city soon after, being received with public demonstrations of joy.[2] Several ladies in Santa Fe, including Mrs. Canby, did some praiseworthy work in caring for the sick and wounded Texans in the hospital in that city. Governor Henry Connelly, with his staff, moved back into the Old Palace. The Stars and Stripes were again raised over the plaza in Santa Fe with an impressive ceremony which was enthusiastically responded to by a large crowd assembled for the occasion. A salute was fired by Captain José Sena's Company of New Mexican Volunteers. Mr. J. Howe Watts responded with a patriotic address. While the *Santa Fe Weekly Gazette* praised the ladies and announced with exultant satisfaction the Governor's return and the flag raising, it sarcastically commented that the only memento the Confederates left the Chief Magistrate was some of General Sibley's proclamations and empty champagne bottles.[3]

Colonel Canby planned when he arrived at Albuquerque to demonstrate with his artillery and infantry in an effort to compel the Confederates to withdraw from Santa Fe. Before his arrival with his column in the vicinity of Albuquerque on April 8, the news of his advance up the river had caused the Texans to leave Santa Fe and march hurriedly to Albuquerque in order to protect their limited supplies located there. The Rebels had fortified the city, placing their artillery and infantry in strategic positions, especially in the eastern end.

Canby immediately ordered a demonstration to determine the full strength of the Texans and the position of their batteries. This was done with Captain James Graydon's spy company and regular cavalry under Major Thomas Duncan. Most of the Union artillery with its infantry and cavalry supports was then posted about one mile east of the city. The opposing forces then engaged

2 *Ibid.*, I, 9:509–11, 664; Whitford, *Colorado Volunteers*, 128.
3 *Santa Fe Weekly Gazette*, April 26, 1862.

in artillery duels and in sharp cavalry and infantry skirmishes along the outskirts of the city for two days. The casualties on both sides were slight, although Major Duncan was wounded in the opening skirmish.

During the cannonading the shots from the Federal guns were more disastrous to the defenseless citizens than to the Confederate soldiers. Colonel Canby requested that the women and children be removed from the city, and when his request was refused, Union gun crews were ordered to cease firing. At night Canby moved his army northeast toward Sandia Mountain, camping at Tijeras, about fifteen miles from Albuquerque. Here they awaited the coming of the troops from Fort Union.

The Federal forces recently engaged in the Battle of Glorieta remained at Fort Union for about a week. On April 5, a courier arrived at the fort with the news that Colonel Canby and his column had left Fort Craig, marching up the Río Grande. The same messenger also carried an order for the command at Fort Union to hasten south to meet Canby. Some of the Colorado Volunteers were provoked at the inconsistency of Canby's orders since they now had to march back over much of the same route that they had been compelled to travel the week before.

On April 6, after leaving a detachment to guard the fort, a majority of the troops moved out of the post under Colonel Paul, Fourth Regiment New Mexican Volunteers. Traveling by way of Las Vegas, Bernal Springs, San José, Kozlowski's Ranch, and Galisteo, the two Union columns were united at Tijeras late at night on April 13. The forced march from Fort Union was grueling, having been made in extreme weather conditions and over a route mostly rough and untraveled. During the last day of the march, the column traveled forty-six miles, with many horses and mules dying from overwork and underfeeding. Some of the infantry were left exhausted along the route. Here Colonel Slough's resignation was officially accepted. In response to a petition from the commissioned officers of the First Colorado Regiment, presented by Lieutenant Colonel S. F. Tappan, Colonel Canby, through a field order, appointed Major Chivington to the position of colonel of that regiment. Captain Wynkoop of the First Colorado, Company A, was advanced to the position of major.[4]

General Sibley, fearing no immediate attack from the Federal troops at Albuquerque for a few days, soon completed plans to evacuate the city. The Confederates hastily buried part of the brass cannon with which the command had originally been supplied from those guns surrendered by General David E. Twiggs at San Antonio, Texas. The carriages were retained for transportation purposes. They kept the six fieldpieces captured from Canby's forces at Valverde. The ammunition for the buried guns was entirely exhausted by this time.[5]

During the morning of April 12, 1862, the evacuation of Albuquerque by the Texans commenced, with Colonel Scurry's Fourth Regiment, a battalion of Colonel William Steele's Seventh Regiment, Major Pyron's battalion, and part of the artillery, crossing to the west bank of the Río Grande by ferry and ford. Colonel Thomas Green's Fifth Regiment was ordered to follow, but finding the ford difficult, moved down the east side of the river to Peralta, opposite Los Lunas, where Sibley had halted the remainder of his army to await Green's arrival.

On April 14, the united Union forces under Colonel Canby left Tijeras and after a march of thirty-six miles southward down the east side of the Río Grande to Peralta, camped unbeknownst to the Texans within one mile of Governor Henry Connelly's ranch. Here the Confederates had taken full possession and were indulging in revelry with liquor, music, and dance until the late

---

[4] Hall, *History of the State of Colorado*, 283; Stone, *History of Colorado*, 716.

[5] Whitford, *Colorado Volunteers*, 129–30, 137, 138; Keleher, *Turmoil in New Mexico*, 207. Several cannon were buried in Albuquerque (Keleher claimed that there were six; Whitford stated that there were eight). On August 18, 1889 (Whitford listed this date as 1892), former Confederate Major Trevanion T. Teel, El Paso, Texas, directed a large group of curious citizens to a spot, five hundred feet northeast of San Felipe Church, where they began digging. Safre Alexander, the landowner, objected and sought a court injunction. George Lail, mineowner, who had previously offered Alexander $100 for any damage to the land that might occur, posted a mining location on the plot. This legalized the prospecting, and the guns were recovered. They were later divided between Albuquerque city government and Colorado Historical Society.

hours of the night. Colonel J. M. Chivington, who had been informed of the situation by scouts, requested permission to surprise and capture this Texan detachment at once. Colonel Canby, "always cautious and now fearful of disaster," denied the request, but Chivington persisted, offering to use his Colorado Regiment to make the assault. Canby refused again, stating that if he could overcome his doubts concerning the propriety of a night attack, he would send for Chivington and let him make the attempt. Chivington knew nothing further concerning Canby's intentions or whereabouts until daylight, when the latter was seen with his servant kindling a fire. Almost simultaneous with the flash of the match to light the fire came the flash of the Rebel guns. The first shot beheaded one of Canby's mules, dangerously close to the Colonel himself. This opened the Battle of Peralta.

Whitford believed that the actions of Canby were evidence of a desire to avoid an engagement and allow the Confederates to retreat so as to conserve the Union supplies which would have been needed for the captives. He also contended that the feeling in the Union ranks against Canby became bitter with suspicion. It was felt that since Colonel Canby was a brother-in-law of General Sibley, the former was injuring the Federal cause while favoring that of the Confederates.[6] Bancroft wrote that Canby was "accused of an unwillingness to kill his old comrades, of jealousy toward the volunteers, and even cowardice."[7]

Later, during the morning of April 15, a seven-wagon Confederate supply train with a mountain howitzer, escorted by a lieutenant and thirty men, was seen approaching Peralta from Albuquerque. A detachment of thirty-three Colorado cavalrymen, followed by two companies of Federal infantry, was sent to capture the train, and accomplished the task with the loss of only one man. Four Texans were killed, six wounded, and the remainder were taken prisoner. The captured wagons and gun with seventy mules and fifteen horses were then brought into the Union camp. Lieutenant Ira M. Claflin used the how-

[6] Whitford, *Colorado Volunteers*, 130–32.
[7] Bancroft, *History of Arizona and New Mexico*, 698.

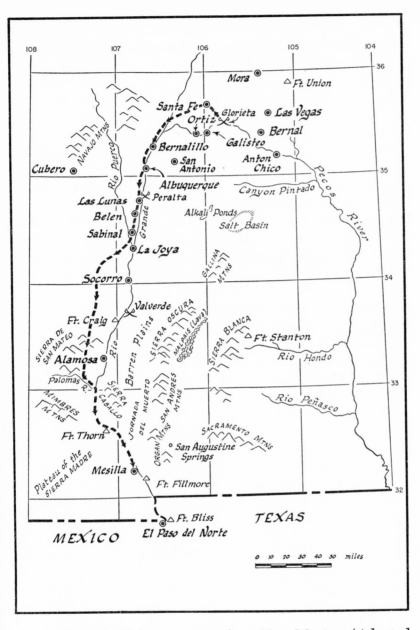

Route of the Confederate retreat from New Mexico. (Adapted from *Battles and Leaders of the Civil War* [1887].)

itzer with his battery during the Union bombardment of the Confederate lines.[8]

To test the strength of the Texans and locate the position of their artillery, Captain James Graydon, with his spy company of New Mexican Volunteers, galloped into the outskirts of Peralta, and after exchanging a few shots with the Rebels, dropped back. Colonels G. R. Paul and J. M. Chivington, each commanding an infantry column, with a section of artillery in the center and three companies of cavalry under Captain R. M. Morris, Third U. S. Cavalry, moved through the woods toward Peralta, driving the Confederates out of Governor Connelly's ranch and from the dense forest of trees which surrounded it. The Union troops then started toward the river to gain the shelter of the timber in a maneuver to retake the town and seize control of the ford.[9]

When General Sibley learned of the critical position of Colonel Thomas Green's Fifth Texas Regiment on the east side of the Río Grande, he sent his entire force, then at Los Lunas, across the river under Colonel Scurry to assist Green, reserving only a sufficient number of men to guard their supply train. Later Sibley crossed the stream himself, but claimed that he was forced back to the west bank "amid a shower of balls." The united Confederate force then entrenched behind adobe walls.[10]

In the meantime, the Union troops were ordered by Colonel Canby to hold their line, but not to advance farther. This resulted in defensive tactics on both sides, consisting mainly of skirmishing and cannonading which continued until after nightfall. During the bombardment Colonel Chivington and one of his captains barely escaped a Confederate cannon ball, which, after skipping along the ground directly toward them, bounded a

[8] Hollister, *Boldly They Rode*, 92–93; *O.R.*, I, 9:551. Canby placed the Confederate casualties during this skirmish at 6 killed, 3 wounded, 22 prisoners.

[9] Hollister, *Boldly They Rode*, 93; *O.R.*, I, 9:551, 672–73. Governor Connelly bitterly complained that during the forty-eight hours the Confederates were in possession of his ranch, they destroyed $30,000 worth of property, much of which was through pure vandalism.

[10] *O.R.*, I, 9:510, 665.

few inches over their heads. Unfortunately, this same ball then fatally struck two Federal soldiers who were walking behind the officers.[11]

Hollister, exasperated at Colonel Canby's lack of aggressiveness, wrote that Colonel Paul, second in command, was eager to bring on a pitched battle. He permitted Major Wynkoop, at his own request, to advance his battalion for that purpose. The cavalry was to charge on the right and Chivington's column was to support Wynkoop when the occasion required. The plan of attack had been inaugurated when Canby came to the front and "squashed" it. This Colorado cavalryman continued:

It was the most harmless battle on record. . . . Canby and Sibley are comrades of old. We lay around on the ground in line of battle asleep. I had ample time to take the fullest notes. . . . The General (Canby) was castigated unmercifully that night. . . . With a superior better appointed force, we had fired a few artillery shots; had been drawn up in line of battle for six hours, just beyond the rifle range of the foe . . . left the ford unguarded and allowed them to put the river between us.[12]

Hall related that Canby ordered the Federal troops to clear the woods of Rebels, but to be sure not to bring on a general engagement. For five hours in the broiling sun, Colonel Paul and his men were drawn up in line of battle receiving the shelling from the Texan batteries under cover of adobe walls and heavy cottonwood timber. The entire day was spent in "standing up to be shot at by the Rebels without the privilege of returning the fire," except when the artillery answered them from the place Canby had occupied in the morning.[13]

During the night of April 15, the Texan troops withdrew from their position and in darkness crossed the Río Grande at Los Lunas. They left behind their dead, and some of their wounded and sick were left without attendants, medicine, and almost

11 Whitford, *Colorado Volunteers*, 132.
12 Hollister, *Boldly They Rode*, 94–95.
13 Hall, *History of the State of Colorado*, 284.

without food. In their haste, while crossing, they abandoned three supply wagons, which fell into Union hands the next day.

By daylight next morning, the Confederate column had advanced five miles down the west side of the stream in their retreat. Whitford wrote that Colonel Canby permitted them to escape unmolested although his force was double that of Sibley. He claimed that the Union people of New Mexico, as well as nearly all of his soldiers, never forgave Colonel Canby for permitting the Confederates to go in peace.[14]

Governor Connelly, although anxious for the capture of the Confederates, was not so critical. He wrote that the cannonading was carried on from both sides without any serious results. He defended Canby by explaining that the position of the enemy was a strong one and dangerous for the infantry to approach because of the enemy's position behind high adobe walls. Against this position, he continued, Canby did not think it advisable to make any demonstration. During the night the enemy silently withdrew.[15]

Morale in the Confederate ranks was now reaching a low ebb. It was reported in the *Santa Fe Weekly Gazette* on April 26 that from 200 to 250 Texans refused to take part in the engagement at Peralta, claiming that they had been induced by misrepresentation to join the expedition. They contended that they had been paid nothing and had had no provisions while in New Mexico except what they had taken from the people. The mutineers threatened to shoot Colonel Scurry if he should attempt to bring them into the engagement.

It is hard to reach an accurate count of the casualties at Peralta since there is nothing said in the Confederate official reports and the Federal sources are incomplete. From what is available, the Texan casualties in killed, wounded and imprisoned totaled about thirty-five. The Union reported loss in killed and wounded was less than ten, with no prisoners.[16]

[14] Whitford, *Colorado Volunteers,* 132.
[15] *O.R.,* I, 9:665.
[16] Hollister, *Boldly They Rode,* 92, Confederates, 4 killed, 6 wounded, 25 prisoners; Union, 2 killed, 1 wounded who died later. Whitford, *Colorado Volun-*

Sibley's brigade was now retreating faster than its couriers could notify the Confederate bases farther south. During the fight at Peralta, twenty-six Texan troopers traveling up the Río Grande from Socorro had bypassed Los Lunas and Peralta. Reaching Albuquerque, where they expected to join Colonel Scurry, on April 16, they were taken prisoner by a Federal detachment of troops.

Instead of following the fleeing Texans across the Río Grande, Canby ordered his troops to advance down the east side of the river, intending to cross farther down. The Union column gradually overtook the Confederates. The Rebel supply wagons and artillery had by this time become such an encumbrance along the rough, sandy road, where there was little forage for the draft animals, that abandonment of either the wagons or the artillery seemed inevitable. On April 16, the armies, now nearly abreast, traveled along on the opposite banks of the stream at about the same speed. Frequently they were within cannon range of each other. That night the two forces camped in plain view of one another on the river between Sabinal and La Joya.

General Sibley's original plan was to push down the Río Grande in advance of the Federal troops and attack and demolish Fort Craig with its reduced garrison. Colonels Green and Scurry and other high officers of command suggested at this time, in order to avoid another engagement in their crippled condition, that a detour be made through the mountains west of the river, thus avoiding Fort Craig and reaching the stream below the post. This proposition was accepted by Sibley. Major Bethel Coopwood, who had commanded a spy company under Lieutenant Colonel Baylor and claimed to know the topography of the region, was chosen to lead the Southern army over the mountainous, trackless route. All of the wagons which could be dispensed with were abandoned. Seven days' provisions were

*teers,* 131–32, 159, Confederates, 6 killed, 3 wounded, 22 prisoners; Union, 4 Colorado Volunteers and 2 Federal (regular) soldiers killed; nothing on non-fatal wounds. Stone, *History of Colorado,* 716, 4 Colorado boys killed, many others wounded. *O.R.,* I, 9:551, Canby reported Confederates, 6 killed, 3 wounded, 22 captured; Union, 1 killed, 3 wounded.

allocated, and the entire remaining Confederate force except the sick and wounded marched out of camp during the night.

At dawn on the morning of April 17, the Yankee commander observed that there was no action in the Rebel encampment, although the campfires were burning brightly. After waiting some time for the Texans to commence their march, Canby sent some scouts across the Río Grande, who soon returned with the information that the Confederate camp was vacant and that it had been abandoned during the night. It was ascertained that Sibley and his men, after leaving behind thirty-eight supply wagons, had left the river and proceeded westward toward the north end of the Magdalena Mountains.

This part of the Confederate retreat was a desperate one. They passed along the west side of the Sierra Magdalena and through the San Mateo Mountains until they reached the dry bed of the Palomas River, down which they trudged until they reached the Río Grande. Here they received supplies which had been sent to them from Mesilla. The men were nearly famished and exhausted. It was over one hundred miles from where they had left the Río Grande until they reached it again. The dreary march was made in ten days on seven days' poor rations. The artillery which they were able to take with them was dragged uphill and lowered by the men with ropes. The undergrowth and brush for several miles was so dense that they had to cut their way through with axes and bowie knives. Nearly everything except what the men could personally carry, including much of their remaining ammunition, was abandoned along the way. A Union army officer who traveled over this route nearly a year later related that "I not infrequently found a piece of gun carriage, a part of a harness or some pieces of camp or garrison equipage with occasionally a white, dry skeleton of a man."[17]

During this phase of the retreat the Confederates were unmolested by Federal troops, with the exception of Captain James Graydon and his spy company, who followed at some distance

[17] Pettis, "Confederate Invasion," *Battles and Leaders of the Civil War,* II, 110–11.

behind the ill-fated expedition, picking up a quantity of service-able articles which had been abandoned. They found three bodies which had been only partially interred, along with the arm of a man half-eaten by the wolves, and reburied them. Wagons, harnesses, camping equipment, and more than sixty dead horses and mules were found along the way. In one place the Texans had blown up and burned six caissons, one twelve-pound howitzer and two mountain howitzer carriages. On an-other occasion nineteen wagons, ten ambulances, six caissons, and three carriages had been burned. At one spot three howitzers were buried and six one-hundred-pound barrels of gunpowder were blown up.

Colonel Canby, on May 4, wrote Washington that the Con-federate force, in rapid transit, had taken a route through a mountainous and difficult country which was destitute of water. From scouts and prisoners he had learned that the retreating Texans were greatly demoralized. They had abandoned every-thing that would impede their flight, including their sick and wounded, whom they left by the wayside. Many of these, he stated, had been brought in and properly cared for. Arrange-ments had also been made to collect the valuable property which had been left behind by the Confederates.

Following the discovery on the morning of April 17 of the sudden departure of the Texans, the Union troops continued their march down the east side of the Río Grande and camped opposite Polvadera. The Federal column rested for a day while Canby determined the approximate location of the detouring Confederates and strengthened the security of his supply train in the rear. William Pelham, former surveyor general, came into the camp with thirty other Confederate prisoners. After taking the oath of allegiance, they were paroled and departed from the Territory. The Northern army then proceeded on down the river and crossed to the west side at Lemitar. Here seventy-five Confederate sick and stragglers were taken. On the march again, the Yankees passed through Socorro and arrived at Fort Craig on the twenty-second of April.

93

During the march down the river the Union command had been divided into three columns, the infantry under Colonels Paul and Chivington and the cavalry under Captain R. M. Morris. When it was learned that the Confederates would probably return to the Río Grande several miles below Fort Craig, Paul, Chivington, and Morris, as well as many of their men, were eager to pursue the Texans and harass them from the rear, but Canby would not consent. The Union army then went into encampment in and around Fort Craig. The force was scattered from the battlefield of Valverde seven miles north to the river bottom three miles south of the post.

Here during the next six weeks they underwent one of the severest tests to which the Union troops were subjected. Canby's command had traveled faster than its supplies and from necessity was put on quarter-rations. Day after day supplies were expected, but to the astonishment and disgust of the men, the first supply wagons to arrive were loaded with nothing but whiskey and vinegar—not a pound of anything else. The only rations remaining were six ounces of flour per day and the poorest of mutton. The men and officers grew cross and morose, and mutiny threatened.[18]

Placing Colonel Chivington in command of the Military District of Southern New Mexico, Colonel Canby, with his staff and some of the regular soldiers, left Fort Craig on April 27 for the Department of New Mexico headquarters at Santa Fe. Colonels B. S. Roberts and G. R. Paul were assigned districts in the central and northern part of the Territory. A communiqué from Washington received about the time he arrived at the capital informed Canby that he had been promoted to brigadier general. With the Confederate army in full retreat and Canby thoroughly conscious of the difficulty of securing supplies in New Mexico, the General now urged Army Headquarters in Washington to send only two of the five regiments originally ordered from the Middle West to the Territory.[19]

[18] Hall, *History of the State of Colorado,* 285.
[19] *O.R.,* I, 9:666, 669–70; Hall, *History of the State of Colorado,* 285.

Colonel Chivington remained at Fort Craig until July 4, when at his own request he was relieved of the command of the Southern District of New Mexico by Colonel Marshall S. Howe, Third U. S. Cavalry. Chivington then reported in person to General Canby at Santa Fe and procured an order to move the First Colorado Volunteers to Fort Union. He also obtained a leave of absence and traveled to Washington to ask that his regiment be changed to a cavalry organization and transferred to the Army of the Potomac. His request was only partially granted. In October, 1862, the War Department directed that the First Colorado be made into a cavalry unit, but for western service only. The regiment arrived back in Colorado in January, 1863, where it was mounted. It continued in service in Colorado and adjacent territories during the remainder of the war.

General Sibley arrived at Fort Bliss in Texas during the first week in May, 1862, while his shattered army was strung out for fifty miles to the rear. He reported to Army Headquarters at Richmond on May 4 that his whole force was comfortably quartered in villages extending from Doña Ana, New Mexico, to Fort Bliss, and that the sick and wounded Texans in hospitals at Santa Fe, Albuquerque, and Socorro were receiving adequate medical attention. He claimed that his campaign had resulted in defeating the enemy in every encounter against all odds. He stated that his troops were well clad and well supplied in other respects and that from being the worst-armed force his was now the best-armed force in the country.[20]

Sibley's appraisal of the Confederate campaign in the Intermountain West was not shared by all of his men. One trooper claimed that the Sibley brigade met its "Waterloo" in the Battle of Glorieta, thus starting a rapid retreat "with every man for himself." He bitterly related that they had walked and staggered along, reeling, hungry, and thirsty, like wretches. The "blood thirsty Dog Canyon" Apache Indians followed, scalping the poor, unfortunate boys whose blistered feet and enfeebled

[20] *O.R.*, I, 9:511–12. Sibley naïvely reported that sufficient funds in Confederate paper had been left to provide comfort for the sick "if it be negotiated."

95

frames made it impossible for them to march farther. While describing how many of the men were kept from starving by the arrival of dried buffalo meat, he regretted that the "drunken individual" (referring to Sibley) who caused all their misfortune was kept from starving.[21]

Another Texan soldier, while trudging south with fifty other paroled prisoners, wrote that the retreat through the New Mexican towns was different from their march north two months previously. They felt like heroes after the fight at Fort Craig, where they had frightened the New Mexican Volunteers away and had driven the regular soldiers into the fort. Then they were confident that New Mexico would soon be controlled by the Southern government and Union communication with California would be cut off. "But what a mistake," he commented. After three battles with Federal forces, all of the Confederate troops who were not killed, wounded, or taken prisoner had to destroy everything they possibly could and "flee to the mountains for their lives and get out of the country, the Lord knows how." He hoped that General Sibley would soon be hanged and urged his brother John back home not to join the Texan Volunteers. He concluded, "Had it not been for the devils from Pikes Peak [Colorado Volunteers] this country would have been ours."[22]

In his report to Richmond on the Confederate campaign into New Mexico made from Fort Bliss on May 4, Sibley did not show the enthusiasm that he had exhibited earlier. He tersely concluded that "except for its political, geographical position, the Territory of New Mexico is not worth a quarter of the blood and treasure expended in its conquest." He stated that his troops had "manifested a dogged, irreconcilable detestation of the country and people," and intimated that they would decidedly object if ordered to return.[23] On May 27, in a letter to General H. P. Bee, commanding in West Texas, Sibley added other rea-

[21] Noel, *Autobiography*, 60, 63.
[22] Hollister, *Boldly They Rode*, 166–70. Excerpts from a letter written by Private George M. Brown at Socorro, New Mexico, April 30, 1862, to his wife in Texas. See note 10 in Chapter IV.
[23] *O.R.*, I, 9:512.

sons for the withdrawal from New Mexico when he wrote that in the absence of all official communication from Richmond or local departments, he was "constrained to abandon New Mexico." Provisions, forage, clothing, and ammunition were completely exhausted.[24]

Although the withdrawal of the Confederate Army from New Mexico was discouraging to the Southern leaders, Sibley was not openly criticized by high officials from Richmond. On June 7, 1862, President Davis congratulated him on the distinguished success of his command, especially considering the field of operations and superior number and means of supply of the enemy. The President of the Confederacy felt confident that, with the assistance of the two regiments being sent from Texas, Sibley would "be able to meet the more immediate and pressing exigencies that may arise."[25] A week earlier General Robert E. Lee in Richmond had notified Brigadier General P. O. Hebert, commanding the Department of Texas, that President Davis had been informed of the critical and destitute condition of Sibley's command in New Mexico. Lee assured Hebert that he was right in sending to Sibley's relief the two regiments of cavalry from Texas which had previously been ordered to Little Rock, Arkansas. Lee suggested that the governor of Texas be called upon to aid the New Mexican expedition with a greater number of men and additional supplies.[26]

When General Sibley retired to Fort Bliss, he left Colonel William Steele with about four hundred troops at Fort Fillmore, where they remained until July, 1862. Two minor skirmishes occurred during the latter part of May. On May 21, a Confederate detachment under Lieutenant Bowman suddenly appeared at Paraje, a Union garrison of forty-five men in southern New Mexico, and demanded its surrender. Captain Joseph C. Tilford

---

24 *Ibid.*, I, 9:714. Sibley's statement on clothing and ammunition does not correlate with his report of May 4, when he wrote that his troops were well clad and were the best armed in the country.

25 *Ibid.*, I, 9:717–18.

26 *Ibid.*, I, 9:716. These two promised cavalry regiments never entered New Mexico.

refused the demand and prepared for an attack. The Confederates fired several harmless shots at long range and then continued their retreat south. On May 23, a Yankee picket, about eight miles below Fort Craig, was attacked by a larger Rebel force, but without loss to the Federals. The Texans lost four men in the encounter. The ill-fated Confederate expedition, during its campaign into New Mexico, suffered severely in dead, wounded, and prisoners. Accounts vary from one-third to one-half of the entire force, or a total loss of from 1,200 to 1,700 men.[27]

On February 28, 1862, while General Sibley's victorious Confederate army, following the Battle of Valverde, was marching up the Río Grande, Captain Sherod Hunter, with his company of mounted Texans, had captured Tucson without a fight. During the occupation of this area, Captain Hunter and his troopers "lived off the country," as Sibley's force was doing in the Río Grande Valley. Using Tucson as a base, the Confederates confiscated food, animals, and other property, including some Northern-owned mines. Some valuable Federal-owned property was destroyed. A few Union sympathizers were arrested, while others, suspected of Federal inclinations, were driven out of the country. The Texans did guard the region, to some extent, against the Apache Indians. Hunter's maneuvers, striking first at one place and then at another miles away, gave some Union leaders the impression that he had a much larger command.

Colonel James Reily, First Texas Regiment, on March 3, 1862, en route to Sonora, Mexico, with a letter to its Governor Ignacio Pesqueira from Sibley, left Tucson, escorted by twenty soldiers under Lieutenant Tevis. This was part of Sibley's plan to negotiate a pact with the state governors of northern Mexico. The governor of Chihuahua had been previously consulted.[28] Reily returned, reporting to Southern leaders that he had made a favorable treaty. Actually little was accomplished except to

[27] *O.R.*, I, 9:608, 666. Loss of 1,200 from the army of 3,000. Pettis, "Confederate Invasion," *Battles and Leaders of the Civil War*, II, 111, wrote that the Confederates started with 3,700 and returned with 2,000, a loss of 1,700.

[28] *O.R.*, I, 4:167–74; I, 9:708.

obtain permission to purchase supplies for gold or silver. The Mexicans refused to accept Confederate currency.

On March 3, Captain Hunter led his command to the Pima Indian villages on the Gila River. Here the Texans arrested Ammi M. White, a Federal purchasing agent, and confiscated 1,500 sacks of wheat which had been accumulated for the Northern Army. The wheat was redistributed among the Indians since the Rebels had no means of transporting it. Hunter and his men carried off White's flour, chickens, and hogs and wrecked his flour mill. They destroyed a considerable amount of hay, distributed by Federal purchasing agents along the route from Fort Yuma on the Colorado River up the Gila River in Arizona for use by the Union forces. It was while in the vicinity of the Pima Indian villages that the Hunter detachment first came in contact with California Volunteers.

# 6

# California to the Río Grande

On July 24, 1861, Secretary of War Simon Cameron authorized Governor John G. Downey of California to raise one regiment of infantry and five companies of cavalry to guard the
Overland Mail route from Carson Valley to Salt Lake City and
Fort Laramie.[1] Mustered in at Presidio in San Francisco and
trained across the bay in Oakland, the infantry at Camp Downey
and the cavalry at Camp Merchant became the nucleus of the
California Column which entered Arizona and New Mexico in
1862 and served there throughout the Civil War. It remained
for another regiment of California Volunteers to guard the Overland Mail route.

General Winfield Scott on August 16, 1861, ordered Brigadier
General E. V. Sumner, commander of the Department of the
Pacific, to lead an expedition from San Francisco by ship to
Mazatlán, Mexico, and then march overland through the Mexican states of Sinaloa, Sonora, and Chihuahua into western Texas
to "regain public property and draw the insurgent troops from
Arkansas and Missouri."[2] General Sumner, although setting in
motion the necessary plans to execute the order, wrote Washington suggesting an alternate plan of going through Guaymas,
Sonora. On September 17, 1861, Senator M. S. Latham of California wrote General Sumner that the War Department had de-
ferred the order for the California expedition to invade Texas
through Mexico.[3]

On the same date, in response to reports that Secessionists
were threatening in Southern California, Sumner ordered the

[1] *O.R.*, I, 50:543. (part 1).
[2] *Ibid.*, I, 50:572 (part 1).
[3] *Ibid.*, I, 50:593–94, 624 (part 1). Latham infers that it was through his
insistence that the order was countermanded.

First California Infantry and Cavalry from their training base in Oakland to the southern part of the state. During the late summer and fall of 1861, other California Volunteers were mustered into the United States Army, many of whom were also concentrated in Southern California. In December, 1861, when it was learned in California that Brigadier General Henry H. Sibley, with a Confederate army, threatened to invade New Mexico and Arizona, Brigadier General George Wright, commanding the Department of the Pacific, received permission from Washington, with the personal endorsement of Major General George B. McClellan, to march an army of California troops into Arizona and New Mexico.[4]

The California Column was then organized, and Colonel James H. Carleton was placed in command. It consisted of the First California Infantry, commanded by Lieutenant Colonel Joseph R. West, five companies of First California Cavalry, under Lieutenant Colonel Edward R. Eyre, five companies of the Fifth California Infantry, commanded by Colonel George W. Bowie, Company B, Second California Cavalry, under Captain John C. Cremony, and Company A, Third U. S. Artillery, commanded by Lieutenant John B. Shinn. There was a total of 2,350 men. The column had the double objective of preventing a Confederate invasion of California and helping to expel the enemy from Arizona and New Mexico.[5]

For several months during the latter part of 1861 and early in 1862, men and supplies were gradually concentrated at Fort Yuma on the Colorado River in preparation for the advance into Arizona. The tedious journey through the desert in southeastern California required many weeks. The scarcity of water in certain areas compelled the troops to march one company at a time, twenty-four hours apart. Frequently they traveled at night.

Military supplies, food, and forage for the animals were very

<hr />

[4] *Ibid.,* I, 50:752–53 (part 1).

[5] *Ibid.,* I, 9:595–96, I, 50:1075 (part 1); Bancroft, *History of Arizona and New Mexico,* 514; Twitchell, *New Mexican History,* 389. The name "California Column" was not officially applied to this army until May 15, 1862.

difficult to transport. Some provisions were slowly hauled overland while others were shipped from San Francisco and San
Pedro down the Pacific Coast, through the Gulf of California,
and up the Colorado River to Fort Yuma. From that post almost
everything that was used by the column, except some wheat
and hay purchased with *manta* from the Pima Indians, had to
be transported by wagons or pack mules.[6]

Before leaving Los Angeles for Fort Yuma, Colonel Carleton
had received dispatches concerning the activities in Arizona of
Captain Sherod Hunter and his Confederate troopers. On March
15, 1862, Carleton ordered Major E. A. Rigg, commander at
Yuma, to send Captain William McCleave of the First California
Cavalry with a detachment into Arizona, using the pretext that
he was going out to fight Tonto Indians. Actually McCleave was
to lead a company of cavalry and one of infantry into that territory. They were to travel up the Gila River to the Bend, cross
country to the Pima Indian villages, then south, where they
would surround and take Tucson before being discovered. Mc-
Cleave, according to the outlined plan of Carleton, would then
"be able to capture and destroy Mr. Hunter and his band of
renegades and traitors."[7] Anxious that McCleave succeed, Carleton wrote him directly with detailed instructions. The Colonel
predicted that if the Union captain was able, by surprise, to
"fall on Hunter at Tucson with his 100 mounted Texans," it
would be an accomplishment for McCleave to remember all the
rest of his life.[8]

Captain McCleave, however, became the victim of clever
strategy himself. Captain Hunter, after capturing Ammi M.
White, the Union agent, and confiscating the Federal wheat,
remained at the Pima villages, planning to seize fifty wagons
reported to be en route for the wheat. Captain McCleave pushed
ahead of the main body of his troops with nine picked men,

[6] George H. Pettis, "The California Column," *Historical Society of New
Mexico*, 7, 8, 12; *O.R.*, I, 50:1052 (part 1). The Indians had no use for regular
money; therefore, *manta*, ordinary cotton cloth, was used as currency.
[7] *O.R.*, I, 50:928–30 (part 1).
[8] *Ibid.*, I, 50:931–32 (part 1).

traveling up the Gila River toward the Pima villages. Arriving at White's residence near the villages at daylight about March 18, with two men, McCleave asked to see Mr. White personally. Captain Hunter, who was sleeping in the house, was awakened, and, representing himself as White, asked McCleave if those were all the men he had with him. The Californian replied that he had six others near by. McCleave, seeing no uniforms, and supposing he was among friends, had taken off his firearms while his men were putting up the horses. Meanwhile, Hunter's men were gathering around. Suddenly Hunter drew his pistol, announced that he was a Confederate captain, and stated that McCleave was his prisoner.[9] McCleave and White were eventually taken to Mesilla on the Río Grande, where McCleave was later exchanged for two lieutenants. White was released later when Colonel William Steele's detachment finally retreated from New Mexico.

Both officers and men of the California Column were eager to push into Arizona and New Mexico and drive the Confederates out. Captain William Calloway, late in March, 1862, started from Fort Yuma with a Union vanguard of 272 men, composed of California infantry and cavalry and a battery of two twelve-pound howitzers. The Federal command had planned that Calloway march up the Gila River to the Pima villages, where a base was to be established. From there the cavalry were to dash forward into Tucson by a cross-country route and surprise the Rebels. Then, if necessary, they could fall back to the Pimas. Special haste was urged in order to recapture Captain McCleave before he could be taken east to Mesilla. When the vanguard reached the Gila River Bend, Union pickets were fired upon by Texan troopers who had been destroying Federal hay along the route. One Californian was wounded. A Yankee

[9] *Ibid.*, I, 9:708; I, 50:940, 966 (part 1). Sources disagree on the date of Captain McCleave's capture. On March 19, Lieutenant James Barrett of Captain McCleave's command wrote Major E. A. Rigg at Fort Yuma announcing that McCleave had been captured. Bancroft, *History of Arizona and New Mexico*, 514, Sloan and Adams, *History of Arizona*, I, 260, and Wyllys, *Arizona*, 148, all place the date of the capture more than two weeks later, on April 6.

cavalry detachment under Captain N. J. Pishan was sent in pursuit, but the Rebels could not be caught.

Arriving at the Pima villages, Captain Calloway learned that a Confederate detachment under Lieutenant Jack Swilling was just leaving the vicinity. Captain Sherod Hunter with most of his Texan troopers by this time was back in Tucson. Lieutenant James Barrett with twelve Union cavalrymen was directed to make a wide detour in order to strike the Confederates on their flank, while Calloway, with the main party, was to attack in front. The retreating Texans were not found in the immediate front, but after traveling several miles, Barrett with his men, on April 15, 1862, caught up with the Rebel detachment of sixteen men at Picacho Pass about forty-five miles northwest of Tucson. The Yankees forced the Texans into the chaparral, where a few minutes of fierce fighting took place. Calloway with the main group of Federal troops charged forward when they heard the rapid firing. Barrett and two of his men were killed and three were wounded. Two Confederates were wounded, three were taken prisoner, and the remainder escaped. The fight at Picacho Pass was the only Civil War skirmish fought in present-day Arizona. It has been referred to by one writer as the "westernmost" battle of the war.[10]

The Union dead were buried a short distance from where they fell. The Federal force then bivouacked on the battlefield for the night. The following day, over the protest of all of his officers, Captain Calloway ordered a retreat back to Stanwix Station, more than one hundred miles away. Here the detachment met a large force of the California Column led by Lieutenant Colonel West.[11] Calloway's troops were much superior in numbers to Hunter's. Had he at that time pushed on, no doubt he could have forced the Confederate captain with his troopers all the way back to the Río Grande.

[10] Wyllys, *Arizona*, 148.
[11] Pettis, "California Column," *Historical Society of New Mexico*, 10. Stanwix Station, according to William C. Barnes, *Arizona Place Names*, 422, located about ninety-six miles east of Yuma. Previous to the Civil War, it was operated by the Butterfield Overland Express.

The Territory of Arizona in 1864.

The united Union force then proceeded to the Pima Indian villages. Here a permanent fortification was built which was called Fort Barrett in memory of the Federal officer killed at Picacho Pass. The fort served not only as a military base, but also as a trading post to obtain wheat and forage from the Indians.

On May 14, Lieutenant Colonel West, with an advance detachment of infantry and cavalry, marched out of Fort Barrett at the Pima villages for Tucson. He traveled by way of abandoned Fort Breckenridge, located near the junction of the Gila and the San Pedro rivers. Arriving on the eighteenth, he and his men reoccupied the old fort. The United States flag was run up again on the flagstaff, amid the cheers of the soldiers and playing of the "Star-Spangled Banner."[12]

Tucson was occupied by the advance guard of the California Volunteers, under Lieutenant Colonel Joseph R. West, on May 20, 1862, without firing a shot. Captain Emil Fritz with Company B, First Cavalry, charged into the town only to find all of the Confederate soldiers gone. Five companies of Union infantry arrived the following day. Captain Sherod Hunter with eighty Texan troopers had evacuated Tucson on May 4, heading east toward the Río Grande accompanied by several Southern civilians. The Secessionists who could not follow Hunter fled across the border into Sonora. While en route near Dragoon Spring, about fifty-four miles east of Tucson, Hunter's party was attacked by Apaches, who killed four men and stole thirty-five mules and twenty horses. The arrival of the Yankees at Tucson, according to Colonel Carleton, was "hailed with great joy by all of the people" who remained.[13]

Tucson was almost a ghost town when the Californians arrived. Gradually most of the citizens returned. Some of them had fled months before when the Confederates occupied the area. Others departed when Hunter evacuated, fearing reprisal

[12] *O.R.*, I, 9:598; Pettis, "California Column," *Historical Society of New Mexico*, 10–11.
[13] *O.R.*, I, 9:553, 50:1088, 1095 (part 1).

from the Federals.[14] The advance troopers were at first quartered in town, but Lieutenant Colonel West soon established a camp outside of Tucson which was named Fort Lowell, honoring Union General C. R. Lowell, killed in Virginia in May, 1862.[15]

Meanwhile, Colonel James H. Carleton with a section of the California Column had marched from Fort Yuma. At Fort Barrett, on May 24, he ordered Lieutenant Colonel Edward E. Eyre to garrison Fort Breckenridge with the First California Cavalry. The name of the post was to be changed to Fort Stanford in honor of the governor of California. Lieutenant Colonel West was ordered to leave Tucson under the command of Captain William McMullen and proceed with Fritz's company of cavalry and a detachment of infantry to old Fort Buchanan, southeast of Tucson. Upon his arrival, West found that all of the buildings had been destroyed. Carleton, a short time later, withdrew the garrison to Tucson since the site had no military importance. The Stars and Stripes were raised again for this brief period to consecrate "the ground anew to the country."[16]

Colonel Carleton reached Tucson on June 7, 1862. His arrival was greeted with a salute from Lieutenant John B. Shinn's entire battery.[17] Carleton immediately took several steps to assert the authority of the Federal government. He declared on June 8 that the Congress of the United States had set apart a portion of New Mexico and organized it into the Territory of Arizona. He designated himself military governor of the Territory and proclaimed martial law. He contended that during the chaotic situation existing in Arizona, without civil authority and with

[14] *Alta California,* July 10, 1862. The correspondent of this newspaper described Tucson as a little old Mexican town, built of adobe, and capable of "containing about 1,500 souls."

[15] Barnes, *Arizona Place Names,* 255; Wyllys, *Arizona,* 149, stated that West's soldiers became too interested in Tucson's *señoritas* to give the proper attention to their military duties; therefore, they were marched out of town to build the camp.

[16] *O.R.,* I, 50:1095–96, 1128 (part 1).

[17] *Alta California,* July 10, 1862. Carleton had maneuvered somewhat in order to achieve this salute. Traveling from Fort Barrett with a detachment, he deliberately chose a longer route to Tucson, thus permitting Shinn, who had taken the shortest road, to arrive on June 5.

no security of life and property, it became his duty to exert the authority of the United States government until the President should see fit to do otherwise. Under this edict all citizens of the Territory were required to take an oath of allegiance to the United States or leave the area.[18]

Carleton, on June 10, reported to Pacific Department headquarters at San Francisco that he was making every effort to establish law and order so that if a man did have his throat cut, his house robbed, or his fields ravaged, he would have at least the consolation of knowing there was some law that would reach the one who did the injury. He ordered the arrest and imprisonment at Fort Yuma of nine men described as "cutthroats, gamblers, and loafers," who had infested Tucson and aroused the fear of all good citizens. He recommended that these criminals be sent to Alcatraz and held there for the duration of the war. Nearly every one of these desperadoes had either killed his man or helped to kill him.

On June 11, Carleton appointed Acting Assistant Adjutant General Benjamin C. Cutler of the California Volunteers as territorial military secretary of state. The following day, Cutler levied a graduated tax, beginning at $5.00 a month, on all business establishments in Tucson except those selling subsistence stores, fruits, vegetables, and forage. Gambling houses were taxed $100 a month for each table used in the games. All saloons were required to obtain a license at $100 a month. The money collected from these revenues was deposited in a hospital fund for the sick and wounded in the California Column. Any violator of the provisions of this decree was subject to a fine and seizure of his gambling devices and liquor.[19] Following the occupation of Tucson, there was little disorder and few signs of discontent. Aside from these regulations, Carleton does not seem to have been unduly harsh, considering the war-torn condition of the country and the frontier problems which he had to control.

[18] *O.R.*, I, 50:96–97 (part 1). Carleton was mistaken when he stated on June 8, 1862, that Congress had established Arizona as a territory. The Organic Act creating the Territory of Arizona was not signed until February 24, 1863.
[19] *Ibid.*, I, 9:692–93.

Some political prisoners were also arrested, including Sylvester Mowry, a prominent mineowner and operator in the Southwest. When Colonel Carleton arrived in Tucson, he received a letter from T. Scheuner, metallurgist at the Mowry mine. In the letter Mowry was accused of being an officer in the Southern rebellion, of furnishing ammunition and other supplies to the Rebel forces, of boasting that he would be governor of the Territory in six months, and that he with twenty Southerners could whip one hundred Northern troops.[20] Acting on this information and a statement by William Pyburn, another citizen of Arizona, that Mowry had furnished Captain Hunter's men with percussion caps, Carleton on June 8 sent Lieutenant Colonel E. E. Eyre with a detachment of troops to Patagonia, a few miles north of the Mexican border. At 3:00 A.M. on June 13, Mowry was arrested and his silver mine and smelter were confiscated. He was taken with twenty-one other prisoners to Tucson.[21] An army board of officers, headed by Lieutenant Colonel Joseph R. West, convened on June 16 and found sufficient evidence to restrain Mowry from his liberty.[22] The prisoner was then taken to Fort Yuma, where he remained until his release on November 4, 1862, by order of the Adjutant General's Office in Washington.[23]

The bitter contest between Colonel James H. Carleton and Sylvester Mowry continued for several years. Carleton was convinced that Mowry was a Secessionist. In addition to the arrest, court-martial, property confiscation, and imprisonment of Mow-

[20] James H. McClintock, *Arizona—The Youngest State*, 164; Keleher, *Turmoil in New Mexico*, 246–47.

[21] *O.R.*, I, 50:1142–43 (part 1), I, 9:694; Bancroft, *History of Arizona and New Mexico*, 515, stated that probably personal jealousies and the spirit of the time, requiring reprisals for some of Captain Hunter's acts, were the real cause of Mowry's arrest. *Santa Fe Weekly Gazette*, August 7, 1864, in discussing the Mowry case, contended that Carleton had acted under orders from General George Wright, who was obeying the U. S. Confiscation Act.

[22] *O.R.*, I, 9:694–95.

[23] 38 Cong., 1 sess., *Senate Exec. Doc. No. 49*, 1–3. The *Alta California*, November 13, 1862, reported, "Mowry is here at Fort Yuma, swearing furiously about General Carleton; boasting of his ability to have cut up the Californians had he been so disposed, and says he will be released in a few days, and intends making Uncle Sam pay dearly for imprisoning him."

ry by orders of Carleton, a court order was obtained from the United States District Court, meeting at Albuquerque, New Mexico, by which Mowry's property at Patagonia, Arizona, was sold at public auction on July 18, 1864, for $2,000.[24] In August, 1864, when it was rumored that Mowry might return to Arizona, Carleton ordered him expelled from the Territory if and when he arrived.

Mowry, in turn, on December 12, 1862, filed a damage claim in California's Fourth District Court for $1,029,000 against Carleton and others involved in his arrest and property confiscation.[25] Mowry induced Senator John Conness of California to introduce a Senate Resolution on May 20, 1864, which resulted in a Congressional investigation. Mowry also was instrumental in having a Concurrent Resolution passed in Arizona's first territorial legislature in 1864 which censured Carleton for expelling Mowry and demanded that he be permitted to return to the Territory.[26]

Colonel Carleton had tried unsuccessfully several times to get a message through to General Canby in New Mexico concerning the progress of the California Column. On June 15, 1862, he sent John Jones, an express rider, Sergeant William Wheeling, First California Infantry, and a Mexican guide named Chávez, ahead from Tucson. While traveling east of Apache Pass on June 18, they were attacked by Apache Indians. Wheeling and Chávez were killed. Their bodies were found later horribly mutilated. Jones, in a running fight, escaped. On June 20, after a hazardous ride of over two hundred miles alone, he reached the Río Grande at Picacho, about five miles above Mesilla. Here he was captured by the Confederates and taken before Colonel William Steele at Fort Fillmore. Steele confiscated Jones's dispatches and had him locked in the guardhouse. From the dispatches the Texans

---

[24] Keleher, *Turmoil in New Mexico*, 270; O.R., I, 41:662, 674 (part 2).

[25] Aurora Hunt, *The Army of the Pacific, 1860–1866*, 113–14.

[26] Arizona Territory, Legislative Assembly, *Acts, Resolutions, and Memorials,* First Session, 1864, 70; Keleher, *Turmoil in New Mexico*, 271. The feud between Carleton and Mowry continued until October 17, 1871, when Mowry died in London, England, where he had gone to raise money to refinance and rehabilitate his Arizona mining property.

learned the strength of Colonel Carleton's command and the intended movement of the column. While in jail, Jones was able to communicate with Union sympathizers on the outside, who sent word to Canby that the Californians were coming.[27]

The vanguard of the California Column had reached Tucson on May 20, and Colonel James A. Carleton had arrived on June 7, but it had taken several weeks longer to get the entire column, except those detailed to garrison the forts along the way, assembled in that town with food and forage enough to make another start.[28] On June 21, 1862, Lieutenant Colonel Edward E. Eyre led a reconnoitering detachment, consisting of 140 men of the First California Cavalry, from Tucson east toward the Río Grande. The detachment followed the route used by the Overland Mail stages before the war, traveling a distance of about three hundred miles, under a broiling sun and over a country where water could be obtained only at intervals of thirty-five to sixty miles.

The command had to be constantly alert for sudden attacks by Indians and Confederates. At noon, June 25, while the troopers were watering their horses at a spring in Apache Pass, four shots, thought to be a signal that Indians were coming, were heard in the vicinity where the horses that had been watered were grazing under guard. At the same time, from another direction, about one hundred Apache Indians were seen approaching, carrying a white flag. The warriors were well mounted and armed with rifles, pistols, and shotguns. Lieutenant Colonel Eyre, with an interpreter, advanced to meet them. He also carried a white flag. A peace talk was held between Eyre and the chief, during which the latter promised that neither the soldiers nor their

---

27 *O.R.*, I, 9:554, 590; I, 50:95–98, 119 (part 1); Pettis, "California Column," *Historical Society of New Mexico*, 12. John Lemon, of Mesilla, provided horses for Jones's escape. Lemon was caught by the Texans and, with a Mr. Marshall, was taken to a tree to be hanged. Marshall was hanged, but Lemon's execution was postponed. Later Jones and Lemon were exchanged, along with Captain McCleave.

28 Carleton received his commission as brigadier general about June 20, 1862. Joseph R. West succeeded him as colonel of the First California Infantry Regiment.

animals would be molested. The Indians asked for and were given tobacco and food. As the two leaders parted, the chief requested that they continue the parley at sunset, but the meeting did not take place. When Eyre returned to the main part of his command, he learned that three of his men were missing. After an hour's search, their dead bodies were found stripped of their clothing and firearms, and one horse had been stolen. Two of the victims had been scalped. These soldiers had wandered away from the main detachment in defiance of orders. The Indians were pursued, but could not be caught. The dead men were buried, and the command moved on. That evening several shots were fired by the Indians into the Union camp, wounding Surgeon Kittridge and killing one horse.

The Californians proceeded toward the Río Grande without further trouble with the Indians. Along the way they met several white people. One party of miners en route to Mesilla was detained temporarily by Eyre so that his troop movements would not be disclosed. Meanwhile, General Canby, having learned of the entrance of the California Column into Arizona, ordered Colonel Chivington, commanding the Southern Military District of New Mexico, to advance one thousand men from Fort Craig to open communications with General Carleton. On June 29, a scouting party from Chivington's command met the approaching detachment under Eyre. This united for the first time the advance columns of Federal forces from California with those of Colorado and New Mexico.

On July 4, 1862, after being en route from Tucson for two weeks, Eyre and his men reached the Río Grande and camped. Appropriate to the occasion, on Independence Day, the national colors were raised over their camp, amid loud cheers of those assembled. This was the first time the Stars and Stripes had floated over the Río Grande below Fort Craig since the Confederates had occupied that area nearly one year before. On July 5, the detachment marched three miles down the river and occupied Fort Thorn, which had been abandoned by the Rebels. Here Eyre was reinforced by Captain George W. Howland with one hundred men of the Third U. S. Cavalry. Eager to strike the retreating Confederates, Eyre and his troops left Fort Thorn and crossed the flooding Río Grande on July 17 in a small boat, in defiance of instructions received from Colonel Chivington and Howe (Chivington's successor), who were acting under orders from General Canby. The Yankee detachment marched south to Doña Ana and then to Las Cruces, where Eyre learned that part of the Texans were still at El Paso, Texas. Eyre's reluctance to disobey orders further kept him from immediately marching on down the river and attacking the fleeing Rebels.

While the Union forces from California were approaching Fort Thorn and the troops from Fort Craig were moving south toward the same point, the Rebels under Colonel William Steele at Mesilla and Fort Fillmore were preparing to abandon the Confederate "Territory of Arizona" and return to Texas. On July 8, 1862, Colonel Steele with about 400 men, the remnants of the C. S. A. Army of New Mexico, retreated to Fort Bliss, El Paso, Texas. Steele, on July 12, while reporting to Richmond his reasons for abandoning Arizona, wrote that 1,500 Californians were approaching, who with the Federals already in the Territory would total 3,000 men against his 400. The Texans were low on ammunition and inadequately clothed. He had only Confederate currency, which the New Mexican population refused to accept. The Texans had been compelled to seize subsistence supplies from the local people and force them to provide part of the transportation for the Rebel troop movements. Bitter resentment and armed resistance resulted. Foraging parties were attacked, and during the various skirmishes one Confederate captain and several men were killed. The Southern troops were so disgusted with the campaign and so anxious to return to Texas that some of them were on the verge of mutiny, threatening to take matters into their own hands unless they were marched back to San Antonio. Before leaving Fort Bliss, Colonel Steele sold all the surplus public property for gold and silver coin, $830 of which was left to care for the Confederate wounded at the hospital in Franklin (El Paso).

On July 10, 1862, a second detachment from the California Column, under the command of Captain Thomas L. Roberts, left Tucson for the Río Grande. It consisted of infantry, a two-howitzer battery and a twenty-two-wagon supply train escorted by cavalry, totaling 126 men. At 12:30 P.M., July 15, as the advance troops neared Apache Pass, they were attacked by Apache warriors; but after a sharp skirmish, the Indians were driven off. One Yankee was killed and another wounded. As the troops moved into the pass approaching a spring for water, Apaches, posted behind rocks along the canyon rim above, started firing at the soldiers. Roberts sent skirmishers up both sides of the canyon. After a stubborn contest, the Indians hidden in the ledges above the spring were finally dislodged by how-itzer shells which burst among the rocks, causing bloody havoc among them. The whites did not gain control of the water until 4:00 P.M. Another soldier was killed in this skirmish.

As soon as their horses could be watered, Roberts sent six troopers back to warn Captain John C. Cremony, who with the remainder of the cavalry was guarding the supply train. When the couriers had proceeded about four miles west of the pass, they were ambushed by Apaches. One soldier and two horses were wounded, and another had his horse shot from under him later in a running battle, but all of the troopers finally arrived at the supply-train camp that night, two of them on foot, their horses having died from wounds along the way.

After getting water, Roberts withdrew the rest of his men from the pass and camped. Then, with twenty-eight picked in-fantrymen, he marched fifteen miles westward back to the sup-ply train, which he found safe. The battle was renewed on July 16, when the entire command, organized by Roberts to provide the best possible protection while marching, proceeded through Apache Pass. As the detachment approached the spring, Roberts had to use his riflemen and howitzers again. The spring was taken and held by the Californians until they left the pass the following morning and marched on toward the Río Grande.

The Battle of Apache Pass, during which the Indians were led by Chiefs Cochise and Mangas Coloradas, was perhaps the largest-scale engagement fought between the Federal troops and the Apache Indians in Arizona history. It was a defeat for the Apaches since the Union troops forced their way through the pass and caused heavy casualties among them. The estimates vary from ten to sixty-three Indians killed and an unknown number wounded as compared with two soldiers killed and three wounded.[29] This battle called General Carleton's attention to the strategic importance of the pass. The long-range visibility in each direction from the pass permitted the Apaches to ambush travelers getting water from the spring. On July 27, 1862, Carleton gave orders to establish a military camp at Apache Pass which was named Fort Bowie. For years its garrison served as escort for travelers, wagon trains, and stagecoaches through the zone of Apache danger.

General Carleton on July 17, 1862, issued orders for the main body of the California Column to march east from Tucson to the Río Grande, fully equipped with military and subsistence supplies to last for several weeks. The scarcity of water in certain areas compelled the column to separate into divisions and to march at intervals. Colonel Joseph A. West, with four companies of infantry and the necessary wagon trains to support these troops, began the trek on July 20. Another infantry company and a battery of mountain howitzers were ordered to join West later. The following day Lieutenant John B. Shinn led from Tucson the second contingent, which consisted of a light battery and two companies of infantry. Two days later a third division, under Lieutenant Colonel Edwin A. Rigg, consisting of four companies of infantry, marched out of Tucson. A large supply train escorted by a company of cavalry and one of infantry followed on July 31.

[29] Wyllys, *Arizona*, 153, stated that more than sixty Apache Indians were killed and an unknown number wounded. General Carleton, in *O.R.*, I, 9:565, reported that ten Indians were killed, but made no estimate of the number wounded. John C. Cremony, *Life Among the Apaches*, 164, was told by an Apache who fought in the engagement that sixty-three warriors were killed by the shells, and, he added, "We would have done well enough if you had not fired wagons [cannons] at us."

Placing Major David Ferguson in command at Tucson, General Carleton started for the Río Grande on July 23. The following day he passed Colonel West with most of the troops. From then on, escorted by one company of infantry and two of cavalry, Carleton led the advance of the column until they reached the Río Grande. The majority of the units in the column moved slowly over the desert, with both men and animals suffering from the heat, but there was no further difficulty with the Indians.

On August 2, Carleton sent a courier with a letter to General Canby at Santa Fe reporting the progress of the column and requesting instructions. "The gallantry of the troops under your command has left us nothing to do on the Río Grande," he wrote. "It would be a sad disappointment" for the Californians to retrace their steps without engaging the Confederates. He suggested that a Federal force be sent into western Texas, where Union sympathizers were reported ready to run up the Stars and Stripes again. General Carleton arrived on the Río Grande about three miles above Fort Thorn on August 7, 1862. The remainder of the California Column, traveling in detachments somewhat as they left Tucson, one or two days apart, arrived at the river by August 15. The strength of Carleton's command when it reached the Río Grande totaled 1,400 men, including teamsters and other civilian employees[30]

On August 9, Carleton and that portion of his troops who had arrived crossed the Río Grande, which was still very high, and marched south to Las Cruces. Arriving there on August 10, he found Lieutenant Colonel Eyre with his detachment strengthened by four companies of the Fifth U. S. Infantry from Fort Craig. Here Carleton received a letter from General Canby, written on August 11, in which Canby attempted to discourage Carleton on the invasion of Texas from the west, but on the following day Canby forwarded another dispatch in which he authorized Carleton to use his own judgment in regard to the disposition of troops in Arizona and New Mexico.[31]

[30]*O.R.*, I, 9:557–59; I, 50:94 (part 1).     [31] *Ibid.*, I, 9:566–67.

While at Las Cruces, Carleton issued an order to his commanders in the towns along the Río Grande between Jornada del Muerto and Fort Bliss, a distance of about one hundred miles, to establish sanitary regulations and require the local inhabitants to clean up the streets and repair their dwellings. Carleton's orders assured the people of the Territory that the era of anarchy and misrule was over and that life and property would be protected. He told them that they could now pursue their avocations unmolested and without fear.[32] Union troops were stationed at Mesilla, Fort Fillmore, and Las Cruces. One company was sent to take possession of Simeon Hart's flour mill at El Paso, Texas. Mesilla was made the headquarters of the District of Arizona. The southern Overland Mail route was reopened.[33]

On August 16, Carleton, with three companies of cavalry, started for Fort Bliss. At Franklin (El Paso), the following day, he found a Confederate surgeon and twenty-five sick and disabled soldiers whom he made prisoners by orders of General Canby. This was only a technical procedure. Actually he furnished them with medicine and provisions. On September 1, Carleton paroled the Texans and sent them to San Antonio with an escort of twenty-five cavalrymen led by a lieutenant. Twelve wagonloads of hospital and quartermaster supplies, which had originally belonged to the United States, were found by the Californians stored at the customhouse in El Paso, Mexico (now Juárez). These were shipped to the supply depot at Mesilla.

Carleton, with two companies of cavalry, then marched one hundred miles on down the Río Grande in Texas. His objective

[32] *Ibid.*, I, 50:144 (part 1).

[33] Pettis, "Confederate Invasion," *Battles and Leaders of the Civil War*, II, 15–16; *O.R.*, I, 50:103, 110 (part 1); *Daily Alta California*, December 6, 1862. Simeon Hart had built the flour mill before the war and made a fortune selling flour at a high price to the army installations in that area. When General Twiggs surrendered in Texas, Hart, a Secessionist, urged Jefferson Davis to send troops into the Territory. When the Texans retreated to San Antonio, Hart went with them, leaving his miller, H. H. Cooper, a Federalist, in charge, who, upon learning of the arrival of the California Column, requested that the mill be seized in the name of the United States.

was to restore the confidence of the people, whom he claimed had been taught by the Texans that the Union Troops were coming among them as marauders and robbers. "When they found that we treated them kindly and paid them a fair price" for their supplies, he wrote, they rejoiced to come under the "old flag once more," through which they could be protected and justly treated. On August 22, Captain John C. Cremony, with a company of California cavalry, reached the abandoned Fort Quitman, over which the Stars and Stripes were hoisted.

On August 23, Captain Edmond D. Shirland, under orders from Carleton, started with a company of California troopers for Fort Davis, one hundred miles farther into Texas. The poor condition of the majority of his cavalry horses compelled him to complete the expedition with a twenty-five-man detachment. When he arrived at the post, it was deserted. The body of a Confederate soldier with bullet and arrow wounds was found in one of the buildings. It appeared that he had been left behind because of illness and later was killed by the Indians. Shirland hoisted the national colors over the old fort and remained there with his small detachment until August 30. On the return trip, his troops had a running battle with Indians, during which four Indians were killed and twenty wounded. Two soldiers were wounded. As a symbol of the return of that portion of the country to the United States, Carleton sent the flags which had been raised over Tucson, Mesilla, and Forts Breckenridge, Buchanan, Thorn, Fillmore, Bliss, Quitman, and Davis to the Department of the Pacific headquarters at San Francisco.

On September 2, 1862, General Carleton received an order from General Canby instructing him to proceed to Santa Fe. Here, on September 18, Carleton assumed command of the Department of New Mexico. Canby at his own request, through friends in Washington, had been called East. He had served as departmental commander for sixteen eventful months. Carleton remained in command in New Mexico for four years.

It had taken General Carleton nine long months to move his troops from Southern California across the hot, dry, sparsely populated desert to the Río Grande and to occupy Arizona, southern New Mexico, and western Texas. On September 20, he wrote the Department of the Pacific headquarters that it was no fault of the troops from California that the Confederate forces fled before the arrival of the column, but was due to the gallantry of General Canby's command and hastened by the advance guard from California. The march across the desert, he continued, in the driest season in thirty years was an achievement creditable to any soldiers of the American army. The General maintained that the success of the California Column could not justly be attributed to his ability, but to the superior physical and moral energies of the officers and men.[34] Surgeon J. M. McNulty claimed the success of the march of the California Column was dependent on the endurance of the soldiers and General Carleton's constant care of his men and meticulous attention to every detail of the expedition. Carleton possessed, the surgeon wrote, "a clear head, sound judgment, indomitable will and perseverance."[35]

On September 21, Carleton published an order in which he expressed appreciation for the conduct and services of the officers and men in the California Column. He wrote that California had reason to be proud of the sons she had sent across the continent to assist in the great struggle in which the country was then engaged. Carleton, at the request of Canby, also declared his gratitude for the fact that troops from the Atlantic and Pacific slopes, from the mountains of California and Colorado, acting on the same cause, impelled by the same duties, and animated by the same hopes had met and shaken hands in the center of the great American continent.[36]

When Carleton assumed command at Santa Fe, the invasion of the Confederate Army of New Mexico was history. Reports received by the Union commanders in the Intermountain West during the Civil War that the Rebels were organizing to retake

[34] *O.R.*, I, 9:569–70.
[35] *Ibid.*, I, 9:602.
[36] *Santa Fe Weekly Gazette*, September 27, 1862.

New Mexico and Arizona kept strong garrisons in the southern and eastern part of the Territory.[37] Late in 1862 the Colorado Volunteers returned to Colorado. Most of the army regulars in the Department of New Mexico were transferred to Union armies in the East. The units of the California Column and the New Mexican Volunteers were assigned to various posts throughout the Department. General Carleton's most pressing problem at the close of 1862 was subduing the Indians in New Mexico and Arizona.

[37] *O.R.,* I, 15:597, 683; I, 50:721 (part 2); III, 2:950; IV, 3:76, 960–62, 1035–36. In October, 1862, and February, 1863, it was reported that John R. Baylor was raising an army in Texas for another invasion of New Mexico and Arizona. Baylor, while a Confederate congressman in 1864, again urged an invasion of the Territory. Lansford W. Hastings in 1864 submitted a plan to Jefferson Davis that was approved and referred to E. Kirby Smith, commanding in Texas, in which Hastings would enlist men in California and Arizona for the conquest of Arizona and New Mexico. None of the plans matured.

# 7

# Indian Campaigns

THE INDIAN WARS in the Rocky Mountain West prior to, during, and following the Civil War were the inevitable result of the contact between the red and white races. It was a mighty struggle for domination of the American frontier. For many years the red men had watched with increasing resentment the steady invasion of their homelands by the white men, first the Spaniards, then the Mexicans, and finally the American explorers, fur trappers and traders, miners, stockmen, and farmers. Intelligent Indians saw in the Civil War the opportunity, while the whites were killing one another, to drive the intruders out of the land of their fathers or exterminate them.

During the Confederate invasion of New Mexico and Arizona, when the Northern and Southern armies were struggling for control of those territories, outlying white settlements were left exposed to the depredations of the hostile Indians. According to one contemporary, the Apaches had come to believe that they had "stampeded the entire white population." On roads and trails they savagely attacked small parties of white men and slaughtered them. It was their boast, he wrote, that they had conquered the American nation.[1] When in 1861 the Federal troops were temporarily withdrawn from the Indian country, we are told that

The Apache marauders swept down from their mountain strongholds and carried death and destruction throughout southern Arizona. Mines, ranches and stock ranges were abandoned and the few whites left in the country took refuge within the walls of Tucson. The

[1] John Ross Browne, "A Tour Through Arizona," *Harper's New Monthly Magazine*, Vol. XXIX (October, 1864), 560.

savages indulged in a saturnalia of slaughter, and the last glimmer of civilization seemed about to be quenched in blood.[2]

When Lieutenant Colonel John R. Baylor created the Confederate Territory of Arizona with himself as governor on August 1, 1861, he found that one of his most serious problems was to suppress the Indians in the Territory. Shortly after he took office, detachments of his command fought Indians with costly results to the Confederates. Near Fort Stanton, which had been temporarily occupied by the Texans following the withdrawal of the Union garrison, a Rebel spy party of four troopers was surprised early one morning by Indian warriors. Three soldiers were massacred while the fourth escaped in a ten-mile running battle. A Confederate lieutenant led fourteen men from Fort Davis, Texas, in pursuit of a marauding band of Indians. The Apaches were trailed to their village, where a desperate fight took place. The entire Texan detachment was killed, with the exception of a Mexican guide, who escaped to relate the incident. These losses caused Baylor to write General Van Dorn in Texas for more troops. He stated that it was impossible to hold the U. S. troops in check and continue to operate against the Indians without reinforcements.

The depredations of the Apaches and the Navahos continued during Baylor's administration in the latter part of 1861 and the first few months of 1862. No stagecoach, mail carrier, or traveler on trail or road was safe. In several other skirmishes with the Indians a number of Confederate soldiers under Baylor and General Sibley were killed. They robbed the Texan supply trains and menaced their military operations. Finally, Baylor determined to adopt a policy of Indian extermination. On one occasion, it was claimed, he ordered a sack of flour poisoned and distributed among the Indians which resulted in the death of about sixty of them.[3] On March 20, 1862, Lieutenant Colonel

[2] Patrick Hamilton, *The Resources of Arizona,* 14.
[3] Sloan and Adams, *History of Arizona,* 250.

Baylor from his capital at Mesilla wrote Captain Thomas Helm commanding the Arizona Guards at Tucson as follows:

I learn . . . that the Indians have been to your post for the purpose of making a treaty. The Congress of the Confederate States has passed a law declaring extermination of all hostile Indians. You will therefore use all means to persuade the Apaches or any tribe to come in for the purpose of making peace, and when you get them together, kill all the grown Indians and take the children prisoners and sell them to defray the expense of killing the Indians.[4]

When informed of the Indian extermination order, President Jefferson Davis removed Colonel Baylor from his position as governor of Arizona. This loss of office and prestige was a keen disappointment to Baylor's aspirations in the West, although by the time the President acted, the Confederate retreat from Arizona and New Mexico had made Baylor a governor in name only. In a letter to General J. B. Magruder, commander of the Confederate District of Texas, New Mexico, and Arizona, dated December 29, 1862, Baylor refused to disavow his conduct toward the Indians even when reproved by the President and removed from his command. Baylor was defended by M. H. Macwillie, later the delegate from Arizona to the Confederate Congress, who in a letter on January 10, 1862, to the War Department stated that it was understood in the Territory that the extermination of hostile savages was the publicly declared policy of the Confederate government. He contended that Baylor's order was justified since the Indians at that time were actually exterminating the white population of Arizona. Baylor, however, was not restored to his former position as governor.

Meanwhile, the Union leaders in northern New Mexico, General Edward R. S. Canby and Governor Henry Connelly, were also having serious Indian trouble which could have developed to the extent that it might have diverted part of the Federal troops from defending the Territory against the invading Con-

[4] *O.R.*, I, 50:942 (part 1).

federates. Governor Connelly reported to Secretary Seward on October 26, 1861, that although the Navaho Indians were in a state of armistice, they were actually committing daily depredations. He proposed exterminating the Navahos "by the sword or by starvation" as the only remedy for the evils they had caused and would continue to cause. He suggested the possibility that the government might place each tribe of Indians on a reservation with farm equipment and a white farmer, a blacksmith, and a carpenter as instructors.

On December 1, 1861, Canby informed the Western Department headquarters of the Union Army at St. Louis, Missouri, that other Indians, as well as Navahos, were raiding the white settlements. The Apaches had become more daring in their inroads. The Kiowas and Comanches had invaded the Territory ostensibly in pursuit of the Utes, but they did not confine their warfare to the Indians. He claimed that the Navaho problem was aggravated by illegal raids from a portion of the New Mexican people and that these white depredations and the Indian retaliations could not be prevented as long as the New Mexican marauders could sell their captives and plunder. He concluded that there was no choice between the extermination of the Navahos or their removal and colonization in an area entirely remote from the white inhabitants of the Territory where the government could protect and assist them.[5]

During the Confederate invasion and Union counteroffensive in New Mexico and Arizona, the Mescalero Apache Indians roamed over eastern New Mexico from Fort Union to the abandoned Fort Stanton and at times on south to Mexico, committing vicious depredations on the white settlements. When possible, the Federal military units pursued the offenders, but circumstances restricted the Yankee soldiers to only small campaigns. In April, 1862, three Apaches who were locked in the guardhouse at Fort Union saw Sergeant Philbrook, First Colorado Volunteers, executed for shooting Lieutenant Isaac Gray, who was a member of the same regiment. A man passing by their cell

[5] *Ibid.*, III, 1:601; I, 4:77.

jokingly told the Indians that they would be shot next. Later, when the guards opened the door to their cell for another reason, the Apaches fired on them with bows and arrows which by some oversight had not been taken from them. The wounded guards were so enraged that they closed the door, lighted fuses of two cannon shells and tossed them through an opening above the door into the cell. All that remained of the Indians after the explosion were a few fragments of arms, legs, and skulls.

Upon assuming command of the Department of New Mexico, Brigadier General James H. Carleton determined to send troops against the hostile, plundering Indians in the Territory. On September 22, 1862, he wrote the War Department that he had ordered Colonel "Kit" Carson with five companies of New Mexican Volunteers to reoccupy Fort Stanton and punish and control the Mescalero Apaches for their depredations on the white settlements in eastern New Mexico. He stated that he had also ordered Lieutenant Colonel J. Francisco Chávez with four companies of the same regiment to move into the Navaho country to the west of Santa Fe to punish them for stealing livestock and killing a large number of white people. Governor Connelly on the same date issued a proclamation calling for a reorganization of the territorial militia for the purpose of securing indemnity for the past and security for the future from the "blood thirsty" Navahos. During 1861, 1862, and 1863, in the Territory of New Mexico, an estimated total of over two hundred citizens, soldiers, and shepherds were killed by the Indians. At the same time a vast number of sheep, goats, horses, mules, and cattle were stolen by them.[6]

6 *Ibid.*, I, 15:576. Frederick Webb Hodge (ed.), *Handbook of American Indians North of Mexico*, Part 1, 63, 66, listed the Apache Indians who roamed over New Mexico, Arizona, western Texas, and northwestern Mexico in seven tribal groups as follows: (1) Querechos or Vaqueros, consisting of Mescaleros, Jicarillas, Faraones, Llarenos, and Lipan; (2) Gila, including the Gileños, Mimbreños, and Mogollones; (3) Arivaipa; (4) Chiricahua; (5) Pinaleños; (6) Coyoteros, comprising the White Mountain and Pinal divisions; (7) Tontos.

The proclamation is from the *Santa Fe Weekly Gazette*, September 27, 1862; and the estimates of persons killed and livestock stolen are from *Report of the Commissioner of Indian Affairs for the Year 1863*, 110.

Carson with his detachment started on his campaign early in October, 1862. En route to Fort Stanton, he received his orders from Carleton, which included a command to kill all the Mescalero Apache men and bring in the women and children as prisoners. No more treaties were to be made for the Indians to break whenever it benefited their interests. Finally, if the Apaches did beg for peace, their chiefs and twenty other leading men were to come to Santa Fe and meet with Carleton. The General justified his order by instructing Carson to inform the Indians who came to ask for peace that when the people of New Mexico were attacked by the Texans, the Mescaleros broke their treaty of peace, murdered innocent people, and ran off their livestock. The Indian agent assigned to this band of Apaches reported that during the month of August, 1862, alone, the Mescaleros had killed forty white men and six children and had carried off a number of other children. They had stolen a large amount of property, including horses, mules, cattle, and sheep.

Colonel Carson's campaign against the Mescalero Apaches was fast and effective. Most of these Indians were armed with bows and arrows. Only a few had rifles, and for these there was little or no ammunition. The Apaches were no match for the Volunteers, who were well armed, clothed, and fed. Within a week after Carson and his troops reached Fort Stanton and again raised the U. S. flag, thirty-two Mescaleros had been killed in skirmishes, among whom were two important chiefs, José Largo and Manuelito, and a large number of Indians had been wounded.

Realizing that they were overwhelmed, some of the surviving Apache chiefs went to Santa Fe escorted by their agent, where they requested peace from Carleton. The Mescaleros were assigned to Bosque Redondo ("round grove") located on the Pecos River about 160 miles southeast of Santa Fe. The site for this Indian reservation and a new fort named Fort Sumner had been chosen by army personnel in response to an order issued by General Carleton on November 4, 1862.

In October, Captain William McCleave with two companies

of the California Column from Fort Fillmore and Captain N. J. Pishon with two companies of the column from Franklin, Texas, were ordered into the Mescalero Apache country in southeastern New Mexico. They were instructed to co-operate with Carson, yet act independent of him, and were to remain in the field until December 31, 1862. Carleton's orders to the Californians were specific. No council or talks were to be had with the Indians. The men were to be killed whenever and wherever found. The women and children were to be taken prisoner. McCleave reported later that they had proceeded through Dog Canyon and the Sacramento Mountains and had intercepted two small parties of Indians, but saw no other signs of Apaches. Pishon wrote that his expedition had scouted the Guadalupe Mountains, but had been entirely unsuccessful in finding Mescaleros. Brigadier General Joseph R. West, their immediate commanding officer, concluded that these two expeditions resulted "in driving (not catching) the Indians."[7] By the spring of 1863, 410 Mescalero Apaches had submitted to Carleton's ultimatum and were living at the Bosque.[8]

Carleton's next move was against the Gila Apaches, who roamed over southwestern New Mexico and southeastern Arizona. It was claimed that their chief, Mangas Coloradas, notorious for his stature and almost absolute leadership over his tribe, had been the cause of more murders, torture, and burning at the stake of white people than all other chiefs put together. The Gila Apaches were wilier, more resourceful, and better-armed than the Mescalero Apaches, but on the battlefield they were unevenly matched against soldiers equipped with late-model rifles, plenty of ammunition, and adequate food.

On January 2, 1863, Carleton informed Washington that unless he learned beyond a doubt that Baylor was leading another Confederate invasion into the Territory, it was his intention to send an expedition to punish the Gilas for their frequent murders

[7] Joseph R. West received his commission as Brigadier General in November, 1862.
[8] *Report of the Commissioner of Indian Affairs, 1863,* 108.

and depredations. He believed that these Indians occupied one of the richest areas on earth. To open up this country for further exploration and protect the miners at Pinos Altos in southwestern New Mexico from additional Indian depredations, he proposed to establish a military post near the mines.

California and New Mexico Volunteers under Brigadier General Joseph R. West, commanding the Military District of Arizona, which included southern New Mexico and Arizona with headquarters in Mesilla, were selected for this campaign that began in January, 1863, and continued periodically in New Mexico and Arizona even after the end of the Civil War. Carleton's instructions relayed through West were similar to his previous Apache extermination orders. There were to be no councils or talks with these Indians, and the men were to be slain wherever and whenever they could be found. West went personally with several companies of troops to Fort McLane, which was used as a base of operations.[9]

On January 14, 1863, Captain Edmond D. Shirland, with a twenty-man detachment of the First California Volunteers, proceeded with orders to find Mangas Coloradas, who was reported to be in the vicinity of Pinos Altos. Four days later Shirland returned to his command at Fort McLane bringing the chief with him. On being questioned, Mangas claimed that he had dominion over all the country ranged by his tribe and complete authority over its members, but when he was charged with the atrocities committed by the Gilas, he protested his innocence and evaded the responsibility. The chief was told that he would be a prisoner of the United States authorities for the rest of his life, but would be well treated. His family could join him. He was not to attempt to escape. At 1:00 A.M. on January 19, Chief Mangas Coloradas, while attempting to escape, was shot and killed by the guard.[10]

[9] McClintock, *Arizona*, 169, 176. Fort McLane, whose site is fifteen miles southwest of Silver City, N. M., today, was used as a base until Fort West was built at Pinos Altos as Carleton had proposed (*O.R.*, I, 50:275 [part 2]).

[10] O.R., *op. cit.*, I, 50:296 (part 2). Other versions of the capture and death of Mangas were: (1) McClintock, *Arizona*, 176–78 (two). (a) A party of

Captain William McCleave, on the same date, with a detachment of Californians, left Fort McLane for the Pinos Altos mines. When they arrived near the mines, the troops met a party of Apaches from Mangas Coloradas' band. In the ensuing fight, eleven Indians were killed and one wounded, the latter being the chief's widow. On January 20, Captain Shirland with his company came upon an Indian *ranchería*. In the surprise attack by the soldiers, nine Indians were killed and a large number were wounded. Thirty-four animals were captured, a portion of which were stolen government mules. On January 29, the Gila Apaches attacked two hunting parties of the California Volunteers near the Pinos Altos mines, killing a private and wounding a sergeant. The Indians were driven off with a loss of twenty killed and fifteen wounded.

On March 22, a band of Gila Apaches stole sixty horses grazing at Fort West. Major William McCleave, leading eighty men in pursuit, followed the warriors' trail for nearly ninety miles until they came upon an Indian *ranchería* at dawn on March 27. A charge on the Gila camp was made by thirty men, on their only serviceable horses, and thirty dismounted cavalrymen. The rest of the expedition, with the exhausted horses and the provisions, had been left in camp several miles back. During the skirmish part of the men on foot rounded up and guarded the grazing horses to prevent the Indians' escape. The Apaches were completely routed in a twenty-minute fight, during which twenty-five Indians were killed and one soldier seriously wounded. Returning with the recaptured army horses and a number of Indian ponies, the soldiers were attacked by Apaches in a canyon. The troops defeated the attackers, but had to ascend per-

soldiers and citizens captured Mangas by trickery. At Fort McLane he was killed by soldier guards and scalped. He was beheaded by a surgeon. (b) He was induced by Captain Sheldon (possibly Shirland) to come to the fort, where he was shot while in an adobe jail by a guard. (2) Keleher, *Turmoil in New Mexico,* 294, quotes J. G. Knapp of Mesilla, opponent of Carleton, who claimed Mangas voluntarily came to the fort, was killed while in the guardhouse by a guard, and later was scalped and beheaded. Still another account is given in Daniel Ellis Conner, *Joseph Reddeford Walker and the Arizona Adventure,* ed. by Donald J. Berthrong and Odessa Davenport (Norman, 1956).

pendicular canyon walls amid a shower of arrows to dislodge their assailants. A lieutenant was wounded and three Indians were killed. The detachment arrived back at Fort West on April 4. Total casualties during the expedition were two soldiers wounded, one dying later; twenty-eight Indians killed and a large number wounded.[11]

Certain civilians in the Territory gave valuable assistance to the military in the campaigns against the Apache Indians. In May, 1863, Apaches assaulted a strongly guarded train of Charles T. Hayden near the Chihuahua line. The Indians were defeated with a loss of eleven killed, including the notorious Chief Copinggan. Carleton later wrote, "Mr. C. T. Hayden seems to have done well in helping punish the savages who delight in roasting their victims."[12]

It was not always a white man's victory. The Apaches struck frequently, mutilating the bodies of many of those killed. In mid-June 1863, about fifty Gila Apaches attacked a small party of New Mexican Volunteers while traveling along the Jornada Trail, southeast of Fort Craig. During the fight Lieutenant L. A. Bargie, a private soldier, and a mail carrier were killed. The mail was destroyed. Bargie's head was carried off by the Indians as a trophy. Captain Emil Fritz with a cavalry detachment pursued the Apaches west across the Río Grande, but could not catch them.

On June 20, Captain Albert H. Pfeiffer, his wife, three civilians, and an esort of six New Mexican Volunteers were assaulted by twenty Apaches while the Captain was bathing in a hot spring near Fort McRae. In a desperate fight and dash toward the fort, two privates were killed, the Captain, a private, and two civilians were wounded. Later Mrs. Pfeiffer and a woman servant were found mortally wounded on a trail. Lieutenant W. H. Higdon, California Volunteers, en route from Fort Stanton to Santa Fe

---

[11] Browne, "Tour Through Arizona," *Harper's New Monthly Magazine*, Vol. XXIX (October, 1864), 701, wrote that because of superstition the Apaches would not remove the bodies of their warriors killed in battle, nor would they approach the spot where their comrades had been slain.

[12] McClintock, *Arizona*, 170.

on June 28, found the bodies of the privates horribly mutilated. One victim had been burned at the stake.

Eight Apache Indians on July 4, 1863, stole 104 army mules
grazing at Fort Craig. Captain N. J. Pishon with twenty-seven
California troopers pursued the warriors. In the ensuing fight
half of the Indians were killed, but the others escaped. Three
soldiers were wounded. The mules were recovered and taken
back to the fort. A week later a four-wagon train under Sergeant E. V. Hoyt with six men was attacked by Apaches in
Cook's Pass while en route to Las Cruces. In a running fight
three wagons and nineteen mules were abandoned. Four Indians
were killed, a number wounded, and four soldiers were wounded.

Lieutenant Juan Marqués with fifteen New Mexican Volunteers on July 19, while encamped on the Río Hondo near its
junction with the Pecos River, was attacked by fifty Apaches.
During the fight, which lasted for several hours, more Indians
kept coming on the field until they numbered nearly two hundred. The red men at first gained possession of the camp, but
were driven across the river. Recrossing, they attempted to seize
the horses and mules, but were again hurled back. The ammunition ran out, and the soldiers were ordered to break their rifles
and try to escape, which they did. One trooper was killed, several were wounded, and all of the army animals and camp equipment were lost. Six Indians were killed, and an unknown number were wounded. Three days later Captains F. P. Abreu and
Emil Fritz led a detachment of New Mexico and California Volunteers from Fort Stanton to overtake the Indians. After trailing
them for forty-five miles, the detachment stormed their camp,
recapturing some of the horses and mules and the plundered
camp equipment, but the Apaches escaped.

On July 19, Lieutenant Colonel W. McMullen's carriage, with
an escort of California Volunteers, was attacked by Apaches near
Paraje, in southern New Mexico. When the fight was over, one
officer and one enlisted man had been killed. Three Indians were
dead, and a number were wounded. Five days later a California
detachment under Lieutenant John Lambert was assaulted by a

large number of Apaches in Cook's Canyon on the Las Cruces road. One soldier was killed, one wounded, and two wagons and twelve mules were abandoned to the savages. The Indian losses were not known. During the remainder of 1863, the Apaches in New Mexico continued their plundering and massacres, in which a number of lives were lost and thousands of head of livestock were stolen. They were pursued by military and civilian expeditions resulting in several minor encounters and the recovery of many of the stolen animals.

During 1864, hostilities continued in central and western New Mexico between the military forces, assisted by the citizens, and the Apaches. Indian expeditions in that part of the Territory were limited because of the demand for troops in other sections of the Department of New Mexico. On January 28 a party of twelve California Volunteers led by Lieutenant Thomas A. Young, while away from Fort Craig on a scout for Indians, was attacked by about fifty Apaches. In a spirited skirmish, seven Indians were killed and five soldiers were wounded. The Californians, not being numerous enough to continue the fight, were forced back to the fort. In the same month, Socorro County militia under General Stanilus Montoya, while on an Indian expedition near Sierra Datil in western New Mexico, killed twenty Apaches and took an equal number of prisoners.

In August, a detachment of First California Infantry, led by Captain Henry A. Greene, advancing from Fort McRae, New Mexico, encountered a band of Apaches. Five Indians were killed, six captured, and some stolen beef cattle were recovered. On August 25, Lieutenant Henry W. Gilbert, with a party of twenty New Mexican Volunteers, part of an expedition into the Sacramento Mountains, walked directly into an ambush as they lead their horses along the trail of some Apaches. The Lieutenant and two of his men were killed, and three were wounded. The rest of the detachment fled, leaving most of their horses and equipment to the Indians. One Apache was killed, and five were wounded. From time to time during the remainder of 1864, the Apaches in New Mexico raided several small white settlements, stole livestock, massacred a number of whites, attacked supply trains, and committed other depredations. Each time the military forces nearest the scene of the crime, according to the strength of the garrison, pursued the savages, recovered much of the stolen property, and continued to carry out Carleton's extermination order. At the close of that year, 405 Mescalero Apaches and 20 Gila Apaches had been settled in the Bosque Redondo Indian Reservation.

In Arizona, the newly created territory, during 1863–64, the Apaches made frequent raids on the white population. At times they also boldly struck at the military units while en route. A company of Fifth California Infantry, under Captain Benjamin F. Harrover, was attacked in Apache Pass on April 25, 1863, by a band of about two hundred Indians, thirty of whom were mounted and several armed with guns. At the first rifle fire by the soldiers, the Apaches fell back to cover, but they kept up the fight for nearly two hours. In this skirmish, three Indians were killed and a number wounded; one soldier was wounded. During the war years and later, it was extremely dangerous to travel through Apache Pass without a large, well-armed escort. One writer related that the bones of the slain oxen, horses, and mules and the wreckage of wagons were strewn on both sides of the road for fourteen miles through the pass. There was a long succession of graves in which the more fortunate immigrants had buried the bodies of their predecessors.[13]

General Carleton's Apache Indian extermination order was carried forward in Arizona with the same determination as in New Mexico. Early in May, 1863, Captain T. T. Tidball, commander at Fort Bowie, with twenty-five California Volunteers and some civilians, after trailing a band of plundering Arivaipa Apaches five days without lighting a fire, hiding by day and traveling by night over an unknown terrain, made a surprise attack on the savages in their *ranchería* in Arivaipa Canyon, southeastern Arizona. Fifty Indians were killed with the loss of only one soldier.

The soldiery did not hesitate to dash into northwestern Mexi-

[13] *Ibid.,* 170.

co, when occasion required, in pursuit of Apaches, outlaws, or Secessionists. Captain Richard H. Orton, with his First California Cavalry, made several expeditions across the line during 1863–64 chasing Indians and white renegades and breaking up Confederate recruiting stations. On one occasion he and his men saved from massacre the people of the Mexican village of Janos which was under siege by the Apaches. In June, 1863, Captain Joseph Tuttle, with a detachment of twenty soldiers and accompanied by Joseph H. Martin, a California deputy sheriff, another civilian, and a Mexican cowboy, pursued a party of California Secessionists through a portion of northern Sonora, southwestern Arizona, and along the Mexican border. A number of the Rebels were finally arrested at Altar Sonora. The others were prevented, for the time being, from proceeding to join the Confederate Army in Texas.

In April, 1864, Captain James H. Whitlock led an expedition of sixty-one California Volunteers a distance of about one hundred miles in pursuit of a band of Chiricahua Apaches who had stolen a herd of horses and mules. At daylight, April 7, the detachment charged into the camp of about 250 Indians, located near Grey's Peak in eastern Arizona. In a spirited fight of about one hour, the savages were routed, 30 being killed, a large number wounded, and the remainder escaped. There were no casualties among the soldiers, although some of them had arrows in their clothing. The entire Indian camp was destroyed, and the stolen animals which had not perished from the forced drive by the Indians were recovered.

Arizona civilians also mobilized against the Apache Indians during the Civil War. There was hardly a week passed during 1863–64 without an encounter between the frontiersmen and the Apaches. The friendly Maricopa and Pima Indians, traditional enemies of the Apaches, who were issued out-of-date firearms and ammunition by the Union Army ordnance, ably assisted the whites at times. On January 24, 1864, a party of thirty white civilians and fourteen Maricopa and Pima Indians, under King S. Woolsey, aide to the Governor of Arizona, attacked a band of Gila Apaches seventy miles northeast of the Pima villages. The Apaches had stolen a herd of horses and mules from Peeples Valley, a white settlement in western Arizona. During the fight, nineteen Gilas were killed and a large number wounded. One civilian was killed. On April 11 of the same year another party under Woolsey, with a small detachment of California Volunteers from Fort Whipple, in western Arizona, assaulted an Indian *rancheria,* and fourteen Apaches were killed in the skirmish.[14]

The Apaches struck again at the troops while on the march. On May 3, 1864, fifty-four California Volunteers under Lieutenant Henry H. Stevens, en route from Fort Cummings to Fort Bowie, were ambushed by one hundred warriors in Doubtful Canyon in the Steins Peak Range near the border of southeastern Arizona and southwestern New Mexico. In a fight lasting nearly two hours, ten Indians were killed and about twenty wounded. The casualties of the Volunteers were one man missing and five wounded, one mortally.

Responding to General Carleton's Apache Indian extermination order, Lieutenant Colonel Nelson H. Davis, during May and June, 1864, led a detachment of 111 men of the California Fifth Infantry and First Cavalry against plundering bands of Gila Apaches. While on the march from May 9 until June 3, the expedition, which was comprised mainly of Captain T. T. Tidball's company, covered a wide area in the upper Gila River Valley and Mescal Mountains in eastern Arizona. Several Indian *rancherías* and a number of wheat and corn fields were destroyed. Fifty-one Indians were killed, including two chiefs, 17 were wounded, and 16 women and children were taken prisoner. A large amount of stolen property was recaptured from the Indians, including $660 in gold coin and a pistol, diary, and a shotgun, identified by the name on each item, which had belonged to white men who had recently been massacred by the Apaches. The expedition's casualty list contained only one soldier seriously wounded.

14 The locality where the fight took place is known as "Bloody Tanks."

In August, 1864, Major Thomas J. Blakeney led a party of California Volunteers on a thirty-day trip through central and eastern Arizona in search of hostile Apaches. In a fight in the wheat fields on Pinal Creek north of the present site of Globe, Arizona, the Californians drove the Indians back with a loss of ten Apaches killed and two captured. Twenty acres of corn and a large quantity of pumpkins and beans were destroyed. These expeditions were typical of a considerable number made in Arizona during 1863, 1864, and 1865 against the Apache Indians in retaliation for similar crimes against the whites and to carry out General Carleton's extermination order.

Soon after General Carleton assumed command of the Department of New Mexico in 1862, eighteen Navaho chiefs called on him at Santa Fe to learn whether he would make a treaty with them. Carleton responded with the question, "What do you want with a treaty?" They answered, "That we may hereafter have peace." "Go home, stay there," was his unexpected answer, "commit no more robberies or murders . . . and you have peace at once. Treaties," the General informed them, "confuse matters, involving a double labor of making and breaking them." The Navahos knew that they never kept their treaties and that Carleton was not a child to be beguiled by them. The chiefs said that they had never been refused a treaty before. They stated that they would return to their country and try to persuade their young men to behave. In a few weeks the robberies, murders, and retaliations began again.[15]

In the spring of 1863 the Navahos informed Carleton that a large portion of them were peaceful. He responded that since they all lived together, he and his men could not distinguish friends from foes. He urged those who claimed to be friendly to leave the others and go to the Bosque Redondo Reservation. The Indians replied that not one Navaho would come. The General informed them through Lieutenant Colonel J. Francisco Chávez, who had arrived with four companies of New Mexican Volunteers at Fort Wingate, northwestern New Mexico, on Feb-

[15] James F. Meline, *Two Thousand Miles on Horseback*, 285–86.

ruary 1, 1863, that they had better reconsider the matter and that July 20, 1863, would be the deadline before which they could peaceably leave their present location and move to the Bosque. After that date any Navaho seen by the soldiers in that area was to be treated as hostile. Orders were given to kill every male Navaho Indian who could be found who was capable of bearing arms and to take the women and children as prisoners. The Navahos responded that they had heard "big talk before that meant nothing" and "had listened for years to the cry of the wolf that came not."[16]

True to his promise, the war against the Navahos opened on the day set by General Carleton, July 20, 1863. On June 15, Carleton issued orders for Colonel "Kit" Carson to lead an expedition into the Navaho country. His command of 736 troops, 260 of whom were infantry, was composed mainly of First New Mexican Volunteers, with a few officers and men from the California Volunteers and regular army. Two mountain howitzers were taken on the expedition. Co-ordinating with Carson was another force of 326 men under Lieutenant Colonel J. Francisco Chávez, commander at Fort Wingate. On July 7, Carson with the advance companies of his column, left Los Lunas, New Mexico, on the Río Grande. Traveling northwest, he was at Fort Wingate on July 10 and reached Fort Defiance in the heart of the Navaho territory on July 20. A band of Ute (Utah) Indian scouts, anxious to fight the Navahos, their traditional enemies, joined Carson at Fort Defiance. They were issued arms and ammunition.

There were no large battles during the Navaho campaign of 1863–64, but it comprised a series of encircling attacks by the expedition under Carson against these Indians in their desert, canyon, and mountain retreats. The plan was to compel them to surrender and go to the Bosque Redondo Reservation or annihilate them. The Navahos were in no condition to defend themselves successfully against the invading troops. They had a few rifles and revolvers, individually owned, a small supply of ammunition acquired from the Mexican traders, and a large

---

[16] Keleher, *Turmoil in New Mexico,* 303.

number of bows and arrows, although they were not expert bowmen. They had sheep, cattle, and horses, yet the horses were never shod or grain-fed to prepare them for exhausting war travel. They raised wheat and corn, but lived from season to season and did not have surplus supplies when Carleton started the war.

With his characteristic aggressiveness, Carson, accompanied by his field staff and seventy men from his command with some Ute Indian scouts, advanced rapidly into the Navaho country on a two-day reconnoiter. While on the trip, the site of Fort Canby was chosen on Río Pueblo Colorado, twenty-one miles west of Fort Defiance in northeastern Arizona, which became a field headquarters. On the return trip, July 24, the Utes killed eight Navahos, making a total of twelve enemy dead since Carson arrived in the country.

The Ute warriors were brave, expert horsemen, good marksmen, and very effective in tracking and killing Navahos, some of whom they scalped. Carson used them with his troops as scouts or they fought by themselves. Typical of the reports of the bloody toll which they took on the Navahos was one on August 11, stating that since the first of that month the Utes killed thirty-three Navahos, captured sixty-six, took 30 horses and 2,000 sheep. On September 5, it was reported that the Utes had killed nine Navahos and captured forty children. The Utes asked permission to keep the Navaho women and children that they captured, intending to sell part of them to the Mexicans. Carson passed the request on to General Carleton who refused, ordering all captives sent to Santa Fe and from there to the Bosque Redondo.[17]

The Navahos struck back by attacking the troops at every opportunity. Soon after Fort Canby was established, a band of Navahos stole some commissary sheep and goats and ate part of them almost within gunshot of the fort. On the same raid

---

[17] *O.R.*, I, 26:233–34, 26–27, 234–35 (part 1). Fort Canby was named in honor of General Edward R. S. Canby, former commander, Department of New Mexico.

the marauders ran off some horses and mules, including Carson's favorite horse. While in charge of a herd of army beef cattle, three New Mexican Volunteers were attacked by Navahos. Two soldiers were killed. The third one, seriously wounded with eight arrows, threw the guns of his dead comrades into a spring. The Indians fractured his skull with rocks and left him for dead, but he recovered sufficiently next morning to go for help. In the fight several Indians were killed and wounded. The survivors drove off the cattle.

Part of Carson's plan was to starve the Navahos into submission as well as to annihilate them. Acting on his orders, a detachment of soldiers under Major Joseph Cummings, on July 24, chopped down several fields of Navaho grain, which would have developed into over 75,000 pounds of wheat, and a large amount of corn. This was hauled from the fields along the Río Pueblo Colorado to Fort Canby where it was fed to the army animals during the following winter.

An August 5, Colonel Carson, with a detachment of 337 men, left his camp on the Río Pueblo Colorado on an extensive scout in the Navaho country to the west and north. Two weeks later he reported to General Carleton that thus far on the trip three Navahos had been killed, twenty-four prisoners taken, 187 acres of corn and 15 acres of wheat destroyed, and 1,100 sheep and 23 horses captured. One commissioned officer, Major Joseph Cummings, had been killed by a concealed Indian.[18] Carson, with his command, left Fort Canby on August 20 for a preliminary survey of the almost inaccessible Canyon de Chelly, the famous Navaho stronghold. Here a party of twenty-five men under Captain Albert H. Pfeiffer stole into the canyon to gather information to be used in a later invasion and to find what Indians they could. The command returned to the fort on August 31, having killed one Indian and wounded two.

In August and September, 1863, New Mexican Volunteers,

[18] When Carleton later established a fort at Cook's Canyon, southwestern New Mexico, on the main road from Mesilla to Tucson, he named it Fort Cummings in honor of Major Joseph Cummings.

under Lieutenant Colonel J. F. Chávez, advanced against the Navahos from Fort Wingate. One company, led by Captain Rafael Chacon, on a two-week scout killed eight Navahos, captured fourteen, and took 1,500 sheep and goats and 17 horses and mules. At the same time Captain Joseph P. Hargrave, with his company of California Volunteers, scouring the area along the headwaters of the Little Colorado River, pursued several bands of Navahos, and captured 500 sheep.

Meanwhile, General Carleton, intent on getting the Navaho Indians to the Bosque Redondo Reservation or having them killed in the field, drew his other commanders into the campaign. On August 3, 1863, he ordered Captain William H. Lewis, commanding officer at Albuquerque, to send a company of infantry on a thirty-day Indian hunt in the near-by Sandia Mountains, with instructions to kill every male Navaho or Apache who was large enough to bear arms. On the same day, Carleton sent similar orders to Captain Samuel Archer, in charge of a post at Los Pinos, commanding him to forward an infantry company to the Manzano Mountains southeast of Albuquerque. In September, Archer was again ordered to send a party of thirty infantrymen into the Manzano Mountains to hunt for Navahos and Apaches. On August 4, Carleton instructed Colonel Edwin A. Rigg, commander at Fort Craig, to send a detachment for thirty days to a Navaho rendezvous west of Limitar in central New Mexico. Here the Indians drove the stolen cattle and jerked the meat. The soldiers' orders were to kill every Navaho and Apache they could find.[19]

On September 27, Lieutenant P. A. J. Russel, with four mounted men and a party of Pueblo Indians, trailed a band of Navahos who had stolen livestock from the Pueblos. The marauders were overtaken near the town of James, west of Santa Fe. During the ensuing fight, eight Navahos were killed, twenty

---

[19] 39 Cong., 2 sess., *Reports of the Committees,* 1866–67, appendix, pp. 122, 123, 138. (Hereafter cited as *Senate Com. Rep.*) During the Civil War there was a Los Pinos about twenty miles south of Albuquerque which should not be confused with Los Pinos, New Mexico, of today, located in the northern part of the state.

women and children were made prisoners and 125 sheep and 2 horses were recaptured. The Pueblos also acted independently against the Navahos. On October 5, it was reported that during a recent campaign the Pueblos had killed twenty-two Navahos, captured fifty-one prisoners, 1,200 sheep and 40 mules, some of which had the U. S. brand.

In August, Colonel Carson was told by Ute scouts that Zuñi Indians were helping the Navahos escape from the net that had been spread out to kill or capture them. Carson informed Carleton accordingly. On September 19, the General answered that, if necessary, six prominent Zuñi men should be seized as hostages. He suggested that the tribe be warned that their village would be destroyed if they aided the Navahos, injured any white men, or stole their animals. During the latter part of September, Carson, with a detachment of troops, visited the Zuñi village and found them friendly to the whites. The Zuñis had killed several Navahos and had captured a number of sheep and goats.[20]

Although the Navaho campaign had its temporary setbacks, and at times in their counteroffensive, Navaho warriors attacked some of the army outposts and supply trains, the morale of these Indians began to falter. The first week in September, 1863, General Carleton was able to report to Washington that the initial assignment of fifty-one Navahos—men, women, and children— had been sent to the Bosque Redondo Indian Reservation.[21] In October a delegation of Navaho chiefs went to Fort Wingate to treat for peace. They were given Carleton's ultimatum contained in a letter to Carson:

Go to Bosque Redondo, or we will pursue and destroy you. . . . You have deceived us too often, and robbed and murdered our people too long, to trust you again at large in your own country. This war shall be pursued against you, if it takes years . . . until you cease to exist or more.[22]

[20] Keleher, *Turmoil in New Mexico*, 307–308; *O.R.*, I, 26:727, 252–54 (part 1).
[21] *Report of the Commissioner of Indian Affairs*, 1863, 112.
[22] *O.R.*, I, 26:728, 29 (part 1); Edwin L. Sabin, *Kit Carson Days*, 430, 431.

As the autumn of 1863 merged into winter, the stern war went on, with the Navahos steadily losing. The campaign against the Navahos was approved by the civilians in New Mexico who worked with the military forces and acted independently on several occasions. In November a party of citizens pursued a band of marauding Navahos beyond Fort Wingate. The Indians were overtaken, and in three skirmishes a total of fourteen Navahos were killed, sixty were made prisoner; twenty horses and mules and twenty-five sheep and goats were captured.

On November 15, Colonel Carson with a detachment left Fort Canby and for three weeks the party scoured the area west of the fort for Indians. One Navaho village and an Indian camp were destroyed. Four Navahos were killed, four were wounded, three were captured, but several escaped. By the middle of November, 188 Navahos had surrendered at Fort Wingate to be transferred to Bosque Redondo. Statistics released for 1863 in the Department of New Mexico, which included the territories of New Mexico and Arizona, revealed that a total of 301 Indians had been killed during the campaigns, 87 known wounded (many were unaccounted for), and 703 captured. About 25,000 animals were stolen by the Indians of which more than 24,500 were recovered. During the year, 17 soldiers were killed in skirmishes with the Indians and 25 were wounded. Sixteen civilians were killed and four who were engaged in the campaigns were wounded, but this did not account for the unknown number of people massacred during the Indian raids along the roads, trails, and at the outlying ranches.[23]

In order to subdue the entire Navaho tribe completely, it was necessary to invade the famed Canyon de Chelly, located about forty miles northwest of Fort Defiance in northeastern Arizona. This stronghold, thirty miles long with walls over one thousand feet high, had been regarded as almost impregnable. Federal troops under Colonel Sumner in 1851 and under Major Canby just prior to the Civil War had entered the canyon for a short time pursuing Navahos, but they were both forced to retreat.

[23] *Ibid.,* I, 26:33-34 (part 1).

On January 6, 1864, an expedition under Colonel Carson marched out of Fort Canby for Canyon de Chelly. He divided his force into two columns. Taking with him 375 men, consisting of New Mexico Volunteers with a few California Volunteers and army regulars, Carson reached the west opening of the canyon in six days. The deep snow which covered the entire area greatly retarded the progress of the troops and the supply trains. Captain Albert Pfeiffer, leading the other column, composed of First New Mexico Cavalry, arrived at the east entrance to the canyon on January 11.[24]

Carson, on January 12, with his staff made a preliminary survey along the south rim of the canyon. On the same day Sergeant Andreas Herrera, leading a detachment of fifty men, skirmished with a party of Navahos, heading for a side entrance to the canyon, with a considerable loss to the Indians. On the thirteenth, Carson divided his command into two columns sending them on a two-day reconnoiter of the canyon rims. Captain Asa B. Carey, Thirteenth U. S. Infantry, led one detachment, accompanied by Carson, along the south rim, and Captain Joseph Barney, First New Mexican Cavalry, led the other along the north rim.

Meanwhile, Captain Pfeiffer and his men with a pack train traveled through Canyon de Chelly from east to west. En route the detachment had several skirmishes with Navahos on both sides of the canyon, some of whom were whooping, yelling, cursing, firing shots, and throwing rocks on the soldiers from their dwellings and fortifications hundreds of feet above the bottom of the canyon. The troops silenced a number of the Indians with accurate rifle fire. The detachment, after toiling through ice and snow, arrived at the west end of the canyon and was united with the remainder of Carson's troops on January 14.

Two days later Captain Carey left camp with a company of New Mexican First Cavalry. Traveling through the canyon from

[24] *Ibid.*, I, 34:76 (part 1). The daring bravery of Captain Pfeiffer during the Navaho and Kiowa campaigns was probably caused, in part, by the hatred of the Indians resulting from his wife's murder in 1863.

west to east, they destroyed Indian property, including a large number of peach trees, and warned the Navahos, then half-starved and naked, to surrender or be annihilated. One hundred and five Navahos voluntarily accompanied Carey back to Fort Canby, which they reached on January 15.

Colonel Carson with his entire command had returned to Fort Canby by January 21. The immediate results of the expedition to Canyon de Chelly were only 23 Navaho Indians killed, 34 captured, and 200 who voluntarily surrendered, yet from that time on the Navahos capitulated in large numbers. By January 23, Carson was able to report that he had 500 Navahos at Fort Canby, who would soon be sent on to Santa Fe. One thousand more Indians were en route to the fort to emigrate. On February 28, Captain Carey reported that there were 2,500 Navahos at Fort Canby awaiting transportation, 500 having been sent from that post since Carson's arrival from Canyon de Chelly.

While the Navaho campaign was in progress in the north, one hundred Navahos drove off a herd of livestock owned principally by Apaches residing on the Bosque Redondo Reservation. On January 5, 1864, a mounted company from Fort Sumner and twenty-five Apaches pursued the marauders in a running battle near the fort, on the Pecos River, during which forty Navahos were killed and twenty-five wounded. The remainder escaped, but the stolen animals were recovered. The only casualties on the other side were two slightly wounded Apaches.

The fighting spirit of the Navaho tribe as a whole finally seemed to be broken. On February 7, 1864, General Carleton wrote Washington that it was his belief that this would be the last of the Navaho War.[25] On May 4, Governor Henry Connelly issued a proclamation stating that hostilities against the Navahos had ceased.[26] During the remaining months of the Civil War, the Navahos continued to surrender and were steadily sent to the Bosque. On January 14, 1865, Carleton reported that there were 8,354 Navahos on the Bosque Redondo Indian Reservation,

[25] *Ibid.*, I, 34:72, 73, 76–78, 78–80, 74–75, 118, 69–70.
[26] *Santa Fe Weekly Gazette,* May 7, 1864.

who, with the Apaches there, made a total of 8,991.[27] On January 30, 1865, the New Mexican territorial assembly passed a joint resolution which expressed appreciation to the United States government, to the soldiers and officers who had participated in the campaign, and to General James H. Carleton for prosecuting the war against the Navaho Indians and placing them on the Bosque Redondo. Carleton had previously highly praised the citizens of New Mexico and officers and men of the militia for their splendid work during the Indian campaigns.[28]

In the fall of 1864, General Carleton was compelled to divert his interest somewhat from the Navaho and Apache campaigns and direct a portion of his troops against the Plains Indians. The Kiowas and Comanches for years had troubled the area which is cornered by the present states of New Mexico, Colorado, Kansas, Oklahoma, and Texas. During the Civil War depredations by these Indians had intensified. Frontier settlements had been attacked, and supply trains along the Santa Fe Trail had been robbed. Determined to punish the Kiowas and Comanches, Carleton, on October 22, 1864, issued orders for an expedition to proceed against them, to be led by Colonel "Kit" Carson.

Cavalry and infantry composed of California and New Mexico Volunteers and army regulars, totaling 335 men, were concentrated at Fort Bascom, eastern New Mexico. Seventy-five Ute and Jicarilla Apache Indian warriors were induced to accompany the troops. The expedition was equipped with two twelve-pound howitzers, firearms, ammunition, and subsistence supplies loaded in wagons to last until December 31. On November 12, Carson led the column east from Fort Bascom toward the old Adobe Fort, two hundred miles down the Canadian River into Texas. It was thought that the Kiowas and Comanches were there in winter camp. Under Carson, the infantry was commanded by Lieutenant Colonel F. P. Abreu, the cavalry by Major William McCleave, the artillery by Lieutenant George H. Pettis, while Lieutenant Charles Haberkorn was in charge

---

[27] *O.R.*, I, 48:523 (part 1).
[28] *Ibid.*, I, 26:32 (part 1).

of the Indians. When the expedition had reached a point about thirty miles west of Adobe Fort, the supply wagons were ordered to proceed slowly, guarded by the infantry. Carson went on with the mounted force and howitzers.[29]

At sunrise on November 25, 1864, a Kiowa Indian village, estimated to have from 150 to 176 lodges, located on the Canadian River near Adobe Fort, was attacked by Carson's men. The surprised Indians immediately abandoned their camp. Indian women, children, and old men hid in the near-by foothills. The retreating warriors took a position about four miles back and stubbornly resisted for a time. Armed with rifles, they charged on the troops, firing from their horses' necks. Carson's Ute and Apache scouts were out in front also shooting from horseback. Several well-aimed howitzer shells and the rifle fire of the dismounted cavalry, deployed in the high grass, soon routed the Kiowa warriors, who retired down the river toward other camps, consisting principally of Kiowas, along with a small number of Comanches, Apaches, and Arapahos.[30]

Reinforced from a village of at least 350 lodges in less than a half-hour, about one thousand warriors, well mounted and armed, had nearly surrounded the troops. The Indians, yelling like demons, made several charges from different positions. The howitzers, blazing away, supported by a galling fire from the skirmishers, drove the warriors out of range with a heavy loss, but they remained threatening in the near vicinity. Carson determined to return and destroy the vacated camp. The Indians sensing his intentions, advanced desperately in the most severe fighting of the day, but the constant firing of the artillery and

[29] *O.R.*, I, 41:939–40 (part 1); 39 Cong., 2 sess., *Senate Com. Rep.*, 200. The Indian scouts had requested and were given sugar and coffee like the other soldiers. They also asked that while they were gone, their families should receive daily rations from the government stores.

[30] *O.R.*, 41:940–42 (part 1); George H. Pettis, "Kit Carson's Fight with the Comanche and Kiowa Indians," *Personal Narratives of the Battles of the Rebellion*, 16–26. Pettis referred to the place of battle as Adobe Walls. A captive white woman and two children were forced by the Indian women to hide with them in the foothills.

cavalry, supported by Ute and Apache scouts, forced the defenders back.[31]

The Kiowas and Comanches, finding it impossible to prevent the soldiers by repeated charges from marching toward the village, set fire to the long grass and weeds. Burning furiously, the fire forced the troops to close in and advance at double-quick time. The Indians would then dash forward under cover of the smoke, shoot, and drop back to safety. As the detachment neared the camp, the Indians made a desperate effort to rescue part of their property, but the howitzer shells again drove them from the field. Carson and his men then set fire to the village and its stores, which included a large amount of dried meat, buffalo robes, part of a cavalryman's uniform, white women and children's clothing, several sets of harness, an army ambulance and a wagon used by Chief Sierrito (Little Mountain) which had been captured by the Kiowas. The Indians, seeing their village in flames, fled to the hills and did not resist further.[32]

The engagement was over about sunset, but the village continued to burn during the night. Two soldiers were reported killed and from 10 to 21 wounded, two of whom died later from wounds. One Ute was killed and five wounded. The loss of the Kiowas and Comanches was estimated from 60 to 100 killed and from 100 to 150 wounded.

Since the cavalry horses were in poor condition and the men were low on ammunition, Carson thought it better not to advance on the remaining Indian villages, but to return to the supply wagons. After dark the detachment traveled about ten miles up the river, where the supply train was found safely camped and

---

[31] *O.R.*, I, 41:941; Pettis, "Kit Carson's Fight," *Personal Narratives*, 26–29, related that during the battle an Indian bugler would answer the army bugler with the opposite call. When "advance" was blown, the Indian would blow "retreat," etc.

[32] *O.R.*, I, 41:941–42; Pettis, "Kit Carson's Fight," *Personal Narratives*, 27, 31–34. During the battle a howitzer shell entered the body of a Comanche's horse while running at full speed. The shell exploded throwing the rider about twenty feet in the air. He then fell senseless to the ground. Two comrades, throwing themselves on the sides of their horses, seized an arm each and dragged him from the field amid a shower of bullets from the skirmishers.

guarded by the infantry. On November 27, the expedition started on the return trip, arriving back at Fort Bascom on December 10. On December 16, Carson requested from Carleton enough more men to bring his command up to one thousand, but no other campaign was undertaken against the Kiowas and Comanches at that time. Carson complained against the Mexican traders who had sold guns and ammunition to the Kiowas and their allies. He was especially critical of Indian Superintendent Michael Steck for issuing permits to the Mexicans to trade with these Indians. Late in December, 1864, Carleton wrote Carson expressing appreciation to him, his officers, and his men for the manner in which they had conducted the expedition against the Kiowas and the Comanches.[33]

In Colorado during 1861 the hostile Indians threatened, but there were no serious depredations. Governor William Gilpin in that year, while sponsoring the Colorado Volunteers and being constantly on the alert for any possible Secessionist movement, was also closely watching the Indians in the Territory. On October 26, 1861, the Governor informed Colonel Canby at Santa Fe that the Indian population west of the Arkansas River, totaling 64,500, was allied with the Georgians in the Territory who sympathized with the Secession. At the same time there were some Indians in that section of the West who enlisted in the Union armies.

Colorado Secessionists, who had enlisted in the Confederate army under General Sterling Price in the Midwest, convinced him that they could easily raise a regiment of Southern sympathizers in Colorado. Commissions were obtained to staff the proposed regiment and the Coloradans, with a few others who expected to become company officers, departed for the Territory to recruit early in 1862. Federal authorities learned of the project and sent a mounted detachment of volunteer Osage Indian scouts with orders to capture or kill the newly commissioned Confederate officers. The Rebel party was intercepted on the plains in southeastern Colorado, where in the ensuing fight every

[33] *O.R.*, I, 41:942–44 (part 1).

Confederate was killed. To show that their instructions had been obeyed to the letter, the Indians cut off all the dead white soldiers' heads and carried them back as evidence.[34]

As the Civil War continued into 1862, the Indians in Colorado became more threatening. By the end of May of that year, it became apparent that Arapaho, Cheyenne, and other Indian tribes were stealthily preparing for war. Their braves devoted much of their time and shrewdness to obtaining firearms and ammunition "to kill buffalo," they said. Openly they still professed friendship for the whites.[35] In the summer of 1862 some Colorado citizens, fearful of an Indian attack, called for the return of the Colorado Volunteers from New Mexico for home defense. Colonel J. M. Chivington did return in August, but he went on to Washington, where he was able to get his infantry regiment transferred to one of cavalry. The entire First Colorado Regiment did not arrive back in Colorado until some time in January, 1863.

On June 23, 1862, reports reached Denver that a band of Indians were raiding the ranches along the South Platte River, north of that city. Governor Evans, Indian Agent Vaile, and a company of Second Colorado Volunteers under Colonel Jesse H. Leavenworth, taking with them a twelve-pound cannon, proceeded to the scene. The frightened Indians accepted the Governor's ultimatum and left immediately for their hunting grounds on the Republican River. Governor Evans in his message to the territorial assembly on July 18, 1862, urged the enactment of a military law which would provide more protection against the Indians. His recommendations became law on August 14.

Federal officials in Colorado in February, 1863, sent a delegation of Arapaho, Cheyenne, Apache, and Ute Indians to visit the Great White Father at Washington. It was hoped that when the chiefs saw the large cities and powerful armies of the white men, they would understand the futility of an Indian uprising. Before leaving, the seven Ute chiefs were housed at Camp Weld,

---

[34] Whitford, *Colorado Volunteers*, 42.
[35] Jerome C. Smiley, *Semi-Centennial History of the State of Colorado*, I, 412.

near Denver, where they displayed a few Navaho scalps "as thick as buffalo hides" which they planned to present to "Father Abraham" when they called upon him at the White House.[36] Ute Chief Ouray was impressed with what he saw in the East and thereafter exerted his great influence for peace, but some of the younger Utes and the Plains Indian chiefs did not share his good judgment.

In February and again in July, 1863, Ute Indians raided the Overland Stage and Mail stations near Fort Halleck in that part of the Colorado Military District which is now southern Wyoming. The marauders stole livestock, plundered the stations and committed other depredations. A company of Kansas Volunteers at the fort pursued them, and on each occasion a spirited skirmish occurred. During the fight in July, which was the more serious of the two, 70 troops faced about 250 warriors. One soldier was killed and six were wounded, while the Indians lost over sixty in killed and wounded. Major Edward W. Wynkoop with four companies of First Colorado Cavalry was sent to the scene with orders to scout the headwaters of the Bear, White, and Snake rivers for hostile Indians, but the Ute marauders had disappeared.

In March, 1863, settlers' ranches near the mouth of Cache la Poudre River in northern Colorado were raided by Cheyenne and Kiowa Indians, who stole every gun and horse they could get but did nothing worse. They were not ready to start killing. During the later months of 1863, Indian depredations were intensified along the South Platte River. The stage companies, freighters, ranchers, and travelers all suffered from systematic plundering by the Indians. Many of the Indians of Colorado obtained firearms and ammunition from Mexican traders of New Mexico and from corrupt, mercenary Americans, and probably encouragement and material aid from the Confederate officials. Governor Evans, sensing the danger of a general Indian uprising, sent a special messenger to Washington, urging more military assistance for the Territory.[37]

[36] *Rocky Mountain News,* February 14 and 26, 1863.

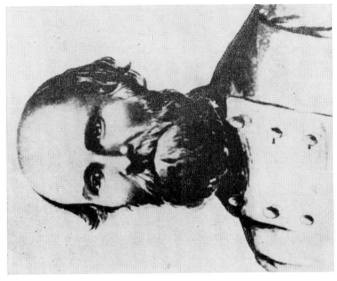

Lieutenant Colonel William R. Scurry, Confederate commander in the Battle of Glorieta.

Colonel John P. Slough, First Colorado Regiment, Union commander in the Battle of Glorieta.

Lieutenant Colonel
John R. Baylor, Confederate
governor of Arizona.

Brigadier General
James H. Carleton,
California Volunteers, Unio
commander, Department of
New Mexico, 1862–65.

Major John M. Chivington
First Colorado Regiment.

The Governor, in September, 1863, sent Elbridge Gerry to invite the Sioux, Arapaho, and Cheyenne leaders to a peace council to be held at the head of the Republican River while Evans, escorted by a company of First Colorado Cavalry, brought food for a feast. Gerry found the Indians insolent and indifferent. They could be neither persuaded nor bribed to attend the proposed conference. When they learned that the Governor wanted them to settle on a reservation and live like white people, they replied that they were not reduced quite that low yet. The attempted meeting was a failure.[38]

Governor Evans had better success with the Ute Indians. During 1863 certain bands of Utes went on several raids, ostensibly after Sioux, but on which they carried off considerable property of white people. In October a commission, among whom were the Governor, Indian Agent Lafayette Head, and John G. Nicolay, President Lincoln's private secretary, escorted by a detachment of Colorado Cavalry, held a council with a large number of Tabeguache Utes at Conejos, in southern Colorado. Through the influence of Chief Ouray, a treaty was made in which the Indians agreed to a peace with the whites and to move from the San Luis Valley to the Gunnison River Valley, west of the Continental Divide. For ten years this band of Utes was to receive $20,000 worth of goods and provisions annually with some cattle, sheep, and horses.[39]

The culmination of the rapidly increasing antagonism between the red and white races in Colorado came in 1864. Late in April, one hundred men of the First Colorado Cavalry, the only military organization then stationed in the Territory, while on a reconnoiter near Fort Larned, western Kansas, were attacked by nearly four hundred Cheyenne warriors. Contrary to usual In-

[37] *O.R.*, I, 22:294 (part 2).

[38] LeRoy R. Hafen, *The Overland Mail*, 254–55. Elbridge Gerry, named after his grandfather, a signer of the Declaration of Independence, residing with his Indian wife on the South Platte River north of Denver, kept Governor Evans informed on Indian developments.

[39] 58 Cong., 2 sess., *Indian Affairs, Laws and Treaties*, Senate Doc. No. 319, II, 856–59.

dian tactics, some of the braves charged on a two-howitzer battery which was blazing away at them. After twenty-five to thirty Cheyennes had been killed and as many wounded by the deadly fire of the Colorado veterans, the remaining Indians scattered over the hills.

On April 12, 1864, a fifteen-man detachment of First Colorado Cavalry, under Lieutenant Clark Dunn, intercepted twenty-five well-armed Cheyenne warriors stealing horses near Frémont's Orchard, in what is now Morgan County, Colorado. Lieutenant Dunn demanded the surrender of the horses and threatened to disarm the Indians. The chief responded with an order to commence firing. Four soldiers were wounded, two of them mortally. As the cavalry horses were nearly exhausted by a previous seventy-five-mile march and the troopers were armed only with revolvers and sabers, the Cheyennes escaped with the stolen animals, but not until eight were killed and twelve wounded.

During the first week in May, 1864, a full company of First Cavalry under Major Jacob Downing was dispatched from Denver with orders to attack any thieving or hostile Indians. At Cedar Canyon, an affluent of the South Platte River, the company attacked an encampment of about three hundred Indians. After a severe fight, the Cheyennes were defeated. Among them were those who had taken part in the raid at Frémont's Orchard. The encampment was destroyed and about one hundred horses were recovered. The casualty reports vary from twenty-five to thirty-eight Indians killed and from forty to seventy-six wounded, while one soldier was killed and one wounded. On May 16, a detachment of Colorado Volunteers under Lieutenant George S. Eayre, was attacked by about four hundred Cheyenne Indian warriors at Smoky Hill between Fort Lynn, eastern Colorado and Fort Larned, western Kansas. After a persistent fight of seven and one-half hours, the troops succeeded in driving them from the field. Three Indian chiefs and twenty-four warriors were killed with an unestimated number wounded. Four cavalrymen were killed and three wounded.

Governor Evans, in June, 1864, alarmed at the threatened

general Indian uprising at a time when one regiment of the Colorado Volunteers had been called to duty in the Middle West, asked General S. R. Curtis at Fort Leavenworth, Kansas, and General J. H. Carleton in New Mexico for additional troops. Curtis replied that none were available, while Carleton could not send any men to Colorado until the last of August, 1864. In desperation, Evans asked the War Department for authority to raise a regiment of hundred-day cavalrymen to fight Indians.[40]

During the first week in June, 1864, a near panic occurred in Denver that spread to near-by towns. This fear was caused by the report that large bands of Indians were approaching to begin a massacre of the whites and destruction of their towns. Governor Evans directed that all business houses close at 6:30 P.M. and ordered all able-bodied citizens to enroll in the home guard for daily drill. Some defenses were thrown up in the outskirts of Denver, and most of the women and children were gathered in the Mint and other brick buildings in the city. There was no general attack on the Colorado towns, and the excitement soon subsided.

At the same time, Indian depredations continued along the roads and trails in the Territory and at some outlying ranches. On June 11, a savage assault was made on a family named Hunsgate at a ranch thirty miles southeast of Denver. The husband, wife, and two children were killed, scalped, and their throats cut by the Indians. The mutilated bodies were later displayed in Denver, where feeling ran high.[41] In mid-July a number of vicious Indian attacks were made on the stage stations and freight wagons along the South Platte River from Junction (now Fort Morgan) to Julesburg, Colorado. Five white men were killed, one wounded, and 130 horses stolen. A detachment of soldiers from Junction pursued the Indians, killed five, and recovered 77 horses. General Robert B. Mitchell, commanding the

[40] Smiley, *Semi-Centennial History*, I, 415; *O.R.*, I, 41:167, 902–903, 644 (part 2).
[41] *Denver Commonwealth*, June 15, 1864.

Nebraska District, ordered all freight trains stopped at Julesburg until a sufficient number could be gathered for the trainmen to protect themselves.

On July 17, there was a skirmish at Fort Larned, western Kansas, between the Indians and Federal troops, some of whom were Colorado Volunteers. The following day Indians attacked a supply train at Walnut Creek, fifteen miles from the fort. They killed eight white men and two Negroes, scalping only the whites. A man and a boy were scalped alive, but they escaped by feigning death and later reached Fort Larned.

Governor Evans, on August 10, 1864, issued a proclamation to the citizens of Colorado appealing to them to organize for the defense of their homes and families against the merciless savages. He claimed that anyone who killed a hostile Indian was a patriot, but warned that there were Indians who were friendly and that to kill one of them would involve the whites in greater difficulty. He urged the Coloradans to fight only hostile Indians.

During the summer of 1864, the Governor sent messengers to Plains Indians in Colorado, thought to be peaceful, inviting them to the nearest military post, where they would receive subsistence and protection. The Indian agents were instructed to draw at the forts supplies necessary to feed them.[42] When the effort met with little or no response from the Indians, the Governor authorized all citizens of Colorado, individually or in parties, to pursue all hostile Indians and to hold for their own use all property belonging to the belligerent Indians which could be captured.[43]

On August 12, Governor Evans finally received authority from the War Department to raise the regiment of hundred-day men to fight Indians. The work of organization was begun immediately. This authority was received in the nick of time, for the situation had now passed from bad to worse. The routes of travel in Colorado were beset by bands of hostile Indians. On August 16, the Indians attacked a stage station on the Arkansas River

[42] *O.R.*, I, 41:963–64 (part 1).
[43] *Rocky Mountain News*, August 11, 1864.

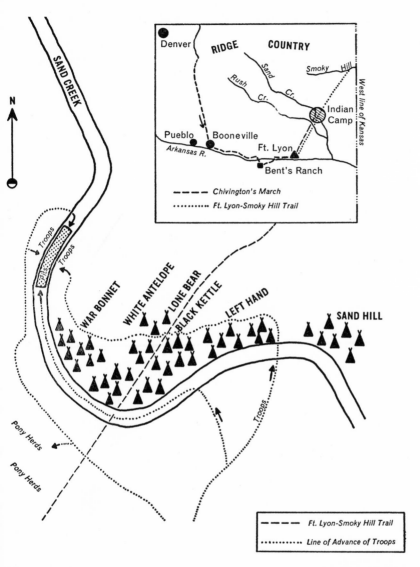

Scene of the Sand Creek Massacre. (From George Bird Grinnell's *The Fighting Cheyennes.*)

route between Bent's Fort and Boon's Station and killed all of the livestock. The next day three men were killed and one woman captured by the Indians on the same route. All mail from the East was interrupted by the summer uprisings. The mail to and from Colorado for a time had to be sent by way of the Pacific Coast and Panama. The halting of supply trains caused prices to soar, and starvation threatened.

A general attack on the Colorado settlements was planned by the principal Cheyenne and Arapaho Indian chiefs for the first week in August, 1864. Friendly Indians notified Elbridge Gerry, who rode sixty miles to Denver to warn Governor Evans. Messengers were sent to the other settlements of the Territory, and defensive preparations were made. The Indians, learning that their plans had been betrayed, refrained from the planned attack.

Early in September, in response to a letter proposing peace, written by George Bent, a half-blood, for Cheyenne and Arapaho chiefs, Major E. W. Wynkoop, commanding at Fort Lyon, with 127 cavalrymen, went to the Indian encampment on Smoky Hill River, in eastern Colorado. A council was held, four white prisoners were released, and seven chiefs, including Black Kettle, accompanied Wynkoop to Denver. At Camp Weld the chiefs met in a peace parley with Governor Evans, Colonel Chivington, Colorado District commander, and others. General S. R. Curtis wired that no peace could be made without his consent and that the Indians should be chastised first.[44] Evans contended that peace could only be made by the military leaders. Chivington left the matter up to Wynkoop until higher authority could be received. The chiefs returned to their people. Wynkoop, acting on Governor Evans' earlier proclamation, allowed the friendly Indians to camp near Fort Lyon, where they were fed government rations. They soon moved to Sand Creek, forty miles northeast of Fort Lyon. Chief Black Kettle with his Cheyennes followed, making a village of about five hundred. These Indians, assuming that they had complied with the white men's terms, felt safe from attack. But other plans were being made.

[44] *Report of the Commissioner of Indian Affairs, 1864,* 221.

About sunrise, on November 29, 1864, Colonel J. M. Chivington, with an expedition of approximately 950 men, composed of Third Colorado Cavalry (hundred-day men), First Colorado Cavalry with two howitzers and a detachment of First New Mexico Infantry, suddenly attacked the Cheyenne-Arapaho village of 138 lodges.[45] Most of the Indian horses, grazing near by, were seized to prevent the Indians' escape. The cavalry and infantry then charged on the village from three directions. The terrified Indians, variously estimated at from 500 to 1,000, consisting of old and young men, women, and children, were shot down indiscriminately as they fled from their tipis.[46] Some of the warriors snatched up their weapons, as they dashed from their lodges, and formed a battle line along Sand Creek about half a mile above the camp. Here they hurriedly dug rifle pits and valiantly defended themselves and some of their women and children for a short time. Overwhelmed by superior numbers and fighting equipment, the braves were steadily forced back from one position to another, until they had retreated more than five miles up the stream. The warriors then dispersed in all directions. The uneven engagement continued until about 3:00 P.M., although a few of the troopers pursued Indians until night. Every Indian that could be found was killed. Orders were given that no prisoners were to be taken.

Chivington and his men then returned and completely destroyed the village, gathering in the spoils of victory in supplies and trophies. About 550 horses and mules were captured. Many of the dead Indians, including old men, women, and children,

[45] *O.R.*, I, 41:948–59, 970–72 (part 1). Colonel George L. Shoup commanded the Third Cavalry. He later served as U. S. senator from Idaho. A battalion of First Colorado Cavalry and the New Mexican detachment were under Major Scott J. Anthony. Lieutenant Luther Wilson was in charge of another unit of Colorado First Cavalry.

[46] 39 Cong., 2 sess., *Senate Com. Rep.*, 41–42, 52, 60. John Smith, interpreter, claimed that when the troops approached, Chief Black Kettle hoisted an American flag over his lodge. Smith, who was in the village, tried desperately to tell the soldiers that these Indians were not hostile, but the troops only fired at him. Indian Agent S. G. Colley testified that Chivington ordered the attack in spite of the advice of several military officers and civilians not to attack the friendly Indians.

were scalped, their stomachs slit open with knives or mutilated in other ways. Some children were shot at their mothers' breasts and their brains knocked out.

The soldier casualties were listed at from 8 to 10 killed and 40 wounded. The reports on the Indian losses vary from 60 to 600 killed.[47] It was estimated that between 300 and 400 Indians escaped and drifted back to their original encampment on Smoky Hill River.[48] The troops remained in the vicinity until December 1. A select detachment pursued a band of Arapahos for several days without results. The regular volunteers returned to their posts and the hundred-day men were mustered out in Denver on December 29, 1864.

At first, news of the victory was highly acclaimed by the white people of Colorado. When the troops arrived on December 22, they paraded before their admiring fellow-citizens. When the facts of the massacre gradually became known, however, public opinion divided into those who still justified Chivington's attack at Sand Creek and those who condemned it.[49] In a short time, reports of the attack reached Washington. A Congressional committee, headed by Senator J. R. Doolittle, after conducting an extensive investigation in 1865, vigorously denounced Chivington and his troops for the indiscriminate slaughter of the Cheyennes and Arapahos at Sand Creek.[50] A military commission presided over by Lieutenant Colonel S. F. Tappan met from

[47] *O.R.*, I, 41:949–59, 960–61, 965, 979 (part 1); Hubert Howe Bancroft, *History of Nevada, Colorado, and Wyoming*, 466. Chivington reported between 500 and 600 Indians killed. Major Anthony placed the Indian dead from 400 to 500. Interpreter Smith reported he counted 60 to 70 dead, most of whom were women and children. Bancroft wrote that 131 Indians were killed, 50 soldiers were killed and wounded.

[48] *Rocky Mountain News*, December 17, 1864.

[49] Irving Howbert, *Memories of a Lifetime in the Pikes Peak Region*, 130–62, defends Chivington, presenting statements that white scalps found in the Indian camp indicated recent depredations on the whites. George Bird Grinnell, *The Fighting Cheyennes*, 164–73, thoroughly condemned Chivington. He cited testimony that the hoisting by Black Kettle of an American flag with a white flag, the absence of defensive precautions, and the peaceful intentions of certain chiefs demonstrated that the Sand Creek attack was unjustified and grossly wrong.

[50] 39 Cong., 2 sess., *Senate Com. Rep.*, 5–6, 26–96. Other members of the committee were Senator L. F. Foster and Congressman L. W. Ross.

February 9 to May 30, 1865, taking testimony on the conduct of Colonel Chivington and his men in the Sand Creek Massacre. A complete report of the proceedings was sent to the Senate by the Secretary of War.[51]

The brutal attack at Sand Creek brought unfortunate results. When other Plains Indians learned of the killing, they were aroused to bitter revenge against the hated whites.[52] By the first week in January, 1865, about 1,500 Cheyenne and Comanche warriors had concentrated at certain areas along the South Platte River. At the same time it was reported that a force of 4,000 Plains Indians were assembled along the headwaters of the Republican River.

On January 7, 1865, Indians plundered the station at Julesburg, northeastern Colorado, and looted a coach and supply train a short distance away. Soldiers at near-by Camp Rankin (later Fort Sedgwick) met the marauders in a spirited skirmish in which artillery had to be used to drive the redskins off. Thirteen soldiers and five civilians were killed in the encounter, while fifty-five Indians were slain. On the same date seventy-five warriors attacked a large supply and immigrant train near Valley Station between Denver and Julesburg. Twelve white men were killed, and all the wagons were burned.

Realizing that Colorado was again nearing a crisis, on January 7, Acting Governor S. H. Elbert urgently telegraphed Governor Evans, who was then in Washington, asking him to obtain 5,000 troops to prevent further depredations, or the white people would be compelled to leave Colorado. The plundering of the supply trains by the Indians created a shortage which boosted the cost of several food items to almost starvation prices. In order to get mail and passengers through the Indians' barrier,

[51] 39 Cong., 2 sess., *Senate Exec. Doc. No. 26*, 1–228. Other members of the commission were Captains E. A. Jacobs and George H. Stillwell, all of the First Colorado Cavalry.

[52] *Rocky Mountain News*, February 1, 1865, printed a letter written by Major Scott J. Anthony repudiating his statement made earlier recorded in *O.R.*, I, 41: 951–52 (part 1), in which he had reported the Sand Creek attack as a success. In contrast, he told the newspaper that the Sand Creek affair disgraced every officer connected with it and the massacre stirred the Indians to revenge.

on January 14, 1865, a train of 105 wagons with 300 men left Denver for the East. The convoy had a strong military escort, equipped with cannon. But such an expedition could not protect outlying mail and supply stations.

On January 15 a simultaneous attack was made by a total of about 500 warriors on the American, Wisconsin, and Godfrey's ranches, stations northeast of Denver. The first two were burned, and the telegraph lines were cut. Seven dead bodies were found in the ruins of the American Ranch. The timely arrival of troops saved the inhabitants of the others.

On January 17, Acting Governor Elbert called for six companies of Volunteer militia to keep the route open from Denver to Julesburg, but before these could be raised, the Indians struck again. On January 28, they concentrated on the South Platte River route, wrecking seventy-five miles of road. They burned stations and ranches, captured freight wagons, and destroyed telegraph lines. On February 2, a large band of Indians again plundered Julesburg, burning all of the buildings. Two supply trains west of that station were captured, the Indians carrying off quantities of flour, sugar, coffee, and clothing.

Martial law was proclaimed in the Territory on February 8, 1865, by Colonel T. Moonlight, commander of the Military District of Colorado and successor to Colonel Chivington. Business houses were closed until 360 men could be raised to open the road to Julesburg. This force was soon raised, the route was opened, and martial law was suspended on February 20. The extreme danger from Indian attacks gradually eased. With the termination of the Civil War in April, 1865, more Federal troops were available to the West, but it was years before Colorado was entirely free from Indian retaliatory attacks.

The Indians in Utah during the first year of the Civil War, 1861, were fairly peaceful. As the war entered its second year, that territory, like other sections of the Far West, became vitally interested in protecting the Overland Mail route and telegraph lines. Plundering Indians in the spring of 1862 had destroyed nearly every mail station between Fort Bridger (then in Utah) and the Platte River bridge in the present state of Wyoming. They burned the coaches and mail bags, ran off the livestock, and killed the drivers. Acting Governor Frank Fuller of Utah, Chief Justice Kinney, and others connected with the mail and telegraph lines recommended to Secretary of War Stanton that James D. Doty, superintendent of Indian Affairs in Utah, be authorized to raise a regiment of mounted rangers from the inhabitants of the Territory. Three days after Fuller's telegram, former Governor Brigham Young, president of the Church of Jesus Christ of Latter-day Saints, wired Utah Delegate John M. Bernhisel in Washington that "the militia of Utah are ready and able, as they ever have been, to take care of all the Indians and are able and willing to protect the mail line if called upon to do so."[53] Delegate Bernhisel conveyed this message to the War Department.

With the need for protection against the Indians demanding immediate action, Brigham Young did not wait for an official call from Washington. On April 24, 1862, he instructed Lieutenant General D. H. Wells, commander of the Utah militia, to send a detachment of militia to escort a passenger and mail train for the Eastern states.[54] A day later, Acting Governor Fuller made an official request for the escort. Wells, in a supplemental order, dispatched Colonel Robert T. Burton with a detachment of twenty mounted men, armed and supplied with thirty days' rations, to guard the coaches and wagons which carried several passengers and a large quantity of mail. The convoy proceeded through the Indian danger zone and arrived safely with the passengers and mail at North Platte River bridge, from which place safe transit was had. The detachment returned to Salt Lake City, having been gone for thirty days and was mustered out of this special service by Acting Governor Fuller.

The War Department did not concur in the suggestion of Acting Governor Fuller and his associates. Department leaders

[53] Edward W. Tullidge, *The History of Salt Lake City and Its Founders*, 252.
[54] *Ibid.*, 252–53. This militia, known as the Nauvoo Legion Militia of Utah Territory was originally organized by Joseph Smith in Illinois. It was sponsored by the Mormon church and took orders from the church leaders.

contended that a regiment would be larger than was necessary. They favored the recommendation of Senator M. S. Latham of California, which would authorize Brigham Young to raise a company of one hundred mounted men to protect the mail route and telegraph lines east of Salt Lake and recover stolen livestock. On April 28, 1862, Adjutant General L. Thomas, by direction of President Lincoln, authorized Brigham Young to raise and equip one completely officered cavalry company for ninety days' service in protecting the stage and telegraph lines and Overland Mail routes in present day southwestern Wyoming. These short-term volunteers were to serve until other U. S. troops could advance to this station in the vicinity of Independence Rock.

On May 1, Brigham Young reported to General Thomas that, in response to his order, a full company of cavalry, totaling one hundred men, had been raised, equipped, and mustered in, and on that date, with ten supply wagons, the company had marched out of Salt Lake City for the section of the Overland Mail route adjacent to Independence Rock. Lot Smith was commissioned as captain of the company.[55] The troops furnished their own horses and equipment necessary for the service. Proceeding to what is now southwestern Wyoming, Captain Smith received orders from Brigadier General James Craig, commander of all U. S. troops along the Overland Mail route, to guard the mail route and telegraph line from Green River to Salt Lake City, a distance of about two hundred miles. Their field headquarters were at Fort Bridger. May, June, and July, 1862, were spent by the Utah Volunteers guarding the mail route and telegraph lines against Indian attacks, rebuilding stations and bridges, and protecting coaches, supply and immigrant trains, and outlying white settlements.

There were no clashes of any consequence between the Utah troops and the Indians until mid-July. During the night of July

[55] Orson F. Whitney, *History of Utah*, 45. It was a curious fact that Lot Smith in 1862 was in charge of a Union cavalry company operating in the same area where in 1857 he had burned wagon trains of a U. S. army, led by Albert Sidney Johnston, in an effort to hinder the column from going into Utah. In 1862, Johnston, now a Confederate general, was killed in the Battle of Shiloh in Tennessee.

15, a band of Indians attacked a white man's ranch six miles from Fort Bridger, driving off three hundred horses and mules. On the following day, Captain Smith with a detachment of sixty men, left the fort in pursuit of the marauders, traveling northward. The troopers, following the trail of the savages, penetrated to the heart of the Indian country along the headwaters of the Snake River and Teton Mountains region. Forced marches were made, part of the time on short rations. The raiders were pressed closely, but were never overtaken. With their horses nearly exhausted and their food supply very limited, the detachment was forced to turn back. The only fatality occurred when one man drowned while swimming his horse across the flooding Lewis Fork of Snake River. With their term of enlistment expired, the Utah Volunteers returned to Salt Lake City on August 9, 1862, and were mustered out of the service on August 14.

In May, 1862, Colonel Patrick Edward Connor with a command consisting of the Third California Infantry and part of the Second California Cavalry, totaling about seven hundred men, was ordered to Utah. Ostensibly this troop movement was for the protection of the Overland Mail route and telegraph lines from Indian depredations. Actually a major determining factor was the belief by high Federal officials that the mail route and the telegraph lines in the area were not secure in Mormon hands, and that a military surveillance should be made in the Territory. The Californians arrived in Utah in October, 1862, and established Camp Douglas (later Fort Douglas) on the bench east of Salt Lake City.[56]

In response to a report that an emigrant boy, whose parents had been massacred by Indians, was being held captive by Chief Bear Hunter's tribe of Shoshonis and Bannocks, Colonel Connor dispatched sixty cavalrymen, under Major Edward McGarry, to an Indian camp in Cache Valley, northern Utah. A sharp skirmish took place near the town of Providence on November 23, 1862, terminating when the Chief agreed to surrender the boy.

[56] *San Francisco Bulletin,* October 30, 31, and November 1, 17, 1862; *O.R.,* I, 50:244–45, 195 (part 2).

This was done, and the troopers returned to Camp Douglas. Three Indians were killed and one wounded. There were no soldier casualties. On December 4, Major McGarry led his men north again to recover stolen emigrant livestock. The Indians, learning of the troop movement, fled with the animals and cut the rope on Empey's ferryboat on Bear River to hinder pursuit. Four Indians were captured and held as hostages, but the livestock was not returned. Thereupon the captives were put to death, and the troops returned to Camp Douglas.

The Mormon policy was to feed rather than fight the Indians, but at times the patience of the Utah pioneers was tried to the limit. During the winter of 1862–63, a large band of Shoshoni and Bannock Indians under Chiefs Bear Hunter, Pocatello, and Sagwitch were camped near Bear River, about twelve miles northwest of Franklin, now southern Idaho. They made life miserable for the Mormon settlers in Cache Valley with demands for supplies and their thievery. In December, 1862, these Indians murdered several miners while en route from the mountains on the north for supplies. There was also reason to believe that they were part of the same general group of Indians who had infested the Overland Mail route for the previous fifteen years until their attacks had become unbearable to the whites.

Colonel P. E. Connor, late in January, 1863, led an expedition of about three hundred men, consisting of California cavalry, infantry, two howitzers, and a supply train, with O. P. Rockwell, Mormon scout, as guide, north from Camp Douglas to the Indian encampment. The trip through northern Utah settlements and Franklin was made in intensely cold weather and deep snow. At 6 A.M. on January 29, after fording the partially frozen Bear River, the cavalry under Major Edward McGarry dismounted and attacked the fortified Indian village, whose fighting power was estimated at from three hundred to four hundred warriors. In front of the camp, located in a sheltered ravine, willows had been thickly woven from where the defenders could fire without exposing themselves.

At first the Californians lost heavily in a frontal attack from the Indian rifle fire and arrows. The savages shouted defiantly and waved scalps of their white victims. The infantry, led by Major P. A. Gallagher, arrived late on the field, having been transported across the icy Bear River by the dismounted cavalrymen's horses. The howitzers, hampered by deep snow, arrived too late to be of service. The men's hands at the beginning of the encounter were so numb it was difficult to load their firearms. In order to cut off retreat, Connor ordered the camp surrounded, but few warriors tried to escape, fighting furiously instead. Frequently the braves fought hand to hand with the troops until the Indians were killed in their hiding places. Attacking simultaneously along the flank and in front, the cavalry and the infantry, with a deadly rifle fire, were finally able to rout the warriors at about 10:00 A.M. Some of the fleeing Indians were shot while attempting to swim the Bear River or killed while hiding in the willows along its banks. Chiefs Pocatello and Sagwitch with between fifty and one hundred Indians escaped. Chief Bear Hunter was slain while making bullets at a campfire, into which he fell when hit.

The Indian casualties, of whom some were women and children, are variously estimated at from 200 to 368 killed. About 160 women and children surrendered, but were released on the field. Fourteen soldiers were killed, 54 wounded, six dying later.[57] Seventy-nine were disabled from frozen feet. About 175 horses were captured. In camp the troops found firearms, ammunition, meat, wheat, and a considerable amount of emigrant plunder. After supplying the released prisoners with some provisions, Connor and his men destroyed over seventy lodges and their contents, except a few items which were taken back to Camp Douglas and sold. On the return trip, the expedition, traveling through the freezing weather, was assisted by the Mormon settlers, who provided teams and sleighs to carry the dead, wounded, and frozen back to the post.

[57] *O.R.*, I, 50:184–87 (part 1). Connor reported 224 Indians killed. Tullidge, *History of Salt Lake City*, 290, quotes two reports from local sources: (1) Logan (Utah) Mormon Branch Records, 200 Indians killed; (2) Colonel Martineau, 368 Indians killed.

The victory completely broke the power of the Indians in northern Utah and southern Idaho and conveyed a threat to them which was never necessary to repeat. The relief from the danger of hostile Indians in Cache Valley was appreciated by the settlers. It helped to make the Overland route safer for emigrants, mail, and supplies.[58] On March 29, General H. W. Halleck congratulated Colonel Connor on the victory and notified him that as of that date he was promoted to the rank of brigadier general.[59]

In December, 1862, by request from the Overland Mail Company to the War Department, one company of California troops was sent from Camp Douglas to Fort Bridger, which was then in the Utah Military District. In July, 1863, a detachment of troopers under the post commander, Captain M. G. Lewis, captured fifty Indians. The fort was garrisoned by California and Nevada Volunteers until the end of the war. Although an occasional expedition against marauding Indians was made, there were no serious encounters in the vicinity during the time. Evidently the presence of troops acted as a deterrent to further depredations. Frequent escorts were made with mail and passenger coaches, emigrant, and supply trains. The telegraph lines were patrolled, and military roads were built.

During the spring and summer of 1863, Indians, principally Pahvants, Utes, and Goshutes, frequently attacked coaches and stations along the Overland route in western Utah. General Connor ordered troops to the vicinity. In March, Indians killed the keepers at Eight Mile Station and shot the driver of the eastbound coach as it approached. While the horses were running, G. N. Mott, U. S. delegate from Nevada, climbed into the drivers seat, took the reins, and drove on to Deep Creek, the next station. On May 19, an Overland coach with its military escort was ambushed, and the driver was killed, but Major Howard Egan drove the coach to the next station. The soldiers' return fire was

[58] Tullidge, *History of Salt Lake City*, 290; Hubert Howe Bancroft, *History of Utah*, 631–32, tersely commented that, "had the savages committed this deed, it would pass into history as butchery or a massacre."

[59] *O.R.*, I, 50:187 (part 1).

Ienry Connelly, governor of
New Mexico during the
Civil War.

William Gilpin, first governor
of the Territory of Colorado.

gham Young, first governor of
: Territory of Utah and second
:sident of the Mormon church.

John N. Goodwin, first governor
of the Federal Territory
of Arizona.

## FOUR GOVERNORS

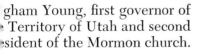

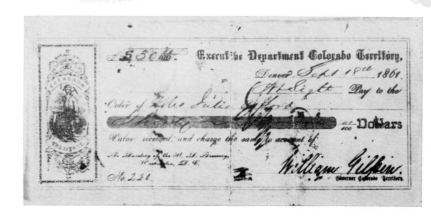

One of Governor Gilpin's sight drafts, which the Federal government at first refused to honor.

ineffective against the Indians, who were hidden behind large rocks. On June 10, 1863, Indians attacked a coach twenty-five miles west of Salt Lake City, killing and scalping the driver and his companion and cutting the mail into pieces. In May and again in June, California troops under Captain Samuel P. Smith met bands of Indians in skirmishes near Willow Springs, west of Salt Lake City, killing twenty-two warriors in one fight and twenty-seven in another. In mid-June, Captain Smith with his detachment killed all ten inhabitants of a small Indian camp— braves, women, and papooses. In revenge for this butchery, Indian warriors attacked Canyon Station on July 8, near Deep Creek. Four soldiers and one civilian were killed, and four of the victims were scalped. One soldier was bald, so the Indians skinned off his heavy beard.

In the spring of 1863, hostile Ute Indians raided areas in central and western Utah. During the last week in March, Lieutenant Anthony Ethier, led twenty-five Second California Cavalrymen through Skull Valley and Cedar Mountains in pursuit of some cattle-stealing Utes. A band of about one hundred warriors was finally encountered at Cedar Fort west of Utah Lake. After a short skirmish, the dismounted cavalry, outnumbered and fearful that the Indians would capture their horses, withdrew from the area. One chief was mortally wounded. On April 2, Captain George F. Price, with a detachment of fifty-one California troopers, joined Ethier. In a search by the combined forces around the south end of Utah Lake, this same band of Utes was located in Spanish Fork Canyon, where a brisk skirmish ensued. The Indians finally retreated up the canyon and were followed by the troops until dark. During the march back down the canyon, the warriors hovered in the rear, discharging their firearms at the soldiers. There were no white casualties reported as a result of the fight. One Indian was known to have been killed and several wounded.

A larger expedition under Colonel George S. Evans was planned against the Utes in Utah County. Guided by the experience at the Battle of Bear River, Lieutenant Francis Honeyman, Third California Infantry, with five gunners and a howitzer concealed in an ambulance, was sent ahead. On arriving at Pleasant Grove, Utah, the cannon was hidden in an adobe house. At 6:00 A.M. on April 12, a band of about one hundred belligerent Utes approached the soldiers' camp. The concealed howitzer went into action. The first shell of grapeshot missed the Indians and killed five government mules. The second cracked the walls of the house. No more artillery shots were attempted. The Indians, firing from behind an adobe fence, kept up the siege until 8:00 P.M., when they withdrew, taking the soldiers' provisions and seven surviving mules. The house was riddled with bullets, but none of the troops were killed. On April 13, the main part of Colonel Evans' command, consisting of 156 Second California Cavalry, arrived at the town and made an unsuccessful search for the plundering Indians in the canyons to the east of the settlement.

Proceeding south and up Spanish Fork Canyon on April 15, 1863, at 5:00 A.M., the Californians encountered about two hundred Ute warriors. The Indians opened fire from positions to the right, left, and front. Dismounted cavalrymen with rifles were deployed on both sides of the canyon and in front as skirmishers. The howitzer, mounted on a knoll, dropped shells into the Indians' positions. The troops, moving in closer, also used revolvers. The soldiers charged forward, and the braves reluctantly fell back. The cavalry remounted and pursued the Indians up the canyon for about fourteen miles, the warriors making their escape in the various outlets. At 11:00 A.M., the troops were ordered to return down the canyon, and the fight was over. Thirty warriors were killed, among whom was a chief, and a large number were wounded. A lieutenant was killed and two sergeants were wounded. Twenty-two horses and mules, saddles, bridles, a number of rifles, and other plunder were captured from the Indians.

During the latter half of 1863, there was a marked improvement in the relationship between the white men and the Indians in Utah Military District. Several peace councils were held and a number of treaties were signed. In June, General Connor, with a military escort, met in council with about seven hundred Snake Indians at Fort Bridger at which time they surrendered 150 stolen horses and mules. On July 2, Utah's governor, J. D. Doty, accompanied by an armed escort, negotiated a peace treaty at Fort Bridger with eastern bands of Shoshoni Indians which was signed by Chief Washakee and other leaders of that tribe. The Indians agreed not to molest the telegraph and Overland Stage lines and to permit military posts to be built along the routes and consented to the construction of a transcontinental railroad through their country. Six thousand dollars' worth of provisions and clothing were distributed among these Indians at the time, and the various bands of Shoshonis were to receive for twenty years an annuity of $10,000 in provisions to be divided among them.

On July 14, 1863, Governor Doty, General Connor, with part of his staff, and an escort of twenty cavalrymen, held a peace council with about seven hundred Ute Indians near the mouth of Spanish Fork Canyon. Presents and food were given to the Indians. Chiefs Antero, Tabby, Kanosh, and Black Hawk were present and expressed their desire for peace and pledged their aid in achieving it.[60] Doty and Connor, accompanied by a military escort, made a treaty in Box Elder County with northwestern bands of Shoshonis on July 30, 1863. Two thousand dollars' worth of goods and provisions were given the Indians. The annuity to the Shoshoni Nation was increased to $15,000. The chiefs present, among whom was Pocatello, agreed to the terms of the treaty made at Fort Bridger pertaining to the Overland Stage and telegraph lines, the military posts, and the future railroad.

Governor Doty and Governor J. W. Nye of Nevada, escorted by troops, on October 1, 1863, negotiated a peace treaty with western Shoshoni Indians at Ruby Valley, Nevada. These Indians agreed not to molest the telegraph and Overland Stage lines, to permit military posts to be constructed along the route

[60] *Ibid.*, 50:527–30 (part 2).

and a railroad to be built through the area they claimed. The Indians consented to allow prospecting for minerals, mines to be worked, mills erected, and agricultural and mining settlements to be formed. For these concessions, these Indians received goods and clothing amounting to $5,000 at the time and a grant of $5,000 in provisions annually for twenty years. On October 12, Governor Doty and General Connor met with the Goshute Indians in Tooele County and signed a treaty. These Indians agreed not to molest the Overland Stage and telegraph lines and to permit the construction of military posts, railroads, mines, mills, and ranches. After signing the treaty, the Goshutes received $1,000 in provisions and an annuity of $1,000 for twenty years in goods and livestock.[61]

Governor Doty on October 21, 1863, wrote the Commissioner of Indian Affairs that through these treaties, the routes of travel through Utah Territory to Nevada, California, and Idaho might be used with safety and that no fears need be held on account of the Shoshoni, Utah, Goshute, or Bannock Indians. On January 11, 1864, a memorial was sent to President Abraham Lincoln by the Utah Assembly, asking that the Indians be moved from the smaller reservations. In the same year Congressional legislation was enacted that authorized the sale of the small reservations in the Territory and the collecting of the Utah Indians on the Uintah Reservation, which had been established by direction of President Lincoln in 1861. During 1864 and in 1865, the Indians in Utah generally were peaceful until the termination of the Civil War, when the Black Hawk War broke out.

[61] 58 Cong., 2 sess., *Indian Affairs, Laws and Treaties, Senate Doc. No. 319,* II, 850–53, 859–60.

# 8

# Political Developments

DURING THE CIVIL WAR DECADE, important political events transpired in the territories of the Rocky Mountains. Colorado, Utah, New Mexico, and Arizona each received their present geographical boundaries during the 1860's. Colorado, under its Organic Act of February 29, 1861, acquired its first territorial government by appointment from President Lincoln. In the same period, through Congressional enactments, Utah's original area shrank more than 61 per cent in favor of Colorado, Nevada, and Wyoming. The Confederates during their occupation of New Mexico, 1861–62, carved from the southern part of the Territory a corridor 670 miles long from Texas to California. They called it Arizona. When the Texans evacuated the Territory, Governor Baylor lost his executive position. In 1863, Arizona received its permanent territorial status from the Federal Government with the boundary line between it and New Mexico running north to south.

## COLORADO

The pioneers of Colorado came from the North and the South and brought with them their sectional sentiments and convictions. The gold discoveries in that area during the three years prior to the Civil War lured miners and fortune hunters from nearly every state and territory in the United States. These frontiersmen united in organizing the Provisional Territory of Jefferson, but the issues of the war had a marked influence on the political developments in the Territory. When the call to arms came, some of the miners threw down their picks and pans and returned to their former homes, where they enlisted in the armies of the United States or the Confederate States.

The physical evidence of the divided allegiance soon appeared among those who remained in the Territory. On April 24, 1861, as has been related, a Confederate flag was unfurled over the store of Wallingford and Murphy in Denver, but it was quickly torn down. In that tense moment it appeared as if there might be a local civil war, but with Union sympathizers in majority, the crowd dispersed without bloodshed. The following day a large Union mass meeting was held in front of the Tremont House. A band played martial music, patriotic speeches were made, and resolutions were adopted which pledged loyalty to the United States government and the Star-Spangled Banner. The chairman of the Union Committee, Richard Sopris, and Scott J. Anthony, secretary, forwarded the sentiments of those assembled to President Abraham Lincoln: "The eyes of the whole world are upon you; the sympathies of the American people are with you; and may the god of battles sustain the Stars and Stripes." Similar meetings were held at Central City, Boulder, and other Colorado towns.[1]

The Colorado Organic Act was signed by President James Buchanan on February 28, 1861, but it remained for President Lincoln, on March 21, 1861, to nominate the first officials for the new territory. William Gilpin was appointed as governor;[2] Lewis L. Weld was chosen as secretary; James E. Dalliba, attorney general; Francis M. Case, surveyor general; Copeland Townsend, marshal; Benjamin F. Hall, S. Newton Pettis, and Charles Lee Armour as judges.

Governor William Gilpin, with other Federal officials, arrived in Denver on May 27, 1861. On June 6, 1861, Governor R. W. Steele of the Provisional Territory of Jefferson, issued a proclamation which declared the provisional government of that Territory at an end. He urged all citizens to support the United States government.[3]

[1] Hall, *History of the State of Colorado,* 265, 275–76. Richard Sopris and Scott J. Anthony also became captains in the First Colorado Volunteers.
[2] William Gilpin was born on the Brandywine battlefield, graduated from West Point, fought in the Seminole and Mexican wars, was a western explorer and resident of Missouri when appointed governor.

Acting under oral instructions received before leaving Washington to do all he could to save Colorado for the Union, Governor Gilpin promptly organized a strong territorial government. Early in June, 1861, the Governor visited the principal settlements and mining camps to acquaint himself with the conditions and needs of the Territory. He had a census taken which showed a population of 25,331. On July 10, Governor Gilpin assigned the Federal Judges to their districts. In some areas their courts replaced "vigilante" committees or "peoples' courts." The following day he divided the Territory into nine Council and thirteen Representative electoral districts. In an election held on August 19, 1861, Hiram P. Bennet, Republican, was chosen delegate to Congress and members were elected to the territorial legislature.

The First Colorado Territorial Legislative Assembly, which consisted of a Council and a House of Representatives, met in Denver from September 9 to November 7, 1861. In his message to the joint session of the legislature, Governor Gilpin recommended that the Territory be divided into counties and that laws be enacted providing for necessary public services. He urged the importance to pioneers of judiciary and military departments, which constituted the "bulwark of their liberties."[4] Most of the session of 1861 was devoted to enacting civil and criminal codes. The Territory was divided into seventeen counties and three judicial districts. The first joint resolution passed was a declaration of loyalty to the United States government. The membership of the assembly was increased to thirteen councilmen and twenty-six representatives, the full number permitted by the Organic Act. Colorado City (Colorado Springs) was designated the capital of the Territory.

Governor Gilpin, with considerable military experience, real-

---

[3] The Provisional Territory of Jefferson was organized by local citizens in 1859. Congress refused to name a territory after a man and changed the name to Colorado. Among other names suggested were Idaho, Montana, and Bill Williams.

[4] Colorado Territory Legislative Assembly, *Council Journal*, first session, 1861, 5–9.

ized that the organization of a strong militia in Colorado was necessary to preserve the Territory for the Union and to aid in repelling the Confederate invasion of New Mexico. In October, 1861, he wrote that there was a "strong and malignant" Secession element, totaling 7,500, in the Territory which had been "ably and secretly organized" from the previous November. "This country," he continued, "can only be defended [and controlled] by a sufficient force."[5] He appointed a military staff, and with leading Colorado citizens he proceeded to raise a Volunteer regiment. He sent agents out among the people to buy arms and ammunition. He ordered the arrest of Confederate sympathizers, who were also buying guns.

To arm, equip, feed, and pay a regiment of soldiers required considerable money. There had been no appropriations from the Federal government for this purpose and there was very little cash in the treasury of the new territory. Relying on verbal instructions received before he left Washington to do what he thought was best for Colorado, Governor Gilpin authorized promissory notes on the United States government totaling $375,-000 to finance Union troops. He fully anticipated that they would be honored by the Federal treasury.[6] The drafts were readily accepted by local merchants and others who furnished supplies, but when they reached Washington, they were not recognized by the War Department.

When the news reached Colorado that the Federal government would not honor the obligations, Gilpin was thoroughly denounced by certain citizens for having issued the drafts without written authority from the War Department. A petition for his recall was circulated. Those who defended the Governor justified his actions to meet the emergency and pointed out that the drafts were being adjusted by a government fiscal agent then in the Territory.

On December 24, 1861, Governor Gilpin left for Washing-

[5] *O.R.*, I, 4:73.

[6] Bancroft, *History of Nevada, Colorado, and Wyoming*, 420. *Colorado Republican and Rocky Mountain Herald*, March 31, 1862, claimed that Governor Gilpin had authority to issue government drafts, if necessary.

ton to defend his action and to obtain recognition for all the drafts he had issued. In this he was supported by Territorial Delegate Bennet and Colorado businessmen. The affair was finally settled. Holders of the drafts who submitted their claims to the Federal government were duly paid. Gilpin was removed from office in March, 1862, for which the Lincoln administration was roundly criticized by the Governor's Colorado friends. The record of the Colorado Volunteers in helping to drive the Confederates from New Mexico in 1862 seem to have justified William Gilpin's financial transactions, even though he may have exceeded the authority ordinarily vested in a territorial governor.

On March 19, 1862, John Evans was nominated by President Lincoln to be Colorado's second governor.[7] At the same time Secretary Weld was replaced by Samuel H. Elbert, and in June, 1862, A. S. Hunt became U. S. marshal in place of Copeland Townsend. Dr. Evans arrived in Denver on May 17, 1862, and served as governor of Colorado until October, 1865.

The second session of the Colorado Territorial Legislative Assembly convened on July 7, 1862, at Colorado City. On July 11, the legislators, becoming dissatisfied with their inadequate living quarters and the place in which they had to meet, moved back to Denver, where they continued the session until adjournment on August 15.[8] Governor Evans' message to the assembly indicated a thorough study of Colorado's statutes and an intelligent tour of inspection of the various parts of the Territory. He recommended changes in the code to strengthen the mining, election, and tax laws, suggested the consolidation of certain counties, and urged a military law to provide protection against the Indians. He advised that a richly endowed school fund be established and legislation passed to facilitate the organization

[7] A friend of President Lincoln, Evans was a resident of Chicago and a successful physician. He helped to establish Northwestern University at Evanston, Illinois, a town named for him.

[8] Colorado Territory Legislative Assembly, *General Laws, Resolutions, Memorials and Private Acts*, second session, 5; Smiley, *Semi-Centennial History*, 368–69. The move back to Denver was accomplished by locking members of the assembly from southern counties in a hotel until the vote for adjournment was taken.

of corporations. He praised Colorado's natural resources and pointed out the need for the Pacific railroad to pass through the Territory.

The lawmakers, in general, followed the Governor's recommendations. In addition, a joint resolution was passed which commended the First Colorado Volunteers to President Lincoln for their services in helping to drive the Confederate invaders from New Mexico. Another was passed which urged the Union Pacific to establish its route through Colorado. A memorial was sent to the U. S. Secretary of Treasury asking that a branch mint be established in Denver. With a majority of the legislators still determined that Denver would not be the capital, Golden City was selected as the seat of government.

Former Governor William Gilpin was not quite out of the picture. Incensed by his removal from office and desiring to continue in leadership, he accepted a call, signed by about three hundred citizens, to become the "Peoples' Candidate for Congress." He was opposed by Delegate Hiram P. Bennet, who was renominated by the "Union Administration" party as the Republicans called themselves. His supporters credited him with locating a U. S. mint in Denver, for obtaining better mail service, new postal routes and wagon roads, securing a land office and another military post in the Territory, payment of the "Gilpin drafts," and laboring for the Union Pacific bill. Gilpin was supported by the Abolitionists, and Bennet was aided by Douglas Democrats. The Breckenridge Democrats nominated J. M. Francisco. Old party lines were almost wholly ignored. After a bitter campaign, Bennet was re-elected by a substantial majority on October 8, 1862.

The Third Colorado Assembly convened at Golden City on February 1, 1864, but four days later the legislators, again because of inadequate accommodations, moved back to Denver, where the session continued until adjournment on March 11. Governor Evans' message of February 3 reflected the acute needs of a frontier territory. He recommended public schools, a territorial library, and the broadening of the incorporation laws. He praised the mining industry, encouraged more agricultural production, and suggested that irrigation water rights be established. He urged that Colorado's soldiers be permitted to vote. He reported the near completion of a road from Denver west to Salt Lake City and expressed hope that the Pacific railroad would be routed through Colorado. He encouraged loyalty to the United States government in the midst of the most "wicked and powerful" civil war in history.[9]

Most of the Governor's recommendations were enacted into law. Legislation passed which strengthened the county governments and courts. Mining, agriculture, school, and tax laws were enacted. Continued road construction was authorized. Traitors and alien enemies were excluded from the courts. A law was passed which provided for joint-stock companies. A joint resolution declared Abraham Lincoln to be an able ruler, a just and honest president, and a worthy successor to immortal George Washington, and recommended him for re-election. Congress was urged in another resolution to pass an enabling act permitting the Territory to become a state in the Union.

During the war years certain leaders in the Territory and in Congress were active in attempting to secure statehood. On July 10, 1862, Representative Charles F. Holley, Boulder County, introduced a statehood bill in the Second Colorado Territorial Legislative Assembly without authority from Congress for so doing. Its sponsors expected that in the midst of the Civil War the Federal leaders would gladly overlook this preliminary technicality and accept the loyal new state into the Union. Other members of the House were not so eager for statehood and later voted to postpone action on the bill indefinitely.

In the Thirty-seventh Congress, on December 22, 1862, Congressman James H. Ashley of Ohio introduced in the House of Representatives a bill to enable the people of Colorado to form a constitution and state government. A similar bill was intro-

[9] Colorado Legislative Assembly, *Council Journal*, third session, 1, 6–16, 216. In order to adjust to the Federal fiscal budget, the Colorado Territorial Assembly did not meet in 1863.

duced by Delegate Bennet. Ashley's bill was given preference but received favorable committee action too late for passage before that Congress adjourned. In the same Congress, Senator James H. Lane of Kansas introduced a Colorado statehood bill which passed the Senate on March 3, 1863, but the House did not concur in it before adjournment. During the Thirty-eighth Congress, Ashley and Senator James R. Doolittle of Wisconsin introduced Colorado statehood bills. Doolittle's bill passed both houses and was signed by President Lincoln on March 21, 1864. In Colorado, Governor John Evans at once issued a call for the election of a constitutional convention to convene on July 4, 1864. The election was held and the delegates assembled at Golden City, but moved to Denver the next day. O. A. Whittemore was chosen chairman and Eli M. Ashley, secretary. The framing of the constitution was completed in one week.[10]

The advocates of statehood were so confident that they decided to elect state officials at the same time that a vote was taken on statehood. A convention was held on August 2 by the Union Administration party, during which a complete ticket was nominated. Daniel Witter became candidate for governor and Colonel John M. Chivington for Congress. It was understood that, should statehood carry, Governor Evans and Henry M. Teller would be the party's nominees for United States senators in the anticipated new state legislature.

An anti-statehood movement developed, and a bitter campaign ensued. Opponents, led by Allen A. Bradford, candidate for Congress, Dr. Worrall, Judge Charles Lee Armour, and Rodney Fench, who were supported by some Democratic politicians, contended that statehood would raise taxes and was an office-seeker's scheme. The citizens of Mexican descent in the southern counties were opposed to any change that would place them under a local government in which they would be a minority.

The statehood leaders argued that with two senators and a

[10] *Cong. Globe*, 38 Cong., 1 sess., 19, 521, 1228. Bancroft, *History of Nevada, Colorado, and Wyoming*, 430–31, contended that Congress was induced to pass the enabling act by the population's being estimated at between fifty and sixty thousand, double what it really was.

representative in Congress who could vote, Colorado would have more control in the national government on such vital legislation as the Pacific Railroad Act, which appeared to be leaving the Territory off the transcontinental route. The proposed federal tax on mining profits could be more effectively fought. Statehood would end the terms of certain unpopular Colorado territorial officials. In the election held on the second Tuesday in September, 1864, statehood lost by a vote of 4,676 to 1,520. Allen A. Bradford, who had come to Colorado as a federal judge, was elected as delegate to the Thirty-ninth Congress, defeating incumbent Hiram P. Bennet.[11]

The Fourth Colorado Assembly met in Golden City on January 2, 1865, and continued there until adjournment on February 10. On January 9, Acting Governor Samuel H. Elbert delivered the Governor's message. He reported on the Indian war then raging in the Territory and of the progress in mining and agriculture. He recommended changes in the code to aid the laws on incorporation, county government, and charity. He praised the war record of the Second Colorado Regiment in Kansas and Missouri, the First Colorado in New Mexico and in the home territory, and the Third Colorado (hundred-day men) for service during the current Indian war.

This assembly enacted laws to provide a school system and a territorial library. It became illegal for gamblers and owners of gambling houses to serve on juries. Legislation was passed to improve county government; courts and county poorhouses were established. Colorado citizens in the army were permitted to vote. To meet the serious Indian depredations, additional military laws were enacted, and President Lincoln was memorialized to create a military district composed of Colorado, Utah, Montana, present-day Wyoming, and western Nebraska and Kansas, with General P. E. Connor commanding.

During the spring of 1865 a second effort for statehood in Colorado gained some momentum, but it was not until 1876 that the goal was attained. Colorado's prospect at the close of the

[11]Bancroft, *History of Nevada, Colorado, and Wyoming*, 434.

Civil War appeared discouraging. Manpower had been reduced by those under arms and by interrupted immigration. Hostile Indians were a constant threat. Placer mines were playing out, and ore refining by reduction had not started. Agriculture and grazing were in their infancy. The Pacific railroad was being built north of the Territory. However, the Territory progressed during the next decade to a position where it was ready to take its place as a state in the Union.

## UTAH

The history of Utah during the Civil War was unique. No Confederates invaded that Territory. Very few citizens sympathized with the South. The vast majority of the Mormons were from the Northern states and the working class of northern Europe whose interests were alien to those of the Southern slaveholders. Yet a regiment of California Volunteers under Colonel Patrick Edward Connor marched to Utah in 1862, encamped on the eastern boundary of Salt Lake City, and remained there during the war, acting in some ways as an army of occupation. Outwardly this troop movement was for the protection of the Overland Mail route and telegraph lines from Indian depredations. Actually a major determining factor was the belief held by certain high Federal officials that the mail route and telegraph lines in the area were not secure in Mormon hands and that military surveillance was necessary.

Had Utah, in its key position on the Overland route, seceded at the outbreak of the Civil War,[12] a dangerous East-West cleavage could have compelled the Federal government to expend considerable money and manpower to reroute the telegraph, mail, and stage lines. It might have been assumed that the Territory would favor secession in the hope of safeguarding its institution of polygamy and securing the principle of popular sov-

---

[12] Whitney, *History of Utah,* 93, claimed that Brigham Young rejected overtures from the Southern Confederacy and from a group which proposed a Pacific Slope Federation, contending that Utah would "stand by the Union."

ereignty in the territories. However, on October 18, 1861, when the Pacific telegraph lines were finally completed to Salt Lake City, Brigham Young, while congratulating J. H. Wade, president of the company on the completion of the line, stated, "Utah has not seceded, but is firm for the Constitution and Laws of our once happy Country."[13] Mormon leaders recognized that the Abolitionists of the North and the slaveholders of the South had interests which did not directly concern the inhabitants of Utah. In a sermon on March 3, 1863, Brigham Young said:

> The rank, rabid abolitionists, whom I call black-hearted Republicans, have set the whole national fabric on fire. Do you know this, Democrats? They have kindled the fire that is raging now from the north to the south, and from the south to the north. I am no abolitionist, neither am I a pro-slavery man; I hate some of their principles and especially some of their conduct, as I do the gates of hell. The Southerners make [slaves of] the negroes and the Northerners worship them.[14]

On July 13, 1859, in Salt Lake City, responding to Horace Greeley's question on the Mormon position on slavery, Brigham Young stated that there were some slaves in Utah. He contended that if the Negroes were brought from the states by their masters, he did not favor their escape. However, he maintained that if Utah were admitted to the Union, it would be a free state, adding that slavery in the Territory was useless, unprofitable, and a curse to the masters. He stated further that he could not afford to own slaves, since he would be obligated to provide for them and their families. He concluded, "Utah is not adapted to slave labor."[15]

The Civil War came as no surprise to the Mormons. On December 25, 1832, twenty-eight years before the firing on Fort Sumter, Joseph Smith, the Mormon leader, prophesied that the Rebellion would begin in South Carolina. He further predicted

[13] Tullidge, *History of Salt Lake City*, 250.
[14] Brigham Young, *Journal of Discourses*, X, 110.
[15] *New York Daily Tribune*, August 20, 1859.

that the Southern states would ask Great Britain for aid and the slaves would be marshaled for war against their masters.[16]

When the war broke out, Alfred Cumming, a Democrat appointee, was governor of Utah. He had served since President Buchanan sent the Utah Expedition under General Albert Sidney Johnston in 1857–58 to quell the alleged insurrection and disloyalty among the Mormons. When Cumming departed in May, 1861, he was succeeded by Secretary Francis M. Wooton.[17]

President Lincoln's first appointments were John W. Dawson, governor; Frank Fuller, secretary; John F. Kinney, R. P. Flenniken, and J. R. Crosby, judges; James Duane Doty, superintendent of Indian affairs; S. R. Fox, surveyor-general. Fuller preceded the others and for a few weeks acted as governor. Lincoln, who had known many of the Mormons earlier in Illinois, when asked about his policy toward them, stated that he proposed to let them alone as much as possible. He compared the Mormon question to a knotty green hemlock log on a frontier farm. It was too heavy to remove, too knotty to split, too wet to burn, and, therefore, like a wise farmer, he proposed to "plow around it."[18]

Governor John W. Dawson arrived in Salt Lake City early in December, 1861. On December 10, he delivered his message to the Utah territorial legislature, in which he expounded constitutional interpretations that were in agreement with those of many of his constituents. He declared that the Compromise of 1850, by which Utah became a territory, recognized that slavery, and all other questions of domestic or local policy, should be decided by each state and territory independent of Congress, so far as consistent with national law and the Constitution.

A movement for statehood was initiated in the legislature during December, 1861. A bill to authorize the election of delegates

[16] *Doctrine and Covenants*, Section 87:1–4, 144.

[17] Bancroft, *History of Utah*, 500, 526–27, 575. Governor Cumming, from Georgia, entered Utah on the brink of war, amid a forced display of welcome, but he left it with the sincere regrets of the citizens, whose respect and admiration he had won by his tact and executive ability.

[18] Whitney, *History of Utah*, 25–26.

for a constitutional convention passed both houses. It was vetoed by Governor Dawson on the grounds that January 6, 1862, the date for choosing the delegates, did not allow time for the people throughout the Territory to be notified and for the act to be submitted to Congress for approval. The legislators maintained, on the other hand, that the act, if signed by the Governor, would have been legal; but since it was vetoed, they were powerless. However, mass meetings were held on the designated date, and delegates were elected to meet on January 20.

Meanwhile, Governor Dawson's moral standards led him to a hasty exit. He was accused of making indecent proposals to Mormon women, one of whom drove him from her home with a fire shovel because of his vulgar abuse of her. On December 31, 1861, he hurriedly departed by stage-coach for the East. At Mountain Dell, a stage station in northeastern Utah, he was severely flogged by a gang of ruffians, led by a relative of one of the insulted women.[19]

Governor Dawson having departed from the Territory, Secretary Frank Fuller again assumed the duties of the executive. Among the legislative measures which received his approval was a memorial to Congress asking for the admission of Utah to the Union. From January 20 to 23, 1862, elected delegates met in Salt Lake City, drafted a constitution, nominated state and national candidates for an election to be held on March 3, and wrote a memorial to Congress asking for the admission of the state of Deseret to the Union. In the election on March 3, Brigham Young was chosen governor, Heber C. Kimball, lieutenant governor, and John M. Bernhisel, representative to Congress. Senators and representatives were also elected for the legislature of the proposed state. On April 14, pursuant to the proclamation of the Governor-elect, the General Assembly met and listened to Brigham Young's message. William H. Hooper and George Q. Cannon were chosen United States senators-elect. Hooper, Can-

---

[19] *Ibid.*, 38. Three of the assailants, also accused of robbery, were shot by Salt Lake County and City officers while attempting to escape. The others were tried in court and punished.

non, and Bernhisel labored diligently in Washington, but the movement for statehood failed.[20]

A clash occurred between June 13 and 15, 1862, when territorial police, under Colonel Robert T. Burton, served a writ, issued by Federal Judge Kinney, on leaders of the Morrisites, a fanatical anti-Mormon group in a fortified camp near Ogden, Utah, for unlawfully imprisoning two men. During the three-day siege and assault on the camp, Joseph Morris, three of his followers, and two posse men were killed, but the besieged survivors surrendered. The event later had an unfortunate effect on the relationship between the Mormons and certain Gentile political leaders supported by the army officers at Camp Douglas. Mormon authorities were unjustly accused of causing the incident when actually the writ had been issued by a judge who was not a Mormon.

President Lincoln again filled Utah vacancies. In July, 1862, Governor Stephen S. Harding and two new judges (there were three districts in Utah), Charles B. Waite and Thomas J. Drake, arrived in Salt Lake City. All were present at the Pioneer Day celebration on July 24, during which Governor Harding's complimentary address on Mormon achievements made a favorable impression on his listeners. Toward the close of 1862, a complete change came over Governor Harding. Certain events may have altered his attitude from friendliness to hostility, such as the arrival and influence of Colonel Connor, misinformation on the Morrisite affair, Congressional enactment of the anti-polygamy bill of 1862, and the realization that, although he was officially governor of Utah, Brigham Young was still "governor" of the Mormon people.

On December 8, 1862, Governor Harding delivered his message to the territorial legislature, in which he thoroughly criticized the practice of polygamy and called attention to the Congressional legislation the previous July which outlawed it in

[20] *Ibid.*, 38–43; Bancroft, *History of Utah*, 605–606; Tullidge, *History of Salt Lake City*, 259; 37 Cong., 2 sess., *House Misc. Doc. No. 78*. If statehood were granted, those sponsoring the movement also hoped that permission would be given to use "Deseret," which was the original name of the Territory before 1850.

the territories. He urged the loyalty of the people to the national government and found fault with the conduct of local affairs.[21] T. B. H. Stenhouse wrote that the manner of delivery was even worse than the matter. Probably no legislature was ever more humiliated and insulted. It was painful to observe the legislators as they sat quiet and immovable, hearing their faith condemned. It was interpreted as an open insult from the executive.[22]

Early in 1863, Judge Waite drew up a bill which would amend the Organic Act of Utah to restrict the selection of juries to the United States marshal and which would authorize the governor alone to appoint militia officers. It was approved by the Governor and forwarded to Congress. When this became known, there was a huge gathering of citizens, on March 3, 1863, in the Salt Lake Tabernacle. Inflammatory speeches were made. A petition, signed by several thousand, was addressed to President Lincoln requesting that he remove Governor Harding and Judges Waite and Drake on the grounds that they were strenuously endeavoring to create mischief and stir up strife between the people of Utah and the government of the United States and between the citizens of the Territory and the soldiers at Camp Douglas. On March 4, a committee of three, appointed at the mass meeting, met with the Governor and Judge Drake, and sent a letter to Judge Waite, who was out of town, requesting all of them to resign. Harding had previously promised to do so if his activities were not agreeable to the people as a whole. Now each of these officials refused to comply. A counterpetition, signed by all of the officers in Camp Douglas and some non-Mormons in Salt Lake City, was sent to the President, urging the retention of Governor Harding and Judges Waite and Drake.

When Colonel P. E. Connor, "prejudiced and biased" against the Latter-day Saints, arrived in Utah in the autumn of 1862, he at once assumed a hostile attitude toward the Mormons. Following a preliminary visit in Salt Lake City, he made a very

21 Utah Territory Legislative Assembly *Journals,* 1863, 93–107. Harding stated that the prevailing opinion of the people of Utah was that the Anti-Polygamy Act of July, 1862, was unconstitutional.
22 T. B. H. Stenhouse, *The Rocky Mountain Saints,* 603.

derogatory report concerning the citizens of the Territory, in which he accused them of being traitors and fanatics. It was his intention, when he arrived with his command, to entrench himself and "say to the Saints of Utah, enough of your treason." Some of the soldiers at the post were also antagonistic toward the Mormons. Many of the Third California Infantry were reluctant to stop in Utah, being so anxious to go on to eastern battle fronts that they offered to pay part of their travel expenses by authorizing a deduction from their salaries. They contended that infantry was of no use in Utah and that cavalry was necessary against the Indians. Brigham Young, they argued, had offered to protect the Overland lines. If it were to keep Mormondom in order, they concluded, Brigham could annihilate them at any time with the 5,000 to 25,000 frontiersmen always at his command. With Camp Douglas completed and the guarding of the Overland Mail and telegraph lines requiring only an occasional expedition against the Indians, the impetuous Connor joined in the quarrel against the Mormons.[23]

Colonel Connor and most of his men were actually miners in uniform. It was very natural that Connor should permit his soldiers to prospect the untapped mineral-rich near-by mountains of Utah. These had remained for the most part undeveloped, since Brigham Young had discouraged nonferrous mining for fear that such activity would deter the development of the more essential industries of agriculture and manufacturing. Connor was quick to see that bringing in Gentile miners would afford an opportunity to secure an economic footing in the Great Basin and break the Mormon monopoly. He had the double motive of acquiring wealth and displacing the power of the Latter-day Saints. Argentiferous galena was discovered in the latter part of 1863 at Bingham Canyon.[24] In the summer of 1864, Con-

[23] *O.R.*, I, 50:119 (part 2). In contrast to Connor's attitude in 1862, ten years later, according to Tullidge, *History of Salt Lake City*, 330, the General offered to provide Brigham Young's bail of $100,000 when Brigham was on trial in the court of Chief Justice James B. McKean. *San Francisco Bulletin*, October 1, 1862.

[24] Tullidge, *History of Salt Lake City*, 697, credits a Mr. Ogilvie with finding the first piece of ore in Utah; Stenhouse, *Rocky Mountain Saints*, 713–14, wrote

nor, under California law, incorporated the Jordan Mining Company, and that same year he built the first furnace in the Territory at Stockton, after which several others were constructed.

The tense situation at Salt Lake City continued through March, 1863, during which the Mormons under Brigham Young and the anti-Mormon faction, led by Governor Harding and Colonel Connor, viewed each other with mutual distrust. Each group placed unfavorable interpretations on the moves of the other. On March 8, Connor telegraphed headquarters at San Francisco that the Mormons were at work making cartridges and that Brigham Young, in fear of being arrested, was guarded at night by three hundred men.[25] Young at this time was accused of violating the anti-polygamy law. It was rumored among the Saints that Colonel Connor, with his troops, was going to arrest the Mormon president and take him to the States for trial.

On one occasion, when Colonel Connor was leaving Judge Waite's home, a Mormon elder standing near by heard the Colonel say, "These three must be surprised." He assumed that the Colonel referred to Brigham Young and his two counselors and hurried to Young. A signal flag was hoisted over Brigham Young's mansion and, within half an hour, one thousand armed men surrounded the premises. In one hour another thousand were armed and on duty. Scaffolds were erected behind the walls of Brigham Young's mansion to permit the armed guards to fire down on the soldiers in case of an attack. Night and day for several weeks there was an armed body of men around the Mormon leaders until it was felt that the danger was over. Stenhouse explained that Colonel Connor had actually been referring to the recent marriage of another man to the three widows of a wealthy merchant, which he thought would provide a good test case of the anti-polygamy law.[26]

On March 10, Brigham Young permitted himself to be ar-

that the wife of a Camp Douglas surgeon (Mrs. Robert K. Reid) made the initial discovery while on a picnic; also that Captain A. Heitz found the first ore vein. Ogilvie was credited with the first mining.

[25] *O.R.*, I, 50:342 (part 2).
[26] *Rocky Mountain Saints*, 604–607.

rested by United States Marshal Gibbs, unaccompanied by troops, and to be taken before Chief Justice Kinney. The defendant was released on $2,000 bail until the next term of court. Later the grand jury failed to indict Young on the grounds of insufficient evidence, and he was released from his bail.[27]

On March 18, General H. W. Halleck at Army Headquarters in Washington, D. C., telegraphed Colonel P. E. Connor that all arms used against the United States were liable to seizure and that the Colonel should use his discretion, but if he did act, he was to do so with "firmness and decision."[28] At that time General Halleck instructed General G. Wright in Sacramento, California, to prepare to reinforce Colonel Connor, but that action never became necessary. When news of the critical situation in Utah reached California, two influential newspapers in that state were decidedly opposed to a collision that might involve Utah and California in a civil war. One paper urged that a "pretty-much-let-alone policy" be adopted toward the Mormons. The other stated that Colonel Connor and his regiment were sent to Utah to protect the telegraph and overland mail and to fight Indians, and not to "kick up trouble with the Mormons or any other class of people."[29]

The excitement gradually subsided only to be revived at 10:00 P.M. on March 29, 1863, when the firing of a cannon was heard at Camp Douglas, accompanied by martial music. The Mormon militia again seized their arms and hurriedly assembled. However, the alarm was false. It had just been learned at the post that Colonel Connor had been promoted to brigadier general. The eleven-gun salute was in his honor.

In March, 1863, in Judge Kinney's court, seven surviving Morrisite leaders were convicted and sentenced to prison for killing two posse men during the siege and assault in June, 1862. Sixty-six other Morrisites were fined for resisting arrest. Gover-

27 Whitney, *History of Utah,* 97–98. Judge Kinney, Secretary Fuller, and other Gentiles who failed to agree with their non-Mormon associates were called "Jack Mormons."

28 *O.R.,* I, 50:358 (part 2).

29 *Sacramento Daily Union,* March 12, 1863; *Alta California,* March 11, 1863.

nor Harding immediately pardoned the entire group. Most of the sect who did not leave the Territory found employment at Camp Douglas. In May, 1863, General Connor, with a detachment of troops, escorted 160 Morrisites to Soda Springs, Idaho, where a settlement and military post to protect overland emigration was established.

President Lincoln endeavored to restore peace in Utah by making concessions on both sides. In June, 1863, Governor Stephen S. Harding was removed. Secretary Frank Fuller and Judge J. F. Kinney were sacrificed to appease the non-Mormon faction. James Duane Doty, superintendent of Indian affairs, was appointed governor; Amos Reed, secretary; and John Titus, chief justice. Utah voters in the next election, August, 1863, expressed their appreciation to Judge Kinney, a non-Mormon, for his fairness by sending him to Congress as a delegate. Judge Waite, in the spring of 1864, resigned in disgust after holding a term of court during which there was not a single case. He was succeeded by Solomon McCurdy. Judge Drake remained at his post for a few years longer, in a hostile "community that had never willingly submitted . . . to Gentile domination."[30]

James Duane Doty served as governor of Utah until his death in June, 1865. He was a liberal and tolerant in his policies and cordial in his contacts with the citizens. Through his excellent statesmanship, he was instrumental in bringing about better harmony between the Federal officials in Utah and the Mormon leaders.[31]

General Connor, on the other hand, continued his anti-Mormon campaign during 1863–64. He sponsored the *Vedette,* a newspaper published in Camp Douglas, which waged a fierce journalistic war against the Mormon people. On July 9, 1864, Connor prompted an incident which threatened the peace of the Territory. He appointed Captain Charles Hempstead as provost marshal of Salt Lake City and detailed a company of Sec-

[30] Bancroft, *History of Utah,* 621.

[31] *Ibid.,* 621–22. Governor Doty, at his request, was buried in Utah, interment being made at Fort Douglas. Business in Salt Lake City was suspended on the day of the funeral.

ond California Cavalry as provost guard; and the troops were ordered to occupy quarters on South Temple Street nearly opposite the Mormon Tabernacle. The General's pretext, as he informed the commander of the Department of Pacific, was that the Mormons were depreciating the national currency in favor of the gold standard. He described Brigham Young as a traitor almost comparable to Jefferson Davis.[32] On July 15 the pugnacious Connor reported that he was prepared to resist any attack, and that the Mormons, knowing their city was at the mercy of his guns, were quieting down some, although infantry and artillery drills were held nightly in Brigham Young's yard.

On July 16, 1864, when Major General Irvin McDowell, new department commander, learned of Brigadier General Connor's most recent tactics, he dispatched Major Edward McGarry from San Francisco with orders for Connor to withdraw the provost guard from Salt Lake City. McDowell warned Connor that a war with the Mormons at that time might weaken the troop strength in the department to the point that the Far West might be an easy target for the actual Secessionists. He reiterated that the California troops were sent to Utah to protect the Overland route and not to attempt to correct alleged territorial problems. McDowell informed Connor on July 20 that it was inadvisable to regulate currency in Utah by military force. On July 23, 1864, General Connor telegraphed department headquarters that he had acquiesced to General McDowell's orders.[33] McDowell, with better judgment than Connor thereby averted what might have become a serious armed conflict in Utah.

Meanwhile, during the war years and soon after, drastic changes were made by Congress in the boundaries of Utah. At the beginning of 1861, the land area of the Territory consisted of 200,196 square miles, which by 1868 had been reduced to 84,476, a loss of 135,720 square miles. Of this, Colorado received 29,500

---

[32] *O.R.*, I, 50:893–94 (part 2). Whitney, *History of Utah*, 110, contended that the people of California (Connor's home state) at first repudiated the government "greenbacks," but Utah and her citizens never did.

[33] *Ibid.*, I, 50:904, 909–10, 914, 916 (part 2).

square miles, Nevada 91,900 square miles, and Wyoming was the eventual benefactor of 14,320 square miles.

In the early part of 1865, as the numerous Union victories indicated that the Civil War was drawing to a close, relations improved considerably between the soldiers at Camp Douglas and the Mormons. A celebration to honor the second inauguration of President Abraham Lincoln was tactfully promoted by Governor J. D. Doty. On March 4, 1865, a Mormon-Gentile civilian and military procession marched before a review stand on which were Federal officials, army officers, and Mormon leaders. General Connor, impressed with the parading citizens who later heartily cheered the speakers, suggested that the differences of opinion be forgotten. He proposed to abolish the newspaper *Vedette*. The officers at Camp Douglas were entertained at the Salt Lake City Hall, where they met the city officials and several leading Mormon authorities. The Nauvoo Legion (Mormon militia) escorted the California Volunteers back to Camp Douglas. The future appeared to be much more peaceful.

## NEW MEXICO

In New Mexico at the outbreak of the Civil War, territorial officials and local citizens, as well as the military, were faced with the immediate decision of allegiance to the United States or to the Confederate States. When hostilities began, the governor of New Mexico was Abraham Rencher, a Democratic appointee from North Carolina. Upon learning of Lynde's surrender to Baylor in July, 1861, the Governor called out the entire territorial militia to act as home guard, a move to influence public opinion in favor of the Union and to keep "restless spirits" under control.[34] The sympathies of Secretary Alexander M. Jackson were unquestionably Southern. He resigned and later served on General Sibley's staff.

On July 9, 1861, President Lincoln nominated Henry Connelly, a resident of New Mexico for years, to be governor of the

[34] Greeley, *The American Conflict*, II, 21.

Territory. He was inaugurated at Santa Fe on September 4, 1861, and held the position until 1866. He was loyal, co-operated with Union commanders, and influenced many of the leading citizens of New Mexico to do likewise.[35] Miguel A. Otero, a former delegate to Congress, was nominated as territorial secretary, but he served only a short time, having failed of Senate confirmation.[36] He was succeeded by James H. Holmes, who served about one year. In turn, W. F. M. Arny became secretary, an office he held until 1867.[37]

Since New Mexico had been recently annexed to the United States by conquest, it may have been assumed that the Spanish-American people would favor the Secession movement. When the test came, however, the majority of the citizens, even at the height of the Confederate victories, especially in the northern part of the Territory, were loyal to the Federal government. Certain prominent New Mexicans, nevertheless, including some members of the Armijo family, did use their money and influence in support of the Confederacy. The most active support for the Secession was in southern New Mexico, where conventions were held in 1861 at Mesilla and Tucson. Twitchell maintained, however, that the masses in the Territory were loyal to the Union.[38] Colonel Canby reported that the people of New Mexico with few exceptions were loyal, but they were apathetic

[35] Twitchell, *New Mexican History*, 381–92. Connelly was a native of Kentucky who resided in New Mexico from 1848 until his death in 1866. Bancroft, *History of Arizona and New Mexico*, 705, wrote that Connelly was a weak man of good intentions, who despite his loyal sentiments made no brilliant record as a war governor.

[36] 37 Cong., 1 sess., *Senate Journal Executive Proceedings*, 472. Greeley, *The American Conflict*, II, 21, accused Otero of circulating an address while he was delegate to disaffect the people of New Mexico toward the Union and incite them to favor the Rebellion.

[37] Twitchell, *New Mexican History*, 391–92. Connelly and Otero were recommended by John S. Watts in whom President Lincoln had great confidence. Connelly's frequent illness required Arny to assume the duties of the executive.

[38] Twitchell, *New Mexican History*, 357–58. Prominent among those who supported the Union were Facundo Piño, José M. Gallegos, José A. Martínez, Donaciano Vigil, Trinidad Vigil, Trinidad Romero, Pedro Sánchez, F. P. Abreu, Miguel E. Pino, J. F. Chávez, Francisco Perea, Manuel Chávez, Rafael Chacon, José D. Sena, and Manuel D. Pino.

in disposition and delayed the plans of the U. S. government by their personal and political quarrels. On August 8, 1861, he suspended the writ of habeas corpus throughout the Department of New Mexico to guard against "treasonable designs" of persons disloyal to the United States.[39] In December, 1861, Governor Connelly reported to the territorial assembly, "I am proud to say that my loyal, patriotic citizens of New Mexico have responded to their Country's call." He placed the number of New Mexicans who served in the Union forces at 3,500.[40]

There was an economic motive in the loyalty of many of the New Mexicans. United States currency which had been used in the Territory prior to and during the Civil War was readily accepted from the Union army purchasing agents and from the soldiers paid in Federal money. Most of the local people on the other hand were suspicious of Confederate currency and refused to take it. During their occupation of the Territory, the Texans on several occasions forcibly seized subsistence supplies from the New Mexicans and compelled them to provide part of the transportation for the Rebel troops. It was normal for the Spanish-Americans to favor the side which treated them most fairly.

On September 2, 1861, following a spirited campaign, John S. Watts was elected delegate to the Thirty-seventh Congress over Diego Archuleta by a large majority. Twelve members of the Council and twenty-one representatives were chosen for the territorial assembly, which met in Santa Fe from December 2, 1861, to January 30, 1862. Lines were sharply drawn on the slavery question.

Governor Henry Connelly, on December 4, 1861, delivered his message to a joint session of the assembly, in which he reported the seriousness of the Texan invasion and the occupation of southern New Mexico. He recommended the repeal of New Mexico's slavery law and urged amendments to other parts of the code to strengthen public administration and the courts. He

---

[39] *O.R.*, I, 4:62.
[40] New Mexico Territory, Legislative Assembly, *House of Representatives Journal*, eleventh session, 1861–62, 21, 23.

deplored the Indian depredations in the Territory and suggested that the red men be placed on reservations. He encouraged mining, manufacturing, and agriculture. He urged loyalty to the Federal government now involved in the Civil War.

The assembly, with a Union majority, repealed the New Mexico slavery act of 1859. The Governor was given extraordinary powers for the defense of the Territory until the emergency was over. The writ of habeas corpus was suspended, whenever necessary, to continue until the enemy was subjugated. Laws were passed to strengthen the administrative and judicial functions of the territorial government and to provide for better health in New Mexico. Arizona County, created by the previous legislature, was abolished, and the region was annexed to Doña Ana County. Congress was memorialized for money to place the Indians in New Mexico on reservations.

In March, 1862, during the Confederate occupation of Santa Fe, Governor Henry Connelly moved the offices of the Executive Department to Las Vegas. The territorial assembly was not in session. While in the capital, the Rebel officers occupied the Governor's Palace, but with the exception of General Sibley, who issued a proclamation at Albuquerque on March 13, none of the Confederate officials attempted to exercise the functions of the governor. Soon after the Texans evacuated Santa Fe during the first week in April, 1862, Governor Connelly, with his staff, moved back into the Palace. The United States flag was again raised over the plaza during a patriotic ceremony.

The Twelfth New Mexico Territorial Legislative Assembly met in Santa Fe from December 1, 1862, until January 29, 1863. Secretary William F. M. Arny, acting for Governor Connelly, away from the Territory on account of illness, gave the message to the legislators. He reported on the Confederate invasion and expressed appreciation to the Federal government, the soldiers from Colorado and California, and the territorial Volunteers for driving the Texans from New Mexico. He recommended legislation favoring education, manufacturing, agriculture, and the lowly peons. He also reported on Indian depredations, especially Navaho, and urged the passage of a stronger militia law to punish the plunderers.[41]

The assembly enacted legislation to aid the administrative and judicial processes. Arizona County was restored, but the failure to re-establish a county government was no loss, since Congress created the Territory of Arizona in February, 1863. Memorials and joint resolutions were directed to the Federal government to restore a portion of southern Colorado with a population of Mexican descent to New Mexico. Appropriations were requested for education, new mail routes, and roads. It was urged that the Indians be placed on reservations to check their serious depredations. In a joint resolution, General Carleton and his California troops were thanked for their rapid march across the desert to aid in expelling the Confederates. Colorado troops were thanked, but the name of the Territory was placed second and no officers were mentioned. Colorado citizens took offense at this injustice, claiming that the Californians had not arrived until the campaign was over. Colorado's Governor Evans complained to New Mexico officials.

The political campaign of 1863 was bitterly fought. Francisco Perea was nominated as the "Union" party candidate for Congress. José M. Gallegos, a priest, headed the other ticket. Assembly candidates were selected by both groups. Statehood, which was the principal issue, was supported by Gallegos. He and his supporters expounded the advantages of becoming a state and accused those politicians who were against statehood of being afraid they might lose their positions. Perea and his followers warned that taxes would be increased and that Federal troops would be removed if statehood were achieved. They accused Gallegos of dishonesty while speaker of the territorial House of Representatives during the previous assembly. On September 7, 1863, Francisco Perea was elected as delegate to the Thirty-eighth Congress by a substantial majority, along with most of those on his ticket. The move for statehood failed.

41 *Ibid.*, twelfth session, 5–176. Army reported that in addition to private property taken, the Confederates had stolen $391 of Territorial funds.

The Thirteenth Assembly was in session at Santa Fe from December 7, 1863, until January 28, 1864. In his executive address, Governor Connelly reported on the Navaho Indian war in which troops under General Carleton were placing these Indians on a reservation. He recommended stronger militia laws to aid in the Indian wars. He advocated a public school system, encouraged manufacturing, and described the mining activities and mineral wealth. He suggested a memorial to Congress to complete the unfinished territorial buildings and one asking for a telegraph line into New Mexico. He urged loyalty to the Federal government.

During this session militia laws to fight Indians were strengthened. Old Spanish and Mexican grants were legally recognized. It became law that minor children could be punished for disobeying their fathers and grandfathers. Criminal and public administration codes were amended. Congress was memorialized to increase the defense against the Indians in New Mexico, complete the territorial Capitol and penitentiary buildings, build additional roads in the area, and see that the transcontinental telegraph and railroad lines were extended into the Territory. The government was urged to make a land survey of New Mexico. A joint resolution stated that it was not the intention of the assembly to place the Colorado troops second to any in the defense against the Confederates. Another urged the advancement of Captains W. H. Lewis and A. B. Carey, U. S. Army, to majors for assisting in the destruction of the Rebel supply train at Glorieta.

The New Mexico Assembly of 1864–65 met at Santa Fe from December 5 until February 2; Governor Connelly again reported on the most urgent problems and needs of the Territory. Stating that there were more than 8,000 Indians on the Bosque Redondo Reservation, he contended that reservations as a solution to the Indian problems were the only alternative to extermination. He urged public education, stricter tax laws, the need for a railroad through New Mexico, and manufacturing in the Territory to process wool and other raw products. He suggested memorials to Congress for more military roads, mail routes, and for the completion of territorial buildings in Santa Fe. He praised the Union forces for their recent victories in the East over the Confederates and encouraged loyalty of the New Mexicans to the Federal government.

The Fourteenth Assembly enacted legislation to aid the mining industry, irrigation, public administration, and the courts. Several new roads were established. A memorial was again addressed to Congress requesting that the southern Colorado counties be returned to New Mexico. Another urged that the route from New Mexico to the Midwestern states be given a large armed patrol to check the marauding Plains Indians. Other memorials requested more mail routes and roads. A joint resolution thanked the United States government, the military officers, and the soldiers for forcing the Navahos and some Apache Indians to occupy the Bosque Redondo Reservation.

With the termination of the Civil War, emergency controls in New Mexico were removed and normal political activities were resumed, but Indian depredations and other needs for military protection in that frontier territory kept the federal troops there for years. Early in 1865, one of the most controversial political campaigns in the history of New Mexico was launched. Congressional Delegate Francisco Perea was again nominated to lead the "Union" party ticket. J. Francisco Chávez was selected by the "Administration" party to head its roster of candidates. The "Unionists" supported the Indian reservation policy in New Mexico, praised General Carleton and the troops participating in the Indian campaigns, recognized the supremacy of the United States government, and condemned Abraham Lincoln's assassination. The "Administration" party opposed Carleton's policy of forcing the Navaho Indians on the reservation at Bosque Redondo. The return of the southern Colorado counties to New Mexico was another major issue. Perea had introduced a bill in Congress in 1864 for the disputed area, but during the campaign he was criticized for not doing more. On September 4, 1865, Chávez was elected by a majority of 2,000 out of a total of 14,000 votes. His supporters interpreted the outcome as a repudiation of Carleton's Indian policy.

## ARIZONA

Arizona was a war-born territory, although for years prior to the Civil War unsuccessful attempts had been made to separate the area known as Arizona from the Territory of New Mexico. Conventions were held in Tucson in 1857 and 1860 which petitioned Congress to authorize the formation of Arizona. The meeting of 1860 proposed taking all of New Mexico south of 33° 40′ north latitude. President James Buchanan in 1857 and 1858 recommended to Congress that a territorial government for Arizona be created. Legislation to create a territory was introduced several times in Congress from 1857 to 1860 without success. Finally the New Mexico Assembly itself in February, 1858, passed a resolution favoring a division with a north-south boundary line along the 109th meridian.

On March 16, 1861, a Secessionist convention was held at Mesilla which declared Arizona to be a territory of the Confederate States. A resolution was adopted which read that

We will not recognize the present Black Republican Administration, and that we will resist any officers appointed to the Territory by said administration with whatever means in our power.

JAS. A. LUCAS, *President of the Convention.*
*Attest*: CH. S. A. HAPPIN, *Secretary.*[42]

Following his victory over Union forces in July, 1861, Lieutenant Colonel John R. Baylor, acting in behalf of the Confederacy, proclaimed the provisional Territory of Arizona. This was to consist of all of New Mexico south of the 34th parallel, extending from Texas to California (670 miles long). He named himself as governor and designated Mesilla as the capital. He selected James A. Lucas as secretary of the Territory; M. H. Mac-

[42] *O.R.*, I, 4:39.

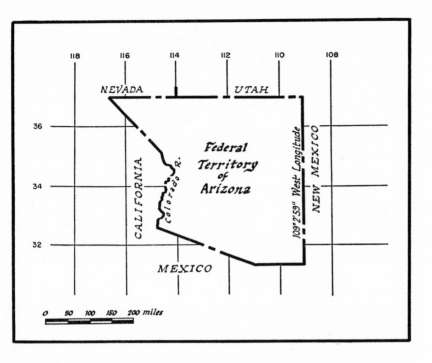

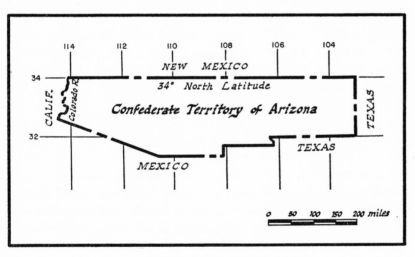

The two Arizonas.

willie, attorney general; E. Augorsteen, treasurer; George M. Frazier, marshal. Baylor also proceeded to establish a judiciary system. He appointed Frank Higgins as probate judge and chose five justices of the peace.

Baylor's hopes were now running high. On August 8, 1861, he reported to General Earl Van Dorn, commanding the Department of Texas, that a provisional government for Arizona had been established. He stated that the Territory, in addition to being an outlet to the Pacific, contained vast mineral resources.

Meanwhile, independent of Baylor, the Rebel position was strengthened in the Southwest. Early in August, 1861, a Secessionist convention was held at Tucson, in which Arizona was declared ready to become a territory of the Confederacy. Granville Oury was elected delegate to the Confederate Congress.

While Baylor proceeded with his military government of Arizona during the later months of 1861, he evidently did not feel as secure as when he had made his proclamation. On October 25, he wrote General Henry H. Sibley urgently requesting reinforcements. He stated that Colonel Edward R. S. Canby was marching down the Río Grande with 2,500 troops which would compel the Texans to abandon the Territory. He reported that the New Mexicans in the area were decidedly Northern in sentiment and that nothing but a strong Confederate force could keep them under control.

The self-appointed governor was anxious to secure assistance from Confederate sympathizers in California. He wrote Major S. B. Davis, assistant adjutant general, Department of Texas, on November 2, 1861, that California was on the eve of a revolution in which many Southern men would join the Rebel expedition in Arizona if they could get through. He suggested that an armed force be placed in western Arizona to watch for the anticipated landing of United States troops at Guaymas, Mexico, thus preventing an invasion of Arizona through Sonora.

On December 14, 1861, General Sibley, at Fort Bliss, Texas, assumed command of all Confederate forces in New Mexico and Arizona. On December 20, he addressed a proclamation to the people of New Mexico announcing that a Confederate army, under his command, was entering the Territory to re-establish a government that would liberate the New Mexicans from the military despotism erected upon the ruins of the former free institutions of the United States. He promised tax reductions, religious, civil, and political liberties, and protection of life and property. On the same day, Sibley decreed that Lieutenant Colonel John R. Baylor would continue as civil and military governor of Arizona.

Early in January, 1862, the Confederate Congress passed an Organic Act officially creating the Territory of Arizona, which was approved by President Jefferson Davis on January 18, 1862. The northern boundary between Arizona and New Mexico was placed at the 34th parallel, with the Texas line on the east, California at the Colorado River on the west, and Mexico and Texas on the south. The Governor and other territorial officials were to be appointed by the President. The legislature, elected by the white male residents over twenty-one years of age, was to consist of thirteen Council members and a House of Representatives of thirteen, which number would increase to a limit of thirty-nine. Military personnel who were not citizens of the Territory could neither vote nor hold office. All legislative and judicial proceedings were to be conducted in English. The legislation passed could be invalidated or modified by the Confederate Congress. Slavery was legalized and was to be protected. Mesilla was designated as the capital. The Territory was permitted to have one delegate in the House of Representatives at Richmond.

President Davis, on February 14, 1862, issued a proclamation declaring the Arizona Territory Organic Act to be in full force and effect. On March 13, he sent the following names to the Senate for confirmation as officials of the Territory: John R. Baylor, governor; Robert Josselyn, secretary; Alexander M. Jackson, chief justice; Russell Howard, attorney; Samuel J. Jones, marshal. Granville H. Oury, first delegate to represent the Territory, was admitted to the Confederate Congress on January 18,

1862, the date the Organic Act was approved, but on March 11, he was replaced by M. H. Macwillie, attorney general in Baylor's military government. The latter served in the House for the duration of the Civil War.

In the spring of 1862, after the Battle of Glorieta, the Texans steadily retreated down the Río Grande Valley into Texas. They were followed by Union forces consisting of the Volunteers from Colorado and New Mexico and army regulars. At the same time the California Volunteers advanced across Arizona to Tucson, where on June 8, 1862, General Carleton proclaimed the provisional Federal Territory of Arizona and established a military government. Most of the Californians then marched on to the Río Grande. In front of each Union army the Confederate officials and most of their supporters hastily abandoned Tucson, Mesilla, and other points in their briefly possessed dominion. The dream of a new Southern territory and an outlet to the Pacific Ocean for the Confederacy was shattered. The Secessionist movement in Arizona almost completely died out.

Meanwhile, important events for Arizona's future were taking place in Washington, where the Arizona Territory bill was reintroduced in December, 1861. With the Southerners then out of Congress there were fewer arguments of a sectional nature. A proviso against slavery was included. Unlike former bills, this one called for a north-south boundary line between Arizona and New Mexico. During the debates in Congress, those favoring the bill contended that the 6,500 whites and 4,000 civilized Indians were entitled to the protection of a civil government, which could not be had under the territorial rule of New Mexico. They argued that the vast mineral wealth of Arizona would justify the necessary expenditure. The opposition claimed that the 6,500 included Mexicans and half-bloods unfit for citizenship. They maintained that the Americans had been driven out and the Territory was in the possession of Rebels and hostile Indians. It was also charged that the bill was a scheme to create political jobs for "party hacks." The bill passed the House of Representatives on May 8, 1862, by a small majority, but the Senate delayed action on it for nearly a year. Finally, on February 20, 1863, the bill passed in the upper house by a twenty-five to twelve majority and became law four days later.[43]

Charles D. Poston, known by some as the "Father of the Arizona Territory," while describing the preliminary wire-pulling in Washington before the act passed, related that there were a number of "Lame Duck Congressmen" wanting to go West who had enough influence to carry the bill through Congress. At an oyster supper sponsored by Poston they made a deal and chose officers for the proposed territory. Late in the evening Poston asked, "What is to become of me?" Gurley (slated for governor) replied, "We will make you an Indian agent." The bill passed, the oyster supper was paid for, and Arizona was launched on the political sea.[44]

The Arizona Organic Act, creating the Territory from the western half of New Mexico, divided along the 109th meridian and provided for a government consisting of executive, legislative, and judiciary departments. The governor with other administrative officials and a supreme court of three judges was to be appointed by the President with the consent of the Senate. The assembly, to be elected by the citizens, was to consist of a Council of nine members and a House of Representatives of eighteen. All legislative enactments previously passed by the New Mexico Assembly, which were not inconsistent with other parts of the act, were extended to the new territory until repealed or amended by future legislation.[45]

In March, 1863, President Lincoln appointed John A. Gurley governor of the new territory, but he died before he had a chance

[43] *Cong. Globe,* 37 Cong., 2 sess., 1341–42, 2023–30, 3093–94; 3 sess., 1125–28, 1306. Delegate Watts of New Mexico and Congressman Ashley of Ohio in the House and Senators McDougal of California and Wade of Ohio in the Senate were its chief advocates. Wheeler of New York in the House and Trumbull of Illinois in the Senate led the opposition.

[44] Charles D. Poston, *Reminiscences,* quoted by Bancroft in *The History of Arizona and New Mexico,* 509.

[45] Arizona Legislative Assembly, *Acts,* first session, 1864, 7. The line was an extension of the Colorado-Utah boundary line south. Later surveys placed the line at 109° 2′ 59″ meridian.

to take office and was replaced the following August by John N. Goodwin. Richard S. McCormick was chosen as secretary; William F. Turner, chief justice, with William T. Howell and Joseph P. Allyn, associate justices. Almon Gage was selected as attorney; Milton B. Duffield, marshal; Levi Bashford, surveyor general and Charles D. Poston, Indian agent. Governor Goodwin with most of the other officials of the Territory of Arizona arrived at Santa Fe on November 14, 1863, and departed on the twenty-sixth. An additional military escort under Colonel J. F. Chávez was furnished by General Carleton.

The Governor's party crossed the eastern boundary of the new territory on December 27, 1863. Two days later the Territory of Arizona was formally inaugurated by ceremonies held at Navaho Springs. Secretary Richard S. McCormick opened the occasion with appropriate remarks and hoisted the Stars and Stripes. Reverend H. W. Read offered a prayer. The oath of office was administered to all of the officials. A proclamation by Governor John M. Goodwin was read which announced that as of that time the Arizona territorial government was organized. The seat of government for the present was to be at or near Fort Whipple, established a month earlier by a unit of the California Volunteers. The officers of the new government arrived at Fort Whipple on January 22, 1864. Near the fort about July 1, 1864, a town was founded, named Prescott, which became Arizona's first capital.[46]

Soon after his arrival, Governor Goodwin with an escort of about eighty civilians and soldiers made an inspection tour of a large portion of the Territory. On April 9, by an executive proclamation, three judicial districts were temporarily created—until the legislature could act and the judges were assigned. During the spring of 1864, U. S. Marshal Milton B. Duffield conducted a census of the Territory which revealed a total white population of 4,573. On May 26, the Governor issued a proclamation for an election to be held. Following a brief campaign, the

---

[46] Bancroft, *History of Arizona and New Mexico*, 522. The capital was named in honor of historian William Hickling Prescott.

first election in the Federal Territory of Arizona was held on July 18, 1864. Charles D. Poston was elected delegate to Congress from a group of five candidates. Nine members of the legislative assembly Council were chosen and eighteen for the House of Representatives. While at Tucson in May, responding to a petition of the citizens, Governor Goodwin by proclamation appointed officials for a much-needed government of that town.

The First Arizona Territorial Legislative Assembly met at Prescott from September 26 to November 10, 1864.[47] Governor John N. Goodwin in his message recommended that a general code of laws be adopted. He urged that the Territory be divided into three judicial districts and into counties for which governments should be provided, and that the time and manner of elections should be set. He asked that the inherited New Mexican laws permitting peonage and debt imprisonment be abolished. He advocated appropriate laws on taxes, minerals, irrigation, and schools and the establishment of a permanent capital. He complimented the troops and the civilians for their campaigns against the Apaches, urged the organization of the Arizona Rangers to fight the Indians, and suggested an Indian reservation on the Colorado River. He urged a memorial to the Federal government for mail routes in the Territory with outside connections, advocated railroad buildings in Arizona, and lauded the Union forces in the East for their victories.

The assembly enacted a general code[48] drafted by Judge William T. Howell. Four counties—Mohave, Yavapai, Yuma, and Pima—were created. Organization of the Arizona Rangers was authorized, as well as a loan to finance a campaign against the Apaches. The Governor was empowered to draft a map of the Territory. Five roads and three railroad companies were incorporated and exclusive rights were granted ferry companies on the Colorado River. Appropriations were made for a school and books for a territorial library. Soldiers were permitted to vote

[47] Arizona Legislative Assembly, *Journals*, first session, 1864, 17–250. Coles Bashford was elected council president and W. Claude Jones speaker of the House.
[48] Based on California and New York laws.

and hold mining claims. Other mining laws were passed. Delegate Poston was urged to secure twelve mail routes and to obtain muskets and ammunition to arm the Arizona Rangers for service against the Apaches. Congress was asked for appropriations to fight Indians, improve navigation on the Colorado River, and establish an Indian reservation on the river. Sylvester Mowry's expulsion by General Carleton was protested. Soon after the First Assembly convened, the fight for the location of the capital started and lasted for years. Nearly everyone wanted it any place but Prescott, but for lack of agreement on another location it remained, for the time being, at Prescott.

When the Civil War came to a close in 1865, Arizona as a Federal territory was only two years old. It was yet in its political infancy. The mineral-rich land areas and opportunities for stock raising offered the principal inducements for immigration. Although the termination of the war permitted additional troops to be sent to the region, the unconquered Apaches continued to terrorize the settlers for years. Despite these difficulties and the rigors of the frontier, the Territory of Arizona continued its political development. Not until the coming of the railroad and the later development of irrigation were the fullest opportunities of its settlers to be realized.

When war came, the majority of the New Mexicans remained loyal. War Governor Henry Connelly co-operated with the Union commanders during the Rebel invasion and repulsion and influenced other citizens, some of whom at first were apathetic, to maintain allegiance. The legislature repealed the New Mexico slave law and strengthened the administrative and judicial processes in the Territory.

There were two Arizonas during the Civil War. Texan Colonel John R. Baylor in 1861 created a territory from the southern part of New Mexico, appointing himself as governor. The Confederate Congress and President Davis followed with the Organic Act of 1862. The movement collapsed with the retreat to Texas of the Confederate troops. Federal Arizona, taken from the western half of New Mexico, became a territory in 1863, and under Governor Goodwin the new territorial government was inaugurated. During the later war years, the legislature enacted a code, organized counties, and established a judiciary system. The termination of the war brought to a close a vital narrative in the history of Western America depicting the Confederate invasion and expulsion, the struggle between the whites and the Indians, and the political development of the Western territories.

# Bibliography

*Public Documents*

Arizona Territory, Legislative Assembly. *Acts, Resolutions, and Memorials,* First Session, 1864. Prescott, Arizona, Office of the Arizona Miner, 1865.

———. *Journals,* First Session, 1864. Prescott, Arizona, Office of the Arizona Miner, 1865.

Colorado Territory, Legislative Assembly. *Council Journal,* First Session, 1861. Denver, Colorado, Thomas Gibson, Colorado Republican and Rocky Mountain Herald, 1862.

———. *General Laws, Joint Resolutions and Private Acts,* First Session, 1861. Denver, Colorado, Thomas Gibson, Colorado Republican and Rocky Mountain Herald, 1862.

———. *Council Journal,* Second Session, 1862. Denver, Colorado, Rocky Mountain News Printing Company, 1862.

———. *General Laws, Joint Resolutions and Private Acts,* Second Session, 1862. Denver, Colorado, Rocky Mountain News Printing Company, 1862.

———. *General Laws, Joint Resolutions and Private Acts,* Third Session, 1864. Denver, Colorado, Byers and Daily Printers, Rocky Mountain News Office, 1864.

———. *House Journal,* Third Session, 1864. Denver, Colorado, Byers and Daily Printers, Rocky Mountain News Office, 1864.

———. *Council Journal,* Fourth Session, 1865. Denver, Colorado, Byers and Daily Printers, Rocky Mountain News Office, 1865.

———. *General Laws, Joint Resolutions and Private Acts,* Fourth Session, 1865. Denver, Colorado, Byers and Daily Printers, Rocky Mountain News Office, 1865.

*Congressional Globe,* 35, 36, 37, 38, and 39 Cong., all sessions. Washington, Office of John C. Rives, 1858–65.

New Mexico Territory, Legislative Assembly. *House Journal,*

Eleventh Session, 1861–62. Santa Fe, New Mexico, Putnam O'Brien Printer, 1862.

———. *Laws,* Eleventh Session, 1861–62. Santa Fe, New Mexico, Putnam O'Brien Printer, 1862.

———. *House Journal,* Twelfth Session, 1862–63. Santa Fe, New Mexico, Santa Fe Weekly Gazette, 1863.

———. *Laws,* Twelfth Session, 1862–63. Santa Fe, New Mexico, Charles Lieb, Publisher of the New Mexican, 1863.

———. *House Journal,* Thirteenth Session, 1863–64. Santa Fe, New Mexico, Thomas S. Tucker, Printer, 1864.

———. *Laws with Joint Resolutions,* Thirteenth Session, 1863–64. Albuquerque, New Mexico, Hezekiah S. Johnson, Printer, 1864.

———. *House Journal,* Fourteenth Session, 1864–65. Santa Fe, New Mexico, Manderfield and Tucker, Printers, 1865.

———. *Laws,* Fourteenth Session, 1864–65. Included in combined statutes up to that date. St. Louis, Missouri, R. P. Studley and Company, 1865.

Richardson, James D., comp. *A Compilation of the Messages and Papers of the Presidents.* 11 vols. New York, Bureau of National Literature. Vol. IV, 1912.

U. S. Congress, House of Representatives. *Misc. Doc. 78,* 37 Cong., 2 sess. Washington, Government Printing Office, 1862.

U. S. Congress, Senate. *Journal of Executive Proceedings,* 36 Cong., 2 sess. (Special), 1861. Included with proceedings from December 6, 1858 to August 6, 1861. Washington, Government Printing Office. Vol. XI, 1887.

———. *Journal of Executive Proceedings,* 37 and 38 Cong., December 1, 1862 to July 4, 1864. Washington, Government Printing Office. Vol. XIII, 1887.

———. *Exec. Doc. 49,* 38 Cong., 1 sess. Washington, Government Printing Office, 1864.

———. *Exec. Doc. 26.* 39 Cong., 2 sess., Report of the Secretary of War. Washington, Government Printing Office, 1867.

———. *Reports of the Committees,* 39 Cong., 2 sess. Washington, Government Printing Office, 1867.

———. *Indian Affairs, Laws and Treaties, Doc. 319.* 58 Cong., 2 sess. Washington, Government Printing Office, 1904. Vol. II.

U. S. Interior Department, Bureau of Indian Affairs. *Reports of the Commissioner of Indian Affairs for the Years 1862, 1863, 1864 and*

*1865* (in separate volumes for each year). Washington, Government Printing Office, 1863, 1864, 1865, and 1866.

U. S. National Archives. *War Records, Military Book, Volume 47.* Correspondence from Assistant Secretary of War P. H. Watson, February 20 and 24, 1862.

U. S. War Department. *The War of the Rebellion. A Compilation of the Official Records of the Union and Confederate Armies.* Four series, 128 vols. Washington, Government Printing Office. 1880–1901.

Utah Territory, Legislative Assembly. *Journals,* Eleventh Session, 1861–62. Salt Lake City, Utah, Elias Smith, Printers, 1862.

———. *Journals,* Twelfth Session, 1862–63. Salt Lake City, Utah, Elias Smith, Printers, 1863.

———. *Acts, Resolutions and Memorials,* Thirteenth Session, 1863–64. Salt Lake City, Utah, Henry McEwin, Printer, 1864.

## Newspapers

*Alta California* (San Francisco), 1861–65.

*Colorado Republican and Rocky Mountain Herald* (Denver), 1861–62.

*Denver Commonwealth,* June 15, 1864.

*Denver Post,* November 6 and 13, 1949.

*Deseret News* (Salt Lake City), 1861–65.

*New York Daily Tribune,* July 16, 21, August 20, 1859.

*Rocky Mountain News,* Daily (Denver), 1861–65.

*Rocky Mountain News,* Weekly (Denver), April 9, 1863 and August 31, 1864.

*Sacramento Daily Union,* March 12, 1863.

*San Francisco Bulletin,* 1862–63.

*Santa Fe Weekly Gazette,* 1861–65, 1868.

## Books

Bancroft, Hubert Howe. *History of Arizona and New Mexico.* San Francisco, The History Company, Publishers, 1889.

———. *History of Nevada, Colorado and Wyoming.* San Francisco, The History Company, Publishers, 1890.

———. *History of Utah.* San Francisco, The History Company, Publishers, 1891.

Barnes, William C. *Arizona Place Names.* University of Arizona *Bulletin No. 2.* Tucson, Arizona, University of Arizona, 1935.

Buel, Clarence Clough (ed.). *Battles and Leaders of the Civil War.* 4 vols. New York, The Century Company, 1887.

Coan, Charles F. *A History of New Mexico,* Chicago, American Historical Society, Inc., Volume I, 1925.

Commager, Henry Steele. *The Blue and the Gray.* New York, The Merrill Company, Inc. Vol. I, 1950.

Coulter, E. Merton. *The Confederate States of America, 1861–1865.* Baton Rouge, Louisiana State University Press, 1950.

Coutant, C. G. *History of Wyoming.* Laramie, Wyoming, Chaplin, Spafford and Mathison, Printers. Vol. I, 1899.

Cremony, John C. *Life Among the Apaches.* San Francisco, Roman and Company, Publishers, 1868.

*Dictionary of American Biography.* New York, Charles Scribner's Sons. Vol. XX, 1931.

*Doctrine and Covenants of the Church of Jesus Christ of Latter-day Saints.* Originally published at Kirtland, Ohio, 1835. Salt Lake City, Utah, Church of Jesus Christ of Latter-day Saints, 1928.

DuBois, John Van Deusen. *Campaigns in the West 1856–1861.* The Journal and Letters of Colonel John Van Deusen DuBois. Ed. by George P. Hammond. Tucson, Arizona, Arizona Pioneers Historical Society, 1949. (The original diary is now in the William Robertson Coe Collection, Yale University.)

Egan, Howard R. *Pioneering in the West.* Richmond, Utah, published by Howard R. Egan Estate and printed by Skelton Publishing Company, 1917.

Fisher, Margaret M. *Utah and the Civil War.* Salt Lake City, Utah, The Deseret Book Company, 1929.

Greeley, Horace. *The American Conflict: A History of the Great Rebellion in the United States of America 1860–1865.* Hartford, Connecticut, O. D. Case and Company. Vol. I, 1864; Vol. II, 1866.

Grinnell, George Bird. *The Fighting Cheyennes.* New York, Charles Scribner's Sons, 1915.

Hafen, LeRoy R. *Colorado and Its People.* New York, Lewis Historical Publishing Company, Inc. Vol. I, 1948.

———. *The Overland Mail.* Cleveland, The Arthur Clark Company, 1926.

Hall, Frank. *History of the State of Colorado.* Chicago, The Blakely Printing Company. Vol. I, 1889.

Hamilton, Patrick. *The Resources of Arizona.* San Francisco, A. L. Bancroft and Company, Printers, 1883.

Harris, Gertrude A. *A Tale of Men Who Knew Not Fear.* San Antonio, Texas, The Alamo Printing Company, 1935.

Hayes, Augustus Allen, Jr. *New Colorado and the Santa Fe Trail.* New York, Harper and Brothers, 1880.

*History of the City of Denver, Arapahoe County and Colorado.* Compiled by the publishers. Chicago, O. O. Baskin and Company, Historical Publishers, 1880.

Hodge, Frederick Webb (ed.). *Handbook of American Indians North of Mexico.* Bureau of American Ethnology, *Bulletin No. 30.* Washington, Government Printing Office, 1910.

Hollister, Ovando J. *Boldly They Rode: A History of the First Colorado Regiment of Volunteers.* Lakewood, Colorado, The Golden Press, 1949. (Original edition published in 1863 entitled *A History of the First Colorado Regiment.*)

Howbert, Irving. *Memories of a Lifetime in the Pikes Peak Region.* New York, G. P. Putnam's Sons, 1925.

Hunt, Aurora. *The Army of the Pacific.* Glendale, California, Arthur H. Clark Company, 1951.

Keleher, William A. *Turmoil in New Mexico, 1848–68.* Santa Fe, New Mexico, The Rydal Press, 1952.

Lane, Lydia Spencer. *I Married a Soldier.* Philadelphia, J. B. Lippincott Company, 1893.

McClintock, James H. *Arizona—The Youngest State.* Chicago, The S. J. Clarke Publishing Company. Vol. I, 1915.

McKee, James Cooper. *Narrative of the Surrender of a Command of U. S. Forces at Fort Fillmore, New Mexico in July, 1861.* Boston, John A. Lowell and Company, 1886.

McMechen, Edgar Carlisle. *Life of Governor Evans.* Denver, Colorado, The Walgren Publishing Company, 1924.

Meline, James F. *Two Thousand Miles on Horseback: Santa Fe and Back.* A Summer Tour Through Kansas, Nebraska, Colorado and New Mexico in the Year 1866. New York, Hurd and Houghton, 1867.

Mowry, Sylvester. *The Geography and Resources of Arizona and Sonora.* An Address before the American Geographical and Statistical Society at New York City, N. Y., February 3, 1859. Published by the Society at Washington, D. C. Printed by Henry Polkinhorn, 1859.

Neff, Andrew L. *History of Utah 1847 to 1869.* Edited and Annotated by Leland H. Creer. Salt Lake City, Utah, The Deseret News Press, 1940.

Noel, Theophilus. *Autobiography and Reminiscences of Theophilus Noel.* Chicago, Theo. Noel Company Print, 1904.

Sabin, Edwin L., *Kit Carson Days.* Chicago, A. C. McClurg and Company, 1914.

Smiley, Jerome C. *History of Denver.* Denver, Colorado, The Denver Times and The Times-Sun Publishing Company, 1901.

———. *Semi-Centennial History of the State of Colorado.* Chicago, The Lewis Publishing Company. Vol. I, 1913.

Sloan, Richard E., and Ward R. Adams. *History of Arizona.* Phoenix, Arizona, Record Publishing Company, 1930.

Stenhouse, T. B. H. *The Rocky Mountain Saints.* New York, D. Appleton and Company, 1873.

Stone, Wilbur Fisk. *History of Colorado.* Chicago, The S. J. Clark Publishing Company. Vol. I, 1918.

Tullidge, Edward W. *History of Salt Lake City and Its Founders.* Salt Lake City, Utah, Edward W. Tullidge, Publisher and Proprietor, 1886.

Twitchell, Ralph E. *Leading Facts of New Mexican History.* Cedar Rapids, Iowa, The Torch Press. Vol. II, 1912.

Waite, Catherine V. *The Mormon Prophet and His Harem.* Cambridge, Massachusetts, Riverside Press, 1866.

Whitford, William Clarke. *Colorado Volunteers in the Civil War.* The New Mexico Campaign in 1862. Denver, Colorado, The State Historical and Natural Society, 1906.

Whitney, Orson F. *History of Utah.* Salt Lake City, Utah, George Q. Cannon and Company. Vol. II, 1893.

Wyllys, Rufus Kay. *Arizona: The History of a Frontier State.* Phoenix, Arizona, Hobson and Herr, 1950.

Young, Brigham. *Journal of Discourses.* Also contains speeches by Brigham Young's Counsellors, the Twelve Apostles, and other Mormon Church leaders. 26 vols. Liverpool, England, Church of Jesus Christ of Latter-day Saints, 1856–84.

## *Articles*

Barker, William J. "Forgotten War for the West," *Denver Post*, November 6 and 13, 1949.

Browne, John Ross. "A Tour Through Arizona," *Harper's New Monthly Magazine*, Vol. XXIX (October, 1864).

Donnell, F. S. "The Confederate Territory of Arizona, As Compiled from Official Sources," *The New Mexico Historical Review*, Vol. XVII, No. 2 (April, 1942).

Ellis, Elmer. "Colorado's First Fight for Statehood, 1865–68," *The Colorado Magazine*, Vol. VIII (January, 1931).

McCoy, Raymond. "The Battle of Valverde," *New Mexico Magazine*, Vol. XXX (September, 1952).

Pettis, George H. "Confederate Invasion of New Mexico and Arizona," Vol. II of *Battles and Leaders of the Civil War*. Ed. by Clarence Clough Buel, *q.v.*

———. "The California Column," *Historical Society of New Mexico*. Santa Fe, New Mexico, New Mexican Printing Company, 1908. Number 11.

———. "Kit Carson's Fight with the Comanche and Kiowa Indians," *Personal Narrative of the Battles of the Rebellion*. Rhode Island Soldiers and Sailors Historical Society, No. 5, Providence, Rhode Island, Sidney S. Rider, 1878.

Teel, T. T. "Sibley's New Mexican Campaign—Its Objects and the Causes of Its Failure," Vol. II of *Battles and Leaders of the Civil War*, *q.v.*

# Index

Abreu, Capt. F. P., N. M. Volunteers: 131, 145, 192 n.
Adobe Fort (Adobe Walls), N. M.: 146
Albuquerque, N. M.: prewar military installation, 6; occupied by Confederates, 38; skirmish between Federals and Confederates, 83–84; Confederates evacuate, 85, 110, 194
Allyn, Joseph P., associate justice, Federal Terr. of Ariz.: 204
Antero, Ute chief: 169
Anthony, Capt. Scott J., 1st Colo. Regt.: 45, 159 n., 172; in Battle of Apache Canyon, 52–54; in Battle of Glorieta, 69–74
Anti-polygamy law: 185, 185 n.
Apache Canyon (N. M.), Battle of: 50–56, 74, 75
Apache Indians: 9, 21, 95, 98, 106, 111, 121–22, 124, 125 n., 130–32, 134–36, 197; Mescalero, 125–27, 133; Gila, 125, 127–29, 133, 135; Arivaipa, 133; Chiricahua, 134; Jicarilla, 145
Arapaho Indians: 146, 149, 156–57; in Sand Creek Massacre, 157–58
Archer, Capt. Samuel (U.S.A.): 140
Archuleta, Diego: 193
Arizona: 10–11, 104, 107, 116, 120, 124, 134, 142, 171, 198–99, 209; Confederate Territory of, 19, 198, 201; Federal Territory of, 195, 202–204, 205, 209
Arizona Guards (C.S.A.): 123
Arizona Rangers (U.S.A.): 205
Arkansas River, Colo.: 148, 154
Armour, Charles Lee: Federal judge, 172; opposes Colorado statehood, 178

Arny, W. F. M., secretary, N. M. Terr.: 192
Ashley, Eli M.: 178
Ashley, Congressman James H., of Ohio: 177, 203
Augorsteen, E., treas., Confederate Terr. of Ariz.: 200

Baker, Lieut. John, 1st Colo. Regt.: 61, 62 n.
Bannock Indians: 163, 208
Bargie, Lieut. L. A., N. M. Volunteers: 130
Barney, Capt. Joseph, N. M. Volunteers: 143
Barrett, Lieut. James, Calif. Column: 103, 104
Baylor, Lieut. Col. John R., Texas Mounted Rifles (C.S.A.): leads invasion of New Mexico, 13, 14; forces Federal surrender, 16–17; proclaims himself governor of Arizona, 19, 122, 198; quarrels with Sibley, 37, 121 n.; removed as governor, 123; appointed governor by President Davis, 201, 209
Bear Hunter, Bannock chief: 163–65
Bear River, Battle of (Utah): 164–66, 208
Bee, Gen. H. P. (C.S.A.): 96
Bennet, Hiram, delegate to Congress from Colo.: 175
Bernal Springs, N. M.: 50, 56, 84
Bernard, Lieut. Reuben F. (U.S.A.): 54
Bernhisel, John M., delegate to Congress from Utah: 161, 183
Black Hawk, Ute chief: 169
Black Hawk War: 170
Black Kettle, Cheyenne chief: 155,

217

# DATE DUE

| | | | |
|---|---|---|---|
| JAN 2 4 '64 | NOV 1 8 '71 | | |
| MAR 1 6 '64 | DEC 8 '71 | | |
| JAN 21 '65 | APR 12 '72 | | |
| APR 2 8 '65 | 08.8 '79 | | |
| DEC 14 '66 | DE 8 '80 | | |
| AR 1 8 '67 | NOV 5 '85 | | |
| DEC 4 '57 | NOV 2 6 '85 | | |
| MAY 7 '68 | NOV 28 '88 | | |
| NOV 1 8 '68 | DEC 7 '88 | | |
| NOV 8 '69 | | | |
| DEC 9 '69 | | | |
| MAR 1 6 '70 | | | |
| APR 2 '70 | | | |
| MAY 6 '70 | | | |
| FEB 23 '71 | | | |
| MAR 1 8 '71 | | | |
| GAYLORD | | | PRINTED IN U.S.A. |